KU-260-663

Working Inter-Culturally in Counselling Settings

Our multi-cultural society is changing the parameters of counselling. *Working Inter-Culturally in Counselling Settings* explores how racial issues can be recognised and worked with in a practical, clinical setting.

The book looks at how the counselling setting can influence practice, and includes chapters in a range of settings, including:

- Counselling training and supervision
- Social work
- The probation service and prisons
- Setting up counselling services in culturally diverse communities.

Aisha Dupont-Joshua, together with contributors of diverse cultural heritage, moves away from exclusive, white models of thought to adopt more of a worldview inclusive of cultural difference. *Working Inter-Culturally in Counselling Settings* will be invaluable for counsellors, trainers, supervisors and other mental health professionals.

Aisha Dupont-Joshua, originally from South Africa, is an intercultural therapist and trainer teaching in Lambeth College, London and Southampton University. She has written extensively in the *BACP Counselling Journal* and has been editor of *RACE* the multi-cultural journal.

Contributors: Elaine Arnold, Angus Igwe, Duncan Lawrence, Isha Mckenzie-Mavinga, Wajiha Mohammad, Samuel Ochieng, Lennox Thomas, Piers Vitebsky, Pam Williamson, Sally Wolfe.

Working Inter-Culturally in Counselling Settings

Edited by Aisha Dupont-Joshua

Brunner-Routledge
Taylor & Francis Group

HOVE AND NEW YORK

First published 2003
by Brunner-Routledge
27 Church Road, Hove, East Sussex BN3 2FA

Simultaneously published in the USA and Canada
by Brunner-Routledge
29 West 35th Street, New York, NY 10001

Brunner-Routledge is an imprint of the Taylor & Francis Group

© 2003 Aisha Dupont-Joshua

Typeset in Times by RefineCatch Limited, Bungay, Suffolk
Printed and bound in Great Britain by TJ International,
Padstow, Cornwall, UK

Paperback cover design by Jim Wilkie

All rights reserved. No part of this book may be reprinted or
reproduced or utilised in any form or by any electronic,
mechanical, or other means, now known or hereafter
invented, including photocopying and recording, or in any
information storage or retrieval system, without permission in
writing from the publishers.

British Library Cataloguing in Publication Data
A catalogue record for this book is available from the British Library

Library of Congress Cataloging-in-Publication Data
Working inter-culturally in counselling settings/edited by Aisha
Dupont-Joshua.
        p.   cm.
    Includes bibliographical references and index.
    ISBN 0-415-22748-8 – ISBN 0-415-22749-6 (pbk.)
        1. Minorities – Counseling of – Great Britain.   2. Social work
    with minorities – Great Britain.   I. Dupont-Joshua, Aisha.

    HV3177.G7 W67 2002
    362.84′00941–dc21   2002025446

ISBN 0–415–22748–8 (hbk)
ISBN 0–415–22749–6 (pbk)

Contents

List of illustrations

Figures

Table

Notes on contributors

Elaine Arnold trained as a teacher before changing career to social worker. She has practised in both professions in Trinidad and Tobago, West Indies, and in Britain. She has supervised work students in Local Authority Social Services, and taught social work to MSW students at Goldsmiths College and Sussex University. She has worked as a training co-ordinator at Nafsiyat Inter-Cultural Therapy Centre for several years.

Aisha Dupont-Joshua is a psychotherapist of mixed race, originally from South Africa. Being part of a minority group in Britain has led her to specialise in working with issues of race and culture in counselling and training. She has piloted an inter-cultural counselling training course at Lambeth College, London, where she works as a counselling lecturer, and she is also a lecturer at Southampton University. She is a professional associate of the Nafsiyat Inter-Cultural Therapy Centre, where she trained. She works as a freelance counsellor, supervisor, trainer and writer. She was Editor of *Race*, the multi-cultural journal, for five years, which prompted her interest in editing.

Angus Igwe is Nigerian by birth and has lived in the UK since the 1970s. He trained through WPF and currently counsels for industry and local organisations. He is a supervisor, trainer and facilitator, experienced in solution focused therapy and an integrative approach in counselling and supervision. He is Director of the Centre for Personal and Professional Development.

Duncan Lawrence is a trainer, consultant and private family practitioner specialising in mental health and human diversity issues. He has practised in the USA, the EU and the Caribbean for several years. He is also Equalities Adviser for the Counselling and Psychotherapy Central Award Body (CPCAB) in the UK. His work has taken him from Alaska to Connecticut to California, and finally to the UK, where he currently resides. His current projects include developing group work programmes for racially motivated offenders, and human diversity projects within the counselling and psychotherapy sectors.

Isha Mckenzie-Mavinga is a creative, transcultural psychotherapist/supervisor Reiki Master and writer. She has contributed to the provision of alternative therapies for African Caribbean mental health. She works as a senior lecturer at Goldsmiths College and runs therapeutic support groups for women affected by domestic violence. She is a published author and has contributed to several anthologies. She has also worked as an artist in education. Her future work will concentrate on transcultural interventions and black issues.

Wajiha K. Mohammad is a part-time lecturer in sociology at Nene University College, and Tutor and Examiner for counselling courses at Northampton College. She has convened National Training Days and acted as Workshop Leader on behalf of RACE for the British Association for Counselling. She is currently researching Indian women's education and career trajectories for her Ph.D. thesis. She researched Asian women and sexuality for her Masters degree. She is aware of the internal and external conflicts which Asians face in Britain. Her other main interests include self-empowerment and spirituality. She lives in Northampton.

Samuel Ochieng is a postgraduate researcher currently working on a research proposal for a Doctoral presentation. He has held the positions of psychologist, counsellor, trainer and lecturer. He is a member of the British Association for Counsellors and Psychotherapists, currently Chairman of the RACE Division within BACP, and a member of the British Psychological Society and of the UK Therapists Group. He has been in the field of psychology for over twenty-five years. He has a psychodynamic background with a special interest in the area of symbols. He has made several presentations in the UK and written articles for US and UK publications. He is a Kenyan by birth and has lived in three continents, where he has gathered a wide knowledge of cultural transition within individuals. He is a trainer in the area of transcultural counselling, and offers workshops and courses in this subject.

Lennox Thomas had a background in childcare, clinical social work and probation before training in psychoanalytic psychotherapy. He was Clinical Director of Nafsiyat, the Inter-Cultural Therapy Centre, and joint Course Director of the M.Sc. in inter-cultural psychotherapy at University College, London. He is now in private practice, working with individuals, couples and families. He is a training therapist, trainer and supervisor for several British psychotherapy training organisations, and a long-standing member of the Association for Family Therapy and GAPPS Group for the Advancement of Psychotherapy and Psychodynamics in Social Work. His published papers are on the effects of ethnicity and difference on the therapeutic process, gender issues, organisational change, communicating with a black child in therapy and multi-cultural aspects of attachment. He is a member of the Intercultural and Equal Opportunities Committee of the UK Council for Psychotherapy. He is currently involved in long-term consultancy and teaching with health organisations in Germany, Denmark and the Caribbean.

Pam Williamson was born in the Midlands to white working-class parents. For the past five years she has been Staff Counsellor at Wandsworth Prison. She works from an existential-humanistic perspective and is also qualified in post-trauma counselling and the clinical use of hypnosis. She developed an interest in reactions to all kinds of loss including 'loss of self' after trauma. She quickly realised she needed to try and understand people not only from an emotional perspective but also within a cultural and social context in order to help them make sense of their experiences and anxieties.

Sally Wolfe is a psychodynamic counsellor and inter-cultural therapist and **Piers Vitebsky** is a social anthropologist specialising in religion and psychology in non-industrial societies. They work as a husband-and-wife team, with white Irish-Scottish and Russian Jewish-Welsh backgrounds respectively. Sally Wolfe is Convenor for the training section of RACE and co-founder of Across Cultures, an inter-cultural counselling group in Cambridge. Piers Vitebsky is Head of Social Sciences at the Scott Polar Research

Institute in Cambridge University. He is the author of many books, including *Dialogues with the Dead* (Cambridge University Press) and *The Shaman* (Macmillan), and has carried out fieldwork in many countries. Together they are working with local organisations on the establishment of counselling services in northern Siberia.

Chapter 1

Introduction

Aisha Dupont-Joshua

What does it actually mean to work inter-culturally? This is a very big question and by way of an introduction into this, I will begin by talking about myself and my involvement in the inter-cultural movement, and why becoming involved with this way of thinking has had so much impact on my life and work. In 1990, I had the privilege of training with the late Jafar Kareem, the founder of the Nafsiyat Inter-Cultural Therapy Centre in London. This training in inter-cultural therapy included anthropology, sociology, and challenged both eurocentric assumptions in counselling (eurocentric being based on European thought and concepts) and psychotherapeutic models of thought. It was revolutionary in counselling training in Britain and was very significant to me in my development, and self-concept as a black woman of mixed race, an immigrant, living and having been brought up in Britain, and as a counsellor. Issues of race and culture had never been on the agenda before in my experience of the counselling world, and this different way of thinking opened up new avenues of understanding for me and has become an essential part of my perception of how I relate to the world. It has also given me an understanding and a willingness to work with the emotional problems facing black and other ethnic minorities, living in a white host society. My training and subsequent friendship with Jafar Kareem gave me tools and a vocation to work with the problems of living in a multi-cultural society.

Jafar Kareem, who was originally from India, founded the Nafsiyat Inter-Cultural Therapy Centre in 1983 to provide a special psychotherapy service for black and other ethnic and cultural minorities, as a result of his experience of working as a psychotherapist in the National Health Service in Britain. Kareem (1992) says that his experience showed him that non-European clients were not responding to the type of psychotherapy being offered and appeared to be rejecting it, as it was practised at that time. This led him to question whether something was wrong with the way it was being practised (rather than taking the point of view of many faltering white practitioners, who came to the conclusion that black people were psychologically unsuitable for psychotherapy) and consequently lead him to explore new ideas that could be relevant to non-European clients.

Kareem (in Kareem and Littlewood 1992) says that a psychotherapeutic process that does not take into account a person's whole life experience, including their race, culture, gender and social values, could lead to a fragmentation of that person. He found that there were huge differences in the concept and expression of mental distress in European and non-European people, that fundamental concepts of personhood were radically different, and this needed to be acknowledged and understood for therapy to be practicable; this included family structures, child-rearing and education, obligations to the community and social hierarchy, morality and spiritual concepts – that people were social beings, woven into traditional structures, rather than isolated individuals. A vivid example was used by Kareem, who described an experience with a Nigerian client of noble birth. The client became stuck when asked to describe his relationship with his mother. After a missed appointment, he came back and declared that he was unable to do this, as he had been fed by nine pairs of breasts. He felt that an understanding of these aspects of people were fundamental to any therapeutic practice; leading him to challenge the assumption that there can be any kind of universal model of the self, as portrayed by the leaders of psychotherapeutic thinking. He felt therefore that cultural patterns needed to be integrated into any therapeutic models.

Kareem (1992) found that there were fundamental differences between individual human beings, physically and/or in their ways of being, and that inner and outer events can deeply affect a person's psyche and become part of their unconscious life. Social and political events in the external world, such as prejudice, racism, sexism, poverty and social disadvantage can shape the lives of individuals, in relation to different societies, and these powerful forces may well become internalised, causing profound distress – these issues, along with inner conflicts, must be addressed as clinical issues. Our work therefore must encompass the inner experiences of the client, together with their total life experience, including their communal life experience before arriving on western soil. Dupont-Joshua (1994) gives the example of Mr J. who had been a respected member of his community, before he immigrated to England, so that his family could escape the degradation of being black in the apartheid system of South Africa. Forced to work a day and an evening job to cover the high costs of living in London with a large family, Mr J. eventually sought help for depression and chronic ill health.

Kareem (1978) defined intercultural therapy as:

> A form of dynamic psychotherapy that takes into account the whole being of the patient – not only the individual concepts and constructs as presented to the therapist, but also the patient's communal life experience in the world – both past and present. The very fact of being from another culture involves both conscious and unconscious assumptions, both in the patient and in the therapist. I believe that for the successful outcome of therapy it is essential to address these conscious and unconscious assumptions from the beginning.

So began the ideas of an inter-cultural therapy that could be used as a bridge to communicate across cultures, so that therapists of totally different life experiences could begin to relate to their culturally different client.

Thinking inter-culturally, it is important to consider what, unconsciously, the white therapist may represent for the black or ethnic minority client, in a historical or social transference – bringing up associations with slavery, colonisation, the Holocaust and other oppressions. It is also important to consider the white therapist's negative counter-transference, for they are part of a society that projects negative images of black people and this might be around feeling their black client to be 'primitive', or being latently violent. Working inter-culturally, it becomes the therapist's responsibility to facilitate the black or ethnic minority client's negative transference, because the client would most probably be in too weak, vulnerable or needy a position to initiate this part of the working relationship. The relationship of mistrust between black and white people in our society can be mirrored in the therapeutic relationship, and black and ethnic minority clients often feel once again in a powerless and vulnerable position.

Working with the emotionally damaging effects of racism forms an important part of inter-cultural work – traditionally, therapy did not work with the effects of racism, as it was felt to be a political or external issue, and that therapy was for working primarily with the inner world. An example could be that racism could be perceived as a state of victimhood in the client, rather than a living reality that many black people have to face on a daily basis. The effects of racism can become internalised, damaging both the victim and the perpetrator, and working and dealing with the very primal and painful emotions evoked for all, by racism, is a very important aspect of our work. It must be understood by the white therapist that for many people of black and minority cultures, the most traumatic feature in their lives is to be black in a white society. Lennox Thomas (1992, p. 133) asks the question 'what makes the dealings in a consulting room between a white therapist and black patient "different"? What are the processes which the therapist needs to go through to disentangle themselves from the structural racism of the society in which they live and were raised?'

Kareem (1992) cites the example of Victoria, a young black woman, who when consulting a white woman therapist because she had become depressed and feared she was going mad, was made to feel that issues of race were essentially her problem. Whenever she tried to bring up anything about her feelings about being black, the therapist always interpreted that as a projection of her inner chaos on to the outside world. Consequently Victoria felt misunderstood and angry that her pain about being in a black/white situation, where she was made to feel powerless, was unacknowledged. She finally sought help from the Nafsiyat Inter-Cultural Therapy Centre because she needed a therapist who could immediately recognise her pain in being powerless and black in a society which is racist. The problem with the first therapist was not that she was white, but that she was unable to look at (or had never been taught to look at) the interrelated themes of race and powerlessness as problems of reality.

Working with the sense of loss is often an important issue when working inter-culturally with black and ethnic minority clients; loss in many aspects: roots, family, environment and social status. For many people of African-Caribbean origin, separation from their parents, especially their mothers, when their parents came to Britain as migrant workers in the 1950s and they were left behind in the Caribbean, has become an important area of work in damaged attachments. Difficulty in forming close and trusting relationships can often be related to this original loss. Elaine Arnold (1998) says that because the reunification of families occurred without social support and counselling, parent–child difficulties often remained unaddressed, leading to behavioural and social difficulties and a disproportionate number of children going into the care of local authorities. The attempts to address these issues with traditional methods of therapy were sadly inappropriate, due to the lack of understanding of the family dynamics of West Indian immigrant parents.

Training in counselling and psychotherapy, where practice begins, has been sadly lacking in racial and cultural components, and this has double-edged consequences. Firstly, white therapists are completely unequipped to work with culturally different clients, and secondly, people of minority cultures often feel reluctant to join traditional training, finding the material unrelated to their experience of life and that they are unable to bring up issues of race, culture and racism, thus perpetuating the cycle of a white-dominated profession. Kareem (1992, p. 31) when talking of his psychotherapeutic training said:

> Such intense training can sometimes be compared to a kind of colonisation of the mind and I constantly had to battle within myself to keep my head above water, to remind myself at every point who I was and what I was. It was a painful battle not to think what I had been told to think, not to be what I had been told to be and not to challenge what I had been told could not be challenged and at the same time not to become alienated from my basic roots and my basic self.

Inter-cultural counselling and psychotherapy training and training components positively take on board these processes and work with validating diverse cultural traditions and expanding therapeutic models to include worldview models.

From 1995 to 2000 I was Editor of the BAC's *RACE* (Racial and Cultural Education in Counselling) multi-cultural journal. This became an important way of communicating inter-cultural ideas and publishing writers of diverse cultures. The experience was a very rich one for me and brought me into contact with so many diverse and interesting writers that the idea of editing this book came as a natural progression of this. The relevance of many of the writers whom I was working with was begging a larger readership, so I took on the challenge of presenting a body of work that would reach a wide range of people working and studying within the caring professions who wish to widen their perimeters and integrate working with issues of race and culture into their work. I am very glad also to be able to include chapters by two of the founder members of the Nafsiyat Inter-Cultural Therapy Centre, Lennox Thomas and Elaine Arnold, who, together with Jafar Kareem, have led the way in inter-cultural thinking. I have tried to present the work in a practical and accessible way, so that people can use the ideas presented in their work setting – I have found that so much of counselling and psychotherapy literature is presented in such a dry, academic way that it is actually quite intimidating and hard to relate to, thus defeating the purpose of communicating with people. In a sense this could relate to a western academic approach, which in some ways perpetuates the exclusive thread which has run through this profession.

The healing properties of the talking therapies are now reaching a much broader spectrum of clientele and are being used in such settings as prisons, social services, the probation service and with disenfranchised groups around the world – I am very pleased to present chapters of working within these areas and others. Here counselling and psychotherapy is no longer adhered to as a religion, with an all-powerful belief system, but as a practical tool that can be adapted to the setting in which it is used and to the culture in which it finds itself. Our multi-cultural society is increasingly demanding that we look at power and spiritual disenfranchisement and that we look at our premises and assumptions. Rather than seeing this as threatening, we can choose to see it as widening our vision and enhancing our practice. As we know as counsellors and psychotherapists, any change requires inner questioning and self-reflection, as well as outer knowledge and action.

Included in this book are nine very varied and original chapters, by people of different races and cultures and working backgrounds. We lost a few contributors on the way due to births, illness and displacement, and the book has changed form in the process, but I hope you will find something stimulating that will be useful in your work and of interest to you. As a way of introduction, I have written a brief synopsis of each chapter. I would like to thank our multi-cultural group of contributors, Isha Mckenzie-Mavinga, Samuel Ochieng, Piers Vitebsky and Sally Wolfe, Wajiha Mohammad, Duncan Lawrence, Pam Williamson, Lennox Thomas, Elaine Arnold and Angus Igwe, for their hard work and co-operation in compiling this book. Isha Mckenzie-Mavinga, a Black British woman of African-Caribbean and European and Jewish heritage, uses the medium of writing as a mirror in her therapeutic work with black women. She runs therapeutic support groups for women affected by domestic violence, has contributed to the provision of alternative therapies for African Caribbean Mental Health and has also worked as an artist in education. She says that she feels that black women have a soul injury caused by patriarchy, slavery and colonialism. Having no therapeutic models to work with in their quest for healing, she feels that black women need to work together in the therapeutic relationship, linked by a common experience and the acknowledgement of common wounds. Through a long process, Mckenzie-Mavinga describes how the difficult work leads to building a positive identity and sense of self, through listening to each other lovingly, turning away from the negative gaze installed by racist images and responding to the eye of the beholder.

The liberation from fear is an important component in Mckenzie-Mavinga's work, and she describes how she uses metaphor as a useful way of locating fear hidden within the texts, and the women are playfully encouraged to face and express their fears in the context of their lives, using their cultural experience and language. Mckenzie-Mavinga says that writing as a therapeutic tool pre-dates psychoanalysis and is a way of understanding the mind, in the same way that writing makes conscious a dialogue with the self and is a way of understanding the internalised self and relationship with others. She feels that it is an opportunity for black women's subjectivity to transfer from the sole attention of her family, to her own self-discovery.

Samuel Ochieng is originally from Kenya, where he trained as a psychologist, and has also lived, worked and trained in counselling in the USA and England. Moving between these cultures, he has found that attempting to apply western psychological concepts to an African setting did not fit and that African cultures and ways of thinking and being needed to be understood in their own right and not be interpreted and translated through western psychological thought. He says that to attempt to mould a person without knowledge of their cultural make-up is to dismiss their heritage – he refers to this as the same mentality as colonisation, where the coloniser brought in his ideas as 'better' and 'more powerful' than those that were inherent in the cultures they colonised.

Ochieng explores important aspects of the African approach to life, including the concept of the group identity, as opposed to the western striving for individuality – how the individual gives meaning to the group and the group gives meaning to the individual – the individual becoming the representation of a clan and carrying with them a tribal and ancestral bonding within them from before birth. He likens African forms of communication with people dead or far away to the western use of the internet, and says that it is essential to understand this natural process of communication that is inherent in a people in touch with nature and who use natural forces for cures and protection as part of the African psychological make-up.

Ochieng gives an overview to the understanding of why witchcraft is a central part of the African psyche. He says that he feels that he is not alone on his journey; his family spirits and clansmen walk with him, to protect him and make themselves known to him on occasion in diverse shapes or forms. To him, it is a deep-rooted energy force outside of the self that may be called on occasionally as a part of natural existence. He likens the merging of the African psychological perspective to stepping into worlds of dualities and has evolved a model that he calls 'Skiatism', which incorporates both western and African thought. Here, symbols are used, just as with Jung, and understood in the 'language' that it is being presented in, so that when an individual appears in the counselling room they bring with them their entire family, both alive and dead. He feels that when working from an African framework a counsellor must acknowledge different realities as a way of life and understand problems in this perspective.

Piers Vitebsky and Sally Wolfe are a husband and wife team, with a Jewish and white British/Scottish/Irish background, respectively – working in Cambridge. Vitesbsky is an anthropologist and Wolfe is a counsellor and inter-cultural therapist, and they have been working together for several years, establishing a counselling service in Yakutsk, Siberia. There they have been working with the Sakha and Even, indigenous peoples who have become psychologically disenfranchised by the engulfing Russian Soviet Union. Vitebsky's experience as an anthropologist and Wolfe's experience as an inter-cultural therapist have been pooled to gain an understanding of the politics, the different cultures, the languages and how to work with the particular problems facing these people.

They have found that some of the standard western procedures, such as assessment, referral and supervision, were largely unknown and they have worked on presenting these procedures for possible adaptation to their setting. Vitebsky and Wolfe discuss at length the impact of the setting in which the counselling is done on the actual therapeutic work, so that the activity is not seen in a void, but rather organically moulded by its setting. Though not many, if any, practitioners reading this piece will be setting up counselling practices in Siberia, some may be attempting to set up counselling practices in diverse communities in Britain or around the world, and I feel a lot can be learned from their work in examining our assumptions and expectations when adapting to counselling in diverse cultural settings.

Having gone through the painful experience of divorce as an Asian woman, Wajiha Mohammad describes at first hand the experience, the stigma, the alienation from her community, the loss of status and poverty she experienced as a single parent. Now a counselling tutor and Ph.D. candidate, studying and working with the effects of divorce on Asian women has become her life's work. The project was her way of resolving her feelings around her divorce, but also to explore the needs of other divorced Asian women and how counselling could be helpful to them.

Mohammad looks at the whole institution of divorce, its implications and relation to societal changes in the western world, and focuses on looking into the attitudes and influences of Islam on divorce and its repercussions. She looks at the effects of divorce on the family unit, especially the children, and explores kinship ties, which are very strong within the Muslim community – economic and material assistance, as well as emotional support, are found in these links. Mohammad's research focuses on six Asian women from a variety of backgrounds, whose experiences form the case studies of her research. She says that although many of her interviewees said they did not require counselling, she felt that they did benefit from off-loading their emotions during the interviews and that there is a need for more education in making Asian women aware of the benefits of counselling. As well as making the recommendation for the employ-ment of more Asian counsellors within mainstream counselling ser-vices, she feels that because white counsellors have limited experience with Asian cultures, they are unable to make the 'therapeutic alliance' with ethnic minority clients, and she gives ten useful recommen-dations for them to build a 'therapeutic alliance' with Asian clients.

Duncan Lawrence is an African-American living and working in Britain. Although growing up in the heart of the civil rights move-ment in the USA in the 1960s and experiencing racism on a daily basis, he was accused of having the 'white man's disease' by a mem-ber of the Inupiaq peoples of Kotzebue, Alaska, when he worked as a village volunteer trainer in the 1980s. Being an urban man and having counselling training that never once looked at issues around working with native peoples left him unprepared for working in this context. When he asked how he could best work with the Inupiaq, he was told by a member, 'get to know our people, they will show you who you are, who their family is and what is wrong or right about them . . . and finally get to know who you are around us.' This statement had a profound effect on Lawrence and his subsequent work in counselling training has led him to work in a way where trainee counsellors can develop skills, knowledge and awareness about their own heritage and assumptions, and gain insight into how this may impact on others of different racial and cultural heritage.

Lawrence makes the point that counselling and psychotherapy are not separate from the rest of society and that one of the important reasons why racial and cultural issues have not been embraced in the counselling world is the same as elsewhere – the quest for power. Schools of counselling and psychotherapy very often wish to maintain the position of disseminating absolute truths and to hold on to this power. Often, being challenged as to their models being eurocentric has proved quite threatening to the lofty power position. Lawrence maintains that, though he does not want to throw the baby out with the bath water, so to speak, for training settings to actively promote worldwide ideas, those who originally made the rules will have to give up their power positions in order to unlock human potential together. While considering models of the self in counselling, which Lawrence describes as mostly eurocentric, he has developed a model of the self which he calls 'The Human Diversity Model of Self'.

Pam Williamson, who is white and British, has worked in London prisons for sixteen years and is currently a staff counsellor at Wandsworth Prison, and it is within this setting that her clinical work in this chapter is based. Her interest in working with cultural diversity has arisen from the increasingly large numbers of black prisoners within the prison system and also the employment of a more culturally diverse workforce. Williamson's philosophy of counselling accommodates different worldviews and values, holding the client's safety by the relationship, which depends on their cultural norms, not hers. To do this, she says that she needs to know something of the client's culture so that she can help them to face what is difficult. She explores how the search for meaning gives rise to values, which roots in our family culture, religious beliefs and the context in which we find ourselves.

Williamson has been involved with race relations training in Wandsworth in which the staff have been sensitised to and interested in other cultures through the means of food and religions. This helped them in their sensitivity towards inmates from different cultures. She uses four very interesting case vignettes within her chapter, two where she gets it 'wrong' and two where she gets it 'right'. I personally did not feel that there was right and wrong involved, only learning to work with different issues, but for the reader it could be very encouraging to see that others, even experts, flounder too. Williamson focuses on the themes of loss and traumatic stress in three case studies she presents from her work, and this seems to be particularly relevant when counselling in a culturally diverse setting that includes some minority ethnic staff who may have experienced many types of losses and are likely to have suffered traumatic stress reactions in response to harassment, misunderstanding and discrimination. She feels that if she continues to keep cultural diversity in the foreground of her work, then she will remain receptive and learn from the richness that cultural diversity can bring.

Lennox Thomas, originally from Grenada, worked as a probation officer for nineteen years. During this period, he also trained as a psychotherapist and began working with Jafar Kareem in developing ideas in intercultural therapy. Upon the death of Jafar Kareem in 1992, Thomas took over the directorship of the Nafsiyat Inter-Cultural Therapy Centre for the next seven years. Thomas says that Nafsiyat, which was set up to provide a specialist service for black and minority clients, was soon receiving referrals from the courts for assistance with offenders, thus pushing the staff with forensic experience to reconsider psychoanalytical application in relation to the meeting of the judicial system process with race, culture, social context and counselling. They realised that they needed to look at a whole picture of a person who had offended against the law.

So began Thomas' interest in working psychotherapeutically with offenders. In his chapter he discusses the different approaches between traditional psychoanalytical therapy and more adapted forms for working with offenders – experts in the field of offender therapy have highlighted the difference between a theory based on neurosis and its inadequacy for working with those who have anti-social tendencies. He also explores the effects of racism on young black British-born people; whereas their parents were generally hardworking and religious, the younger generation often struggle in an antisocial way with a system in which they find themselves at the bottom of the pile.

Elaine Arnold, originally from Barbados, began her involvement with social work as a response to being a primary schoolteacher in the West Indies. Her experience as a teacher led her on to a preference for working with the whole context in which people function, with their developmental stages and also with the impact of social factors which affected their well-being and that of their families. In her chapter Arnold explores the context of social work, its historical background, the function of social services in Britain and, together with the social planning tasks of the social worker, Arnold focuses on their role as a counsellor.

As well as the need for introspection from the social worker, Arnold explores another important factor – the distrust which poor and disadvantaged clients may have towards the well-educated and middle-class social worker. A black client may doubt whether a white social worker could ever understand their experience of discrimination, and a white client presented with a black social worker may fall into social stereotypes and feel that the worker is inferior. Arnold says she feels that the powerful social factors which impinge on the individual cause severe pain and that prejudice, racism, poverty and discrimination are very real to the client, especially people of ethnic minorities, and must be taken into account in the process of counselling. Some of the important inter-cultural tools that Arnold explores are the use of interpreters, work with attachment theory, where separation and loss are involved, and the self-development of the social worker.

Angus Igwe is a counsellor and supervisor originally from Nigeria, now living and working in Hampshire, a predominantly white, middle-class county. His minority status has meant that the majority of clients/supervisees, looking for a black male counsellor/supervisor, are referred to him. In his chapter Igwe focuses on working with the impact of race and culture in the supervision process. He says that working with these racial/cultural interfaces has given him a wide field of exposure to both organisational and individual cross-cultural issues.

Igwe says that he feels that many supervisors are aware of the impact of the supervision process, but that there is a difference between this and having a real awareness which leads to a reduction in the inappropriate use of certain models of supervision, and that the lack of this real awareness is dangerous. He says he believes that real awareness becomes a process of examining and changing principles and beliefs where and when necessary, and stresses the importance of examining entrenched beliefs.

References

Arnold, E. (1998) 'Issues of Reunification of Migrant West Indian Children in the United Kingdom', in J. Roopnarine and J. Brown (eds) *Caribbean Families – Diversity Among Ethnic Groups*. London: Jai Press.

Dupont-Joshua, A. (1994) 'Inter-Cultural Therapy'. *Counselling Journal* 5 (3), August.

Kareem, J. (1978) 'Conflicting Concepts of Mental Health in a Multi-Cultural Society'. *Psychiatrica Clinica* 11: 90–95.

Kareem, J. and Littlewood, R. (1992) *Intercultural Therapy*. Oxford: Blackwell Scientific Press.

Thomas, L. (1992) 'Racism and Psychotherapy', in J. Kareem and R. Littlewood *Intercultural Therapy*. Oxford: Blackwell Scientific Press.

Chapter 2

Creative writing as healing in black women's groups

Isha Mckenzie-Mavinga

For two black women to enter an analytic or therapeutic relationship means beginning an essentially uncharted and insecure journey. There are no prototypes, no models, no objectively accessible body of experience other than ourselves by which to examine the specific dynamics of our interactions as black women. Yet this interaction can affect all other psychic matter attended profoundly. It is to scrutinise that very interaction that I sought you out professionally, and I have come to see that it means picking my way through our similarities and our differences, as well as through our histories of calculated mistrust and desire. . . . I can't tell you how many good white psychwomen have said to me, 'Why should it matter if I am black or white?' Who would ever think of saying, 'Why does it matter if I am female or male?' I don't know who you are in supervision with, but I bet it's not with another black woman.

I have troubled areas of self that will be neither new nor problematic to you as a trained and capable Psychperson. I think you are a brave woman and I respect that, yet I doubt that your training can have prepared you to explore the tangle of need, fear, distrust, despair and hope which operates between us, certainly not to the depth necessary. Because neither of us is male or white, we belong to a group of human being that has not been thought worthy of that kind of study. So we have only who we are, with or without the courage to use those selves for further exploration and clarification of how what lies between us as black women affects us and the work we do together.

(Lorde 1984: 161)

In this excerpt from a letter written by the late Audre Lorde to her therapist, she shares her thoughts about setting up a therapeutic relationship with another black woman. Audre published the letter herself, sharing her feelings, much empathised with by other black women when journeying into therapy, particularly where the therapist may also be a black woman. It is the awareness, understanding and connectedness with the black woman's experience that fundamentally contributes to her healing. As we share Audre Lorde's writing we can see how black women sharing through writing become facilitators of each other's healing. Through similar experience black woman may have the disposition to facilitate each other's healing, yet we are faced with our different yet similar wounds. It is these contradictions that create the conditions for healing. As we enter into the dynamic that separates us we enter into the dynamic that bonds us, and unrequited love becomes a thing of the past.

Words that cannot be said may be written, even between the lines

In this chapter I shall be sharing with you how the practice of creative writing in a therapeutic group setting has enabled black women to share and heal their stories. I am using the term "black" to identify women of colour who have African and Asian origins. The majority of women attending are from African and Caribbean backgrounds. Many of them have inherited mixtures but identify as black. My empathy with black women emanates from the duality of race and gender oppression that we suffer.

In these groups I use the ethos that words which cannot be said may be written, even between the lines. The work I do is influenced by the writers I have mentioned, particularly the research of Carole Boyce Davies who addresses the issue of 'oppression of self'. The idea of black women coming together is based on the intention to heal the 'oppression of self' through the mirroring of responses to similar oppressions attached to the experience of blackness and femaleness.

The effects of patriarchy, slavery and colonialism have meant that the black woman inheriting the trauma of these experiences may be subjected to oppression of self over long periods of time. This 'oppression of self' more commonly known as 'internalised oppression' is a recurring theme within the transcultural debate.

As Lorde says, *'Why should it matter if we are black or*

White?' (ibid.) For as we choose each other we are making the decision to heal. Not only does our maternal and menstrual bleeding bond us; the blood of slavery and racism also bonds us. As sisters, mothers and lovers. Without this coming together we are forever waiting to address our likeness, differences, our blackness and womanhood. In addition to this bonding, issues of separation and loss can be re-experienced and processed during groupwork.

The use of writing as a tool for healing

On cathartic writing Gillie Bolton says,

> This is when you shout or weep onto the page. You may be gripped by anger, pain, hurt, or fear. You may be feeling incomprehension at what life has dealt you, or guilt or shame or remorse or anxiety. Or you may need to shout what you think from the soapbox of your diary. So often there is nothing we can do with these extreme human emotions, except break a window, hurt someone else or knead some bread (this makes excellent bread, since the more it is knocked about, the better it tastes). None of these deal with the feelings; they only release the pressure.
>
> (G. Bolton 1999: 39)

Literature research suggests that way back in the eighteenth century creative writing appeared to act as a means of catharsis and a potential tool for healing trauma and emotional hurt. Phillis Wheatley, an African who was enslaved at the age of eight years old, was said to have expressed her feelings of loss of her family and homeland and the brutality of slavery through her writing:

> Should you my lord, while you peruse my song
> wonder from whence my love of freedom sprung.
> Whence flow the wishes for the common good?
> by feeling hearts alone best understood,
> I young in life, seeming some cruel fate
> Was snatched from Afric's fancied happy feat.
> What pangs excruciating must molest,
> What sorrows labour in my parent's breast?
> Steel'd was that soul and by no mistry moved
> That from my father seized his babe beloved,

Such, such my case. And can I then but pray
Others may never feel this tyranny sway?
(Phillis Wheatley, in Sheilds 1988: 74)

Careful analysis of Phillis Wheatley's writing by Sheilds has
shown that she survived from one poem to the next, sharing and
expressing her story. Similar forms of survival through the expression of writing may be seen in centuries of literature produced by
other black women. Their writing has given me the impetus to bring
the experience of healing and writing together in the development
of therapeutic writing groups.

Jackie Holder, in her book *Soul Purpose* on 'The Art of Writing'
expresses how sharing through writing assisted her healing:

> Part of my healing, as I wrote *Soul Purpose*, was the realisation
> that I was not alone, that to all intents and purposes everything
> had been said and done before. But it had not been said and
> shared by me. It is our collective voices, and all our individual
> stories that really count.
>
> (Holder 1999: 13)

Hearing black women's voices

> Then we know that the oppression-of-self which is the final task
> of all oppression, is in operation. For this reason, I affirm cat-
> egorically the right of Black women to speak out of their many
> realities and be heard out of the variety of their experiences and
> locations. And it is for me there that Black women's writing
> attains its agency.
>
> (Boyce Davies and Ogundipe-Leslie 1995: 7)

This is a quote from Carole Boyce Davies in her book *International
Dimensions of Black Women's Writing*, where she affirms the
expression and strengthening of experience through black women's
writing. She has deduced from her conversations with writers such
as Merle Collins and Beryl Gilroy that they put their own emotions
into their characters in a search for identification and rites of
passage. This creates an expression of African womanhood and
empowerment.

About the groups

Some of the women are accustomed to writing, while others attend the groups because they want to change their lives and feel confident about their writing. It is not a group where the writing itself is under scrutiny. The writing is not judged. The writing is a tool for expression and sharing. The women are required to write within the group and between groups. They are also required to be willing to share their writing and use it for processing and learning how they might change their lives.

Black women usually attend the group to enrich their self-knowledge and retreat into their neglected world of black womanhood. In the shared world of the group, she discovers her visibility and centredness, the depth of her forgiveness and love. A way to cope with inherited attitudes, behaviours and anxieties that she has been burdened with.

Building experience

In my early days as a writer I tutored a class which was particularly challenging. The sessions were set up to attract black women. Although most of the women insisted that they seriously wanted to attend the training, there was consistent lateness which disrupted the sessions. All of them had other pressing concerns that prevented them from attending a full session or completing the whole programme. I challenged them to write about making a space in their lives to write. There were varied responses, but most of them were disturbed by the challenge of rearranging their lives so that they could attend to their own creative needs. We carried out an exercise where I invited them to talk to the thing that was in the way of their rearranging their lives. Most of the women expressed anger at the blockages they were up against: mainly domestic restrictions and lack of family support.

Another difficulty arose when we started to work on issues of language. What languages were we going to use to understand each other? The course was being offered as part of a university curriculum. It included assessment procedures, which led to certification. My eurocentrically trained mind led me to believe that the only way to assess the women's writing was the way that I had been taught myself within the eurocentric education system.

One of the women had begun to create new concepts and

terminology to express her cultural heritage. She was using literary phrases outside of the vocabulary that I was familiar with and words not accessible in the regular dictionary. I anticipated some difficulty with the assessment because there were no reference points within the curriculum from which to understand the language she used to represent her experiences. I asked her to include explanations of the concepts. Some conflict arose between us, which I can now understand. I believe that my response triggered some anxiety related to the experience of institutional racism, where the black woman has to explain and justify her originality to white professionals.

Ten years down the road, I can see how my difficulties with difference between us as black women created separation rather than connectedness. My eurocentric training and my role as an academic tutor created conflict because of the deep need for connection between us as black women. On reflection I now understand how my assimilation into the eurocentric education structures may have been part of the oppression. In order to increase my skills for facilitating with other black women's emotions it was necessary to work through the process of relationship between us. I had to deconstruct my totally eurocentric approach and integrate my understanding of the links between us emanating from our history and socialisation.

I have learned that to support the process of black women's creative writing it is necessary to be open and aware of racial and cultural dynamics that may come between us. Taking for granted that we know each other because we identify as black is not helpful. It is important to have a non-judgemental setting with awareness of our feminine, African or Asian spirituality and personal heritage, also an openness to the diversity and cultural influences which may be expressed through writing. These elements are selectively explored throughout the dynamics in the creative writing groups.

There is a working through and an expression of feelings linked to traumatic experiences of eurocentric socialisation, education and separation from our origins. All this happens within the process of reproducing and discussing each woman's experience in text. The text acts as a means of evidence that feelings and reactions to the experience are no longer hidden. The writing also acts as a means of reflection.

In the excerpt below, Maya Angelou in writing about 'Art for the Sake of The Soul' shares through her writing the contradictions of self-oppression through language and the need for positive reflection for black people.

> Some White people actually stand looking out of their windows at serious snow falling like cotton rain, covering the tops of cars and the streets and fire hydrants and say, 'My God, it sure is a black day'. So black people had to find ways in which to assert their own beauty.
>
> (Angelou 1998: 133)

The struggle for reflection and cultural empathy

In the first instance the women are supported to deal with their issues about writing. Their previous experiences of writing in educational settings were based mainly on the structural components of writing and a pressure to reproduce eurocentric forms of language expression. They complained of lack of sensitivity to the emotional issues of writing. They shared experiences of poor attitude towards learning from their families and carers. In the main they recalled incidents of racism and chastisement. The wounds of education were still festering.

In preparation for the sessions we discussed the act of writing and all that it meant to them. There were issues of secrecy and disclosure. Some women were raised in communities where nothing was sacred, others where they would be scorned for 'washing their dirty linen in public' if they told their stories. There was the issue of shame to write about and deal with, black female shame.

Some women felt scarred by experiences of being put down and discouraged from self-expression in their creative activities, especially writing. One woman told a story of repeated chiding and bigotry from a schoolteacher for being left-handed. She wrote about an incident where she was given detention for asking the teacher for a pair of left-handed scissors in a craft session. Because the teacher made a spectacle of her she became prey to bullying and suffered particularly from racism. She was a bright child who suffered from ignorance and injustice in the education system. These experiences stayed with her, and she developed a distaste for writing and creative activities. Instead she became a workaholic. Prior to joining the group she had listened to some poetry written and produced by some local black women. The performance had moved her to want to write about some of her own experiences as a black woman. She had also remembered some feelings of shame associated with her education. She gained some cultural empathy with the black women performing at the event. She recognised this through her connection with the experiences described in their presentations. This had motivated her to join the therapeutic writing group.

I asked the women questions about exploring emotions in their writing. They wrote about this. They were starting a journey where they would have to write about everything. What did they feel about sharing with others? In the group they were required to break their secrecy and use the help available to express issues of secrecy, disclosure and shame. The explanation of these issues is fundamental to the therapy.

Exploring the subtext and subliminal process

We found that within the subliminal process lay oppressive messages about being black and female. Below is an excerpt from writing by Cecile:

> When I was growing up in Jamaica, I grew up in a very protected environment. I come from the country. I come from a very close family group. My parents worked hard. I had mother and father in the house. That's not always the case at home. I was fortunate that we grew up like a nuclear family and I had a very good education before I left home, which continued here. I am putting this in context. I left boarding school in Jamaica and came to England. I realised later on in my life, that I was never exposed much. I would leave boarding school at the end of term, and go to my aunt before returning to the country. That was as much of the exposure. *Especially if you are a girl child, they wouldn't let you out of their sight they think that you are going to get pregnant. Therefore, I realised that I was not really exposed at all.* So when I went back to Jamaica, there were some areas in Kingston called Shantytown, I visited that I had heard about before but never seen them. So as a black woman returning home I have a responsibility to really go and meet and talk with people in those areas. I may have been more fortunate and had more privileges but they are my people and part of me. I wanted to meet them on their territory, on their ground and not from some lofty heights up there. I asked, could I help in any way? *They*

looked at me with suspicion because my accent is different and they said. 'You come from foreign eh?' I say 'no man I come from Jamaica, I come from down the road'. They say, 'Yea but yu travel, no tru?'

Cecile's writing shows her awareness of internalised cultural messages and identity issues about being a black Jamaican woman who has lived part of her life in England and returned home.

The women are encouraged to work out how some of these internalised messages have turned into behaviour and attitudes that have become harmful to them. They are also supported to research the link with these attitudes and their ancestry. This work is more extensive than traditional European therapies because it pays attention to a whole spectrum of influences which reach back into the woman's heritage. The inherited oppressive messages are linked to all areas of womanhood, including spirituality. We found that some of these messages were hidden between the lines and in the subtext of the writing. It was the discussion of the writing that revealed this.

Below are some excerpts from the discussion, which followed the presentation of Cecile's writing. Cecile spoke about her experience of oppressive messages as a black female. She had been experiencing low self-esteem and this had affected her career. She talks about influences in her relationship to literature, identity issues, and her awareness of internalised cultural messages in black women (I have italicised these issues in the above text).

Cecile: In school, we would read a story and discuss what the author was saying, but then, the teacher would say, 'This is what the author meant' and give their version of the story. At the end of the day, the teacher had the answer. So I grew up believing that everything in the books was true. So even though I was getting good results, I questioned everything that I was doing and I believe this contributed to my low self-esteem.

I always write Black British, Black African, Black Caribbean. I am a bit like a refugee. I don't feel British. In Jamaica where my family come from, they see me as a foreigner. What I am saying is that all three of these identities are important, because I can't say that I am not British, because I am. My family are from Jamaica and originally we came from Africa. I am on a discovery, trying to find out about my heritage.

Isha: I know it raises a lot of issues, for me as well.

Cecile: On my diploma training, a black woman used to streups her teeth [pursing her lips and making a rubbishing sound by sucking air through her teeth.] And a white woman said that she was offended by it. The woman denied that she ever sucked her teeth and changed her body language. Then after the meeting, people came and told her that they thought the woman who challenged her was terrible. I couldn't believe what I was seeing.

Isha: They were colluding with her.

Cecile: They were colluding with her. She was very upset and in supervision I told her that I have seen her do it and more importantly to understand what this is about. *For example, when my mum sucks her teeth, what is she saying, I can't be bothered to talk. Going back to slavery again.* [Cecile links the other woman's experience to her family experience and identifies internalised cultural messages].

Isha: You were not allowed to talk. You would be in trouble.

Cecile: Exactly, we were not allowed to talk, we would be in trouble. And what I notice with black people is that sometimes they are not talking and you can read something on their face. With my sister and me, we do a small glance at each other and we know what we are talking about, we are both thinking the same thing. Sometimes you see somebody kicking their lip up.

This excerpt shows how empathy and experience are shared without speech. This would suggest an ancestral link, which Cecile identifies. Slaves found various ways to send messages to each other when the masters were watching them.

Cecile: This woman was obviously embarrassed about it and tried to deny it, so again, I went back to what was it about, where did it come from.

Isha: Did she talk with you about it in the end?

Cecile: No, even after all that discussion, she said she was not aware of it, and I don't believe her, she must be aware that she does it at home. It's too much of our culture for her not to be aware of it.

Isha: You don't believe her, but you have brought this to her awareness by challenging it, and it's also a common expression, so it's not just about her one doing it. [Here I attempted to bring Cecile's attention to her own issues and link these with the other women's issues.]

Cecile's work brought her in touch with other black women who reflected some of the oppressive behaviours that she was familiar with and had begun to work through herself.

During the group sessions we would use some of these examples to relate to the personal experiences of the women. I asked the women to write down the experience of 'the woman who streupsed' in a humorous way. This helped to highlight some of their own subliminal messages and place them in the context of their history.

We decided that the woman had a vexation which was being triggered by dynamics in the group she was in. She was trying to conceal it with a habit she was accustomed to and declared that she was unaware of. It had become unconscious and therefore part of her normal behaviour. By examining this process we discovered many habits, idiosyncrasies and behaviour patterns that previously the women in the group had concealed, for example, nail biting, lip biting, chewing the cud, throat clearing, blinking, itching, looking over the shoulder, twitching, eye widening, squinting, sniffing armpits, humming, eye rolling. There were other, more intense habits like soap washing, ignoring the doorbell and phone, keeping blinds closed, obsessive cleansing, fear of being seen without hair tidied or make-up on, toning and treating skin to lighten it, wearing black.

Cecile disclosed that she had a habit of responding to conversation with the term 'Uh hum'. In this part of the discussion Cecile began to reveal some of her own subliminal messages and link this realisation to the other women's shared experience of heritage. We went on to write about the anxiety and stress that lay behind the behaviour. Next we traced the experiences which had caused the anxieties.

Cecile: The one that I find more difficult in England is the one where black men find it so hard to stay in a monogamous relationship. Why do they have to go out and have two or three relationships? The children suffer because invariably there are children who suffer in the end because he cannot provide for the children. In Jamaica there's a lot of that going on, but it's more linked to class. Mainly middle- and upper-class women. British classification. They have husbands who have money and a good socio-economic status, but must have two or three women out a street. It is when she finds out that all hell lets loose and it's either, get rid of the other ones or else. More often or not, it's the or else that happens because the man has no intention of changing things, because his friends will laugh at him, because of the macho elements in society, they must be seen to be in charge. Although women are in charge really. So my own anger had a lot to do with relationships with men and their expectations of me. I know I have a strong personality and I was being suppressed. I was being put into a role that is not me, which is the little housewife, staying home and looking after the children. 'Why you want to go after all this education business,' you know? [Cecile revealed that the issue of not being able to talk outlined in her writing had deeper implications. Placing this experience in context helped her to realise that she had always felt not listened to by men.]

In the women's writing it became clear that deeper feelings were not written down. This happened for various reasons: fear, taboo, lack of awareness, and sometimes they edited out issues they felt concerned about sharing. This is like being in a submissive role as a writer. Submission can be linked to unconscious feelings about not valuing yourself.

Finally we made links with characters from folklore, stories and the women's ancestry. One of the folklore characters we discussed was Diablesse. She is characterised as a she-devil with a cloven hoof. She is feared by men and revered by women, as she would seduce and lead straying husbands to their doom. Listening for her cloven foot and the symbol of a cross could thwart her powers. These folklore characters had been passed down through generations of story-telling and shared experience in African village life. Some of the women had grown up with them. The women likened Diablesse to their feelings of anger and revenge at betrayal in relationships: 'All mythology, every fairy tale, expresses the truth of transformation and change – and that therein lies the chance of our own renewal, our making new' (Hartill, in Hunt and Sampson 1998: 49)

Using mythology and folklore enabled the women to visualise

stories and rhymes from their past and endow the characters with their own emotions. The stories could be based on recall or fabrication. The outcome was very positive and transformative in that a lot of ancestral patterns (cultural baggage from the past) were acknowledged. The exercise alleviated the shame and embarrassment the women feel when their behaviour patterns are disclosed. Developing these issues through creative writing seemed a natural process for the women. It gives them a focus for their issues and a useful passage to their emotions. Working with the subtext and subliminal can be likened to working with the unconscious in the writing.

This is what Cecile had to say about her progress in the final group meeting.

Cecile: For a number of years of my life I have allowed myself to be in the submissive housewife role. Now I have woken up. I got out of bed and shook myself and said Cecile, what the hell do you think you are doing to yourself? You cannot be of any value to anyone else unless you value yourself more. And slowly but surely I have begun to work on myself, reclaim myself, take hold of my internal power and I articulated to my partner that I will never be any good to you until I take care of me. My partner said to me, 'that's a very selfish attitude'. I said 'no I think it is a good attitude' and I said 'I think that selfishness in that respect is positive'. I will encourage people to think about the word selfish in a positive way. It is not always negative because when you begin to take care of yourself other people who have difficulty with that say you are selfish and mean it in a negative way. It has to do with deciding to no longer assimilate. It is time to be accepted for me. What makes me angry is when my colleagues say to me, 'I don't see that you are black.' When they say this I am being done a disservice although I know it is their way of saying to me 'you are OK, Cecile'. It is very racist. I used to start feeling very angry and I functioned well as a professional but the more I interacted with white people, from a personal level, anger built up about what has been done to our people and continues to be seen as unimportant. When you think that you have worked through stuff, you discover that you have more to work on. If I go at the racism with a sledgehammer it will not work, so I will continue to chip away at it now I have become more aware.'

Within these deep places, each of us holds an incredible reserve of creativity and power of the unexamined and unrecorded emotion and feeling. For each of us as a woman there is a dark place within, where hidden and growing our true spirit rises. 'Beautiful and tough as chestnut/stanchions against/[y]our nightmare of weakness'.

(Lorde 1984: 36)

Unexamined emotion and description.

Through identifying patterns within their writing, women become aware of their unconscious processes. At this stage the editing out of personal information becomes a thing of the past. The women are encouraged to write in an uncensored way and to include their whole experience. Every woman arrives at a point where she can no longer hide herself. She is opening up. Messages about not sharing, not crying, being the strong woman, can no longer be harnessed within the psyche. The unsaid and unshed has to be revealed. The act of self-disclosure in a safe, confidential setting is a priority in the group process. We must not underestimate the detrimental effects of isolation. (Putting on ice as in the freezing of an emotion.)

There are mountains of issues that have been kept in solitude within the mind of the black woman. Black women have been beaten, ridiculed and starved into silence. In the group, silence is contradicted by the use of description. Description helps with expression.

With mutual support the women have found the courage to describe some of the following issues: Sexual violence, domestic violence, incest, non-heterosexual and non-monogamous sexual practice, addictions, undisclosed anger towards deceased loved ones, experience of colourism, disappointment and betrayal towards loved ones, exclusion from the family and other women when awareness of self develops, detachment from family during the assimilation into patriarchal and European society, the pain and loss of loved ones and elders through immigration and death, menstrual and maternal bleeding, grief and crying, love and relationships, inter-cultural and transcultural relationships, cultural heritage and identity, success and joy, self-expression, racism and sexism.

We found that description opened up the raw elements of an issue and allowed the topic to become shared by others as they began to associate similar experiences.

I have identified three focus areas in the group-writing process.

1   *Thought and fantasy*. The production of free-flowing thought. The women are encouraged to write anything that comes to mind, no matter how outrageous it may appear.

An example of thought and fantasy. Judy wrote about her feelings of loss and family disintegration. Her family had grown out of the habit of meeting every Sunday for a family meal. Judy also wrote about her wish to be like Diana Ross, who has a family yet travels the world as a star and always appears flamboyant. Diana Ross expresses herself through writing, and gains public attention and admiration from thousands of people wherever she goes.

2   *Inspiration or (inspirition)*. Information that is disclosed as a result of discussion about the writing. This is where feelings, the senses and description are given attention.

An example of inspiration. Writing about loss of family inspired Judy to talk about closeness and cultural heritage. Writing about Diana Ross inspired Judy to talk about issues of identity, who she wanted to be and how can she be more of herself? (**Inspiri**tion.) This is the process by which we gain insight and create new ideas and images in our minds. To complete the picture we add feelings and emotions, which allow us to connect with others' experiences. We are then connected spiritually through empathy.

The discussion which started with Judy's wish to be like Diana Ross progressed from inspirition to an examination about what kinds of images about our personalities and lives we try to project on to others and how we attract attention for feelings and emotions. So issues of confidence, assertiveness and depression became paramount. The group worked together on strategies to ask for help, get attention and break isolation, and grow closer to family or friends.

3   *Publication*. The shift from inspiration to publication is similar to the shift from unconsciousness to awareness. The shift is brought about by group relationship with attention to the writing process. Each woman is expected to make this

shift. I hold this as an expectation because in my experience the act of disclosure helps to break through the oppressions. It operates like a coming out, a being more visible.

Publication requires the individual to be explicit. We discussed issues of loss of the family and all the women wrote about their fantasies of Diana Ross.

An example of publication. I requested that the women use their descriptive skills to emphasise the skin characteristics and physical features of the main character within their story and to read out their stories.

Shared reading in the group brought to light the issue of oppression due to difference within the black community and within women's groups. On becoming aware of this issue, Judy revealed her suspicion of me as the facilitator. She linked this acknowledgement to an experience of psychological abuse due to being the darkest in her family. The oppression continued through her working life, and her relationships with other black women had been conditioned by this experience. She also became aware of her fears that I would reprimand or ridicule her in the group as she had experienced in the past. Judy had displayed cautiousness through her writing and we examined this. During the discussions a dynamic began to evolve between myself and Judy which culminated in some annoyance displayed by me in my tone of voice. A group member had noticed my annoyance when speaking to Judy and pointed this out to me. In the moment I had to be real and admit to what seemed like incongruence as a group leader. I discussed the situation in my own supervision and therapy. On returning to the group and acknowledging my part in the dynamic the situation was resolved. The resolution came through attending to the wounds of the past that separate us as black women. My own history of ridicule and pain due to being lighter skinned came to the forefront within that moment of truth. If the truth is not faced then we remain disconnected from each other.

In the previous paragraph I described the effect of publication (in this instance sharing within the group). In the above example publication brought about a shift in the dynamic set-up as a result of colourism. The group supported Judy to break through her difficulties about being noticed. The underlying issue seemed to be her isolation linked to the effects of racism. We also discovered the powerful dynamics of difference within the group and between Judy and myself. Isolation often becomes normal behaviour when someone has been hurt deeply in the past. Isolation is a common factor of mental ill health.

Isolation, blocks and mental health

Each woman has been given an opportunity to break her isolation, and as she adds the experience of others to her own the silences are broken and the group works collectively on the issues.

It is common for women to become stuck because of the intensity and volume of their issues. Many of them have not been used to having the time or attention needed to evaluate the pain in their lives. There has been little time to locate the joy. Their lives have been conditioned by attempts to mask the pain. They have grown used to conforming. Their beauty has been reflected by European stereo-types and weighted against products to make them more female and less black. They have lived in fear of annihilation. It has been dif-ficult to stay clear in thought through the tiredness and striving. This often leads to mental breakdown.

The women in the group were encouraged to share unedited material and write about blocks rather than bulldoze through them, so we used their writing to explore what the blocks were about. Much of the emotional material and terror was harboured within these blocks. I was familiar with this process in my own work as a writer. I rarely feel that my writing is worthwhile. I get distracted easily, I am often faced with my isolation and I know the terror of speaking out. Relief comes with the awareness that others who read my work find affirmation, share in the challenges and connect empathetically with my experiences.

My blocks are the emotional channels to my writing. I am aware that these blocks can lead to emotional distress and bouts of depres-sion, but some of my most creative writing has happened when I have been sick. The challenge is not to get too sick to write. Getting too sick to write brings me close to the edge of madness. Having worked closely with black women using psychiatric care I have become familiar with this experience.

Some of the women had experiences of the mental health service which had impacted on their lives. The issue of medication, depres-sion and being shut up for life were subjects of their writing. This was revealed in descriptions of attack and fear of annihilation. Some of the women believed that they were driven mad while in psychiatric care. Others believed that they were depressed by the oppressions they experienced throughout their lives. Mental breakdown was a common family experience. They had very little knowledge of the treatments they had been given and of the long-term effects of medication. I continued to encourage the women to write about anything. They revealed through their writing that they had rarely encountered opportunities to discuss mental health issues. Their awareness came by realising that they had previously felt helpless in their relationships with statutory organisations. Many of the women had immediate or second-hand experience of racist or domestic violence and murder to someone whom they knew. These experiences lay at the core of their distress and they had been harbouring a lot of fear due to this.

It is not always easy to have a clear mind, and writing became a way of clearing the mind. With each new bout of awareness the women expressed feeling more centred and confident. The lid had been raised on stored emotions and the healing had begun. Within the mire of hopelessness and raised awareness was the continuous striving for an understanding of self and a wish to feel comfortable with identity.

Search for self and the black female gaze

It could be said that black women return their personal and collective 'gaze' through writing, and that their writing acts as a medium for the shared experience of racism and sexism. It also assists in the expression of their particular, interracial and gender experience.

It is clear that responses to black self-image have become distorted by a negative gaze installed by racist images and responses in the eye of the beholder, a process that was normalised in the main by education and upbringing. The effects of this negative gaze may be considered endemic in the relationship dynamics of black people in the western world. Here we have to consider issues of past reflection, internalisation and renewed reflection. The group writing process assists the renewal of the gaze and of a positive black identity. Women attending the group have realised that they have been living in fear of exposure and repercussion. The danger of truth about their history and upbringing.

The search for self begins with the black woman's connection to others. Building identity is an essential part of this. There are many stories to tell and each must be listened to lovingly. Words to express the self have been dressed in the unfamiliar. Affection has been disguised as sexualisation. Black Women have had to barter for real love.

Within Alice Walker's writing of 'Possessing the Secret of Joy' (in Adams 1996: 169) is an example of discovering self after the trauma of sexualisation, through a process of reflection and writing it out. In the story, Tashi has a recurring dream signifying the experience of genital mutilation. Tashi eventually consults a fantasy therapist 'Jung'. She repeatedly returns to the scene of her trauma, and a world where she can express the secrets of pain and desexualisation is portrayed. It appears that the writer's 'better world' is achieved through her character's story. Women in the group find their better world through the process of sharing and writing.

Mother tongue

During the process of sharing and writing the women are encouraged to give their characters a global experience of language. I encourage them to use any languages that they have been familiar with throughout their lives. The reason that I focus on language is because it has been one of the ways in which we have been oppressed. During the process of slavery the tongues of our ancestors were psychologically tied. Slaves were not allowed to communicate in their native languages. They were not allowed to use their African names, so they became distanced from their origins. Their communication was conditioned by enslavement, but they found ways to express themselves. Colonisation and assimilation have perpetuated the suppression of language. The black woman's search for self is embroiled in language differentiation.

The women shared a range of African languages, including Spanish, French and patois. Their language becomes a signifier of their repressed experience. Many of the women can recall the time when they or their parents arrived in Britain. I encourage them to associate the period in their lives when they were ordered to speak proper Queen's English and suppress their mother tongue. They are also encouraged to identify symbols and reflect on images within their writing. In doing this they are able to explore between the lines. What has not been written becomes shared and expressed. The writing becomes a vehicle for shared experience and this process mobilises collective healing.

The women are encouraged to rewrite their story in their own languages and to include the expressions of anger and fear that they associate with their experiences. The story becomes redrafted and through collective processing the group takes ownership of the story. It becomes a shared experience and not an isolated one.

Beka had shared a piece of prose that she had written. During the discussion, some angry feelings were located that she had not specifically identified in her work. Women in the group also noticed that there were voice changes when she verbalised her anger. She lapsed into patois, her mother tongue.

> Every black woman in America lives her life somewhere along a wide curve of ancient unexpressed anger. My black woman's anger is a molten pot at the core of me . . . a boiling hot spring likely to erupt at any point, leaping out of my consciousness like a fire on the landscape. How to train that anger rather than deny it has been our major task of life.
>
> (Lorde 1984: 152)

Lorde aptly writes about the boiling pot of anger.

Women in the group are encouraged to express their anger and overcome the denial of their need for each other and their shared traditions and stories. Lorde suggests the writing acts as a medium for closeness to others. This is the premise from which I encouraged the women to explore their anger. In the above example, Beka was aware that she did not use her mother tongue in situations where she was in the minority as a black woman, such as while she was at work. She was able to switch into patois when she felt a degree of familiarity in the group she was in. She had been operating this method of censoring and selective expression for as long as she could remember. Her parents communicated in a similar way. It had become normal. What was new for her was the realisation that strong emotions such as anger were attached to her voice changes. The group sharing of their own experiences of language and emotion supported her new awareness of self-expression. This was a useful way to locate and explore patterns of concealed feelings such as anger. Her parents, who also expressed themselves in patois when excited or angry, influenced Beka, a gaze through which she learned how to assimilate her language. The search for self is wrapped up in the experience of the gaze (the way we see ourselves based on images reflected to us by other people).

Metaphor and liberation from fear

Like the gaze, the expression of fear is discouraged. Fear is con-
tagious; if one person shows it others will follow. Fear has led to
prejudice, challenge, power, rebellion, revolution, madness and
death. There is great fear of expressing fear. Like a revolving door
these experiences lead to more fear. We are used to dressing up fear
to make it presentable; we disguise it with laughter, embarrassment,
smiles, game playing, shyness, hesitation, lateness, avoidance,
irrational thoughts, sickness and bizarre behaviour often mistaken
for madness.

The therapeutic nature of the groups has enabled available support and concentrated attention to feelings. Using metaphor has
been a useful way of locating fear. Unless there is a disaster, fear is
often disguised or dressed up in everyday life, like the censoring of
language in Beka's experience.

In the groups we approach fear from two directions. First, I ask
the women to underline places in each other's text where fear might
be hidden. Then I ask the owner of the text to create metaphors for
the fearful experience. This enables the women to face any possibility
of unexpressed fears in their writing.

Metaphor is a playful way of confronting an issue that a woman
may be well rehearsed in distancing herself from. She is playfully
encouraged to face and express her fears in the context of her life.
Again I encourage the women to use the full range of their cultural
experience and language. There are many folklores, tales and invoca-
tions which link fearful experiences culturally. The women are
encouraged to invent their own metaphors for fear. After this exercise,
the women are given an option to work more deeply on their fears.

> For we have been socialised to respect fear more than our own
> needs for language and definition, and while we wait in silence
> for that final luxury of fearlessness, the weight will choke us.
>
> (Lorde 1984: 44)

Healing and the final draft

The final draft must include details of each woman's attempts to
challenge and change the role to which she became accustomed after
the experience that made her suppress her feelings. Thus the group
can reflect each member's process to empowerment.

In the therapy groups women are encouraged to tell their story using memory, fantasy, myth or wish. Again I encourage them to use characters from familiar stories, folklore, poetry, songs and dreams. This is a way of linking history with the present. The approach also helps the women to heal through common experience. The isolation is broken and they are encouraged to look outward towards more positive relationships in their lives, rather than solely inward concerning their pain and depression.

It works because lyric, verse, invocation, ritual and oral traditions belong in the heritage of the black woman. Her search for self is affirmed by the experience of her ancestors and these methods of expression that they too used to tell the story and heal their pain. The recognition of writing as a therapeutic tool predated psychoanalysis and was a way of understanding the mind. In the same way that writing makes conscious a dialogue with the self, it is self-conscious. It is a way of understanding the internalised self and our relationship with others. It is a journey from the unconscious to the conscious. It is a journey from silence to language. The journey from ignorance to recognition, from the margins to the centre. It is an opportunity for the black woman's subjectivity to be transferred from the sole attention of her family to her own self-discovery.

It is clear that the process of therapeutic writing has helped black women towards a greater understanding of themselves and their coping skills. It has worked as a tool for reflective process and a means of externalising hidden messages which create low self-concept. Through this process she has become more visible.

These issues are raised as weekly themes for writing and discussion. Each woman presents her own experience of the issue. I challenge the women to exaggerate and make up whatever they cannot recall. This helps with any blocks. Then conversion happens. This is where they exchange the bad experiences for joyful ones. They are encouraged to use the group to turn the situation around. Many have developed hopelessness patterns. Some believe that this is the sum total of their reality and that it will never change. Through fantasy writing they become aware of how much control they have in managing their own stories. We invent and write about rituals that help to eliminate pain. What makes it work is the sharing, acknowledgement and guidance that happens in the group. The experience once shared becomes the common language of oppression and expression. Celia Hunt in *The Self On The Page* says that writing in itself without a collective, reflective process may not be therapeutic (Hunt and Sampson 1998: 184).

The exercises shared in this chapter are not exclusive to therapeutic work with black women. I have used them with mixed racial and mixed gender groups. I have presented the work with black women to show how working actively with a shared experience functions to assist healing. In diverse groups there has to be a common theme to generate collective empathy. The disposition of black women's groups shows that there is likely to be collective empathy present as the group starts with the shared experience of race and gender. In other situations the starting point would depend on other factors.

> For me then the act of writing is an act of resistance, a drive towards self-knowledge as I locate my voice in relationship to my community, the Caribbean, Africa and the world. As a woman, writing is part of my refusal to be completely trounced by male dominated culture; as a black person it is part of my resistance to being fascinated and tyrannised by the brute power of European and Euro-American Philistinism.
>
> Marion Bethel, in Boyce Davies and
> Ogundipe-Leslie 1995: 78)

Other applications

The organising of selected groups always raises questions about discrimination and openness to difference. Readers may wish to know how the work that has been done with black women facilitated by a black female, can be applied to other types of therapeutic writing groups, Such as those with a mixture of black and white participants, or where the culture and identity of the therapist is different from that of the group members.

The starting point in any transcultural setting will require the facilitator to be aware of their cultural heritage and of the oppressions that operate about difference. The British education system, history and the influences of the Empire on writing and self-expression can be a useful starting point. This must be done without assuming a hierarchy of learning and literacy. The majority of participants, whether black or white, male or female, will have been influenced by British culture, whereas each group member will have their own personal history of race and gender issues to share in their writing. It is important to find ways to assist each individual to present their own history and experiences.

Second, many of the issues dealt with in this chapter are not exclusive to the black woman's experience. There will be troubled pasts influenced by war, disaster, immigration, loss and the influence of eurocentric society. On the other hand, there may not be a duality oppression of gender and race. All this and more can be expressed and explored through the text. In some cases there may be empathy within similar experiences, while at other times the differences – especially if interracial or gender-based – may provoke discomfort and feelings of inadequacy for both the participants and the facilitator.

Both black and white people are hurt by racism either as a victim or as a member of the oppressor group. Writing as a tool for healing can be useful for anyone within a diverse group. It is the contradiction of that difference which can provide a 'who am I?' predicament.

The pressure to conform to the predominant status quo can be challenged and supported by writing it out from the standpoint of each individual's experience and personal history. Participants can be encouraged to share experience of difference and ownership through language and images. Gaelic, Norwegian, German, Cockney, Northern or whatever significant codes of communication are fundamental aspects of writing out the lives of individuals: experiences of war and refuge from Eastern Europe and Africa, the commonalities of religion, festival and ritual, the links between myth, folklore and fairy-tale, intergenerational conflict and threads that bind members as citizens of the world. All these aspects of personal and social development can be useful focus points for expression through writing in a mixed group. It is important to use each focus point as a stepping stone for the next piece of writing, which can then be explored, redrafted and used as a reflective healing tool for each individual.

Acknowledgements

Thanks to Joyce Thompson and Beryl Coley.

References

Adam, M. (1996) *The Multicultural Imagination*. London: Routledge.
Angelou, M. (1998) *Even The Stars Look Lonesome*. London: Virago.

Bolton, G. (1999) *The Therapeutic Potential of Creative Writing*. London: Jessica Kingsley.

Boyce Davies, C. and Ogundipe-Leslie, M. (1995) *International Dimensions of Black Women's Writing*. London: Pluto Press.

Holder, J. (1999) *Soul Purpose*. London: Piatkus.

Hunt, C. and Sampson, F. (1998) *The Self on The Page*. London: Jessica Kingsley.

Lorde, A. (1984) *Sister Outsider*. New York: The Crossing Press.

Sheilds, J. (1988) *The Collected Works of Phillis Wheatley*. Oxford: University Press.

Chapter 3

Working with an African perspective in counselling practice

Samuel Ochieng

The subject of cross-cultural counselling seems to buckle the very institutions that western counselling psychology methods are based upon. For this reason it is approached with caution and trepidation by those of the 'more conforming' schools of thought. What I will attempt to do in this chapter is to open doors and show that the fears are due to misconceptions. Leading through this train of thought is that the banner of 'political correctness' should not be upheld by those who do not embrace the concept of differences within counselling formats and to accept that they have been caught short in this area. Freud, Maslow, Jung, Rogers, Millinowski, Fechner, Bell, Binet, etc. all had a good understanding of the psychology of their worlds and are to be credited in every sense for the schools of thought they left behind. In no manner or form are these figures and their institutions denied any due recognition. At the same time, there needs to be the acceptance that the world is now a smaller place, people travel faster, information is more readily available and communication takes place at the touch of a button. In our present age one wonders why more counsellors have not been taught the psychological perspectives of the likes of Soyinka, Ogot, Mboya, Akuti, Obeyeaekere, Marambi Ani, Nkruma and Saro Wiwa. There are many more who can be mentioned who are not of the eurocentric mode. It should also be mentioned that long before the European cultures 'discovered' 'counselling psychology' to the rest of the world, it was a functional practice within non-European models. At the same time it should also be appreciated that the process of counselling also existed in European cultures before the schools of thought made it into a formalised text, to enable the eurocentric existence to become a formal labelling method.

We are in the year 2002, and the aim of this chapter is to produce a 'wake-up' call to present-day counsellors, therapists, psychologists and related fields that there is a broadening of interest in difference, as opposed to the current labelling. Here would be a good starting point for our journey towards understanding a different approach from an African context. It is like sampling 'different flavours'. Many streets in Britain today have, along with the traditional pubs, many cafés, Chinese and Indian restaurants, burger bars and Afro-Caribbean products in supermarkets. A whole variety of differing dishes supplied from different places. The secret of appreciation is to sample a taste. Whether or not one likes the taste is a different matter. At least they will have something to compare it to and they will remember the flavours, whether appealing . . . or not. Not having sampled a taste and saying that you have no liking or disliking for it is pointless. When enquiring about a counselling approach that will give some understanding of an African view in the western counselling world, there should be a focus towards the fusing of western ideas and African belief systems, which are surrounded in witchcraft, possession, soul travel and genes.

To attempt to apply the western psychological perspective straight into the African setting is to miss the understanding of different individuals. It may be taken to mean that African cultures cannot be understood in their own right and therefore need to be translated through interpretation of western thought; a process that dismisses the whole process of communication. On the other hand, to attempt to understand the psychological make-up of an individual without any knowledge of their cultural make-up is to dismiss cultural heritage – a process that is currently prominent in counselling approaches to non-western clients.

There has been the process of modelling, where non-western concepts and attitudes were referred to in western terms and not understood in their own right. This was the same mentality of colonisation, whereby the coloniser brought in his ideas as 'better' and more 'powerful' than those that were inherent in the cultures they colonised. In blind appreciation, those colonised accepted the 'power' of the coloniser and in turn 'gave away' their own, a belief in an illusion that still carries on, some three hundred years after the first encounter with the coloniser. What was forgotten or misguided in the transformation was the 'truth of the matter'. That was the ancestral identity of the culture. Those colonised strove for the power of their colonisers through their materialistic ends. This ultimately created a confusion and fragmented an identity, a problem of today's reality in a eurocentric existence.

In an attempt to recapture a cultural past in terms of meaning, and carry that into a western setting without losing the identity of that meaning, there needs to be an approach on common grounds, beyond translation, power and the 'colonised mind'. In its application towards African consciousness, there has to be an understanding of the interrelationships of symbolism that are being used, and to rework the symbols of similarity in both African and western psychological approaches. This chapter will examine the possibility of a format that can be used towards the comprehension of an already existing African psychology, come to understand its symbolism, and demonstrate how this can be used to understand the processes that occur in therapy without interpretational biases.

First and foremost, most symbols have diversification because they are viewed from a cultural perspective. They are culturally orientated and culturally formulated. However, there are those that are inherent in all human beings and therefore become transculturally formulated. The process of simplified communication is the very basis, through working with symbols. Take the idea of travelling through different countries without understanding the languages and cultures. The first thing that comes to the mind is that things are different and that one is away from 'items of association and similarity', the strongest being food and then language. There is another part that reaches further than the 'outer person': the feeling of being separated from a common bonding, a 'psychic pool'. The harsher this separation is, the greater the fragmentation of this bonding and the more the individual feels 'alone'. This is a basic part of being human. The 'reality' of an individual depends upon how that individual bonds with his cultural surroundings. An example of this would be sewing a patchwork. Each piece is sewn in to form a flowing pattern. However, if a piece is be sewn in which does not blend in, it stands out. If this was then torn from the patchwork, it might damage itself and the surrounding patches.

In terms of an African consciousness as a part of being, there is a part of the individual that carries not only their personal expectations, but also the expectations of the immediate family, the extended family and the clan. In this, the individual becomes a representative of the clan and not the 'individual' as understood in a western model. The individual is a part of a greater whole; that is, they themselves represent the whole and, at the same time, when it is encompassed within the whole, it gives more meaning to that representation. In this manner, although the individual is in other cultural surroundings which are vastly different from their own, and they are physically 'alone', they are not alone on a 'psychic plane', for they carry an ever-present tribal and ancestral bonding instilled in them from birth. This concept goes further than that of individual identity, which is the main focus in western psychology.

Within the African consciousness, time and place is expanded infinitely and 'here' and 'now' take on different meanings. Communication becomes faster than the Internet; the Internet being a western mechanism for what the African has been doing for centuries, namely communicating through the means of 'electrical pulses' with people not immediately, physically present; as also many cultures that are outside of the western concept of time, space and being are able to do. It is beyond the wording of psychic communication, a labelling that applies only to western thought processes. To attempt to give a 'proper' label to the term, in a western context, the 'true' meaning is lost. Therefore, in not having a suitable western reference, the closest label would be 'psychic', which then becomes an interpretation and not the actual process. This begs the question: How does one explain a 'natural' process of communication between those who are in tune with nature, to those who are so out of tune with their own bodies that they suffocate the very life force that feeds them? This then becomes the important focus point when beginning to understand the African psychological make-up. Understand this and one begins to understand the 'language' that is being spoken without interpretation. When an African says they have spoken to a relative who is either dead or far away, this is not dementia, paranoia or schizophrenia. It is a fact. A fact of an ancient past that must be understood in it own right. This is the 'food'. As I said before, in a strange land, the first notable items are not the people but the food and the language.

I would like to like to pause and reflect upon a memory. Many years ago when I was in San Diego, I remember a friend of mine with whom I had travelled, and it was his first visit to the United States. He had remarked about the food and said that it had neither taste nor texture. I told him that it was indeed different, and that soon he would get used to it. Several months elapsed and the subject of food invariably recurred. Obviously, the conversation went back to the earlier conversation, and my friend said that he would ask his relatives to send him some ingredients for 'real' food. After a month or so the ingredients came and were used heartily, and yet to my friend there was still something missing. He decided that he would have a small gathering at his apartment to make more of an occasion of this event. Now, food has a particular attraction, and soon, from a small group we had a full-fledged party, which my friend enjoyed tremendously, eating and reminiscing about Kenya – home. The point here is that my friend was lonely and had to reaffirm his cultural bonding, and the mechanism that was used was food.

Just a thought . . . .

Now in this strange and different land, another element that came to light was that everyone ate separately, sat separately and that there is a strange emphasis on the individual – that concept of 'I'. The African is never 'alone', so everything that is done is done in a communal manner. Eating takes place with members of the family or 'family' – those who are close enough to be considered brothers and or sisters, although they do not share the same parents or household. This is other than the extended family. In the traditional manner, each takes a portion from a common plate and in some cases shares a plate with each member. There is a closeness that this brings which only those who have shared a meal in this manner can relate to. It is a complete submission of trust, acceptance and a bonding that surpasses the thought of 'I' as a single entity. There is a group presence and a binding bond not just with the meal, but also with the process of eating. Each member is a 'fractile', giving the group a greater meaning, and in turn the group acknowledges that without that particular individual there would be a missing component, although in itself the group would be complete.

In order to come to terms with the processes that make up the African 'psyche', a eurocentric model must accommodate the inevitable fact that in the twenty-first century the psychologist/counsellor or therapist will have to take on a whole different set of rules. The plate upon which the food is served is still round, but the meal is 'different', and therefore the manner in which it is eaten is also different. The taste of the meal may be 'familiarly strange'.

The African in Europe, as in all other non-European cultures, gives a complexity to a structure that has been self-generating for generations. The eurocentric model is eurocentric because it is in Europe. One does not enter another's house and immediately rearrange the furniture. Take this concept outside of this container and it ceases to function, at least in its normative form. In the same manner, add anything, any ingredient to it and it will measure that ingredient by the only measuring tool it has, the alternative being that it will classify any irregularities as an anomaly, to which it will set a label that best suits its institutions. On a functional and logical level, there is nothing wrong with this. This is how systems cope with people, the operative word being people. They relate to what they know, and that which is unknown to them or uncomfortable to them is treated with suspicion. However, 300 years is a long time to be suspicious and a lot of mislabelling. As with anything, at first there will be mistakes, then lessons are learned, and more mistakes and so on. But with each mistake we should learn more, become more familiar, be less frightened, and at some point there is a shift from guest to a member of the household. . . . Or is it a case of the guest who has overstayed his or her welcome? If this is so, then we have learned nothing and nothing has been understood.

Up to this point, I have been using the term 'African' in a very general sense. I will attempt to be more specific. The make-up of the African continent comprises some hundreds of languages and thousands of dialects, offering many other complexities. A prime example would be a place like Kenya. It is approximately five times the size of the United Kingdom. It embraces some fifty tribes inherent to the country and a multitude of dialects. It is not uncommon for an urbanised Kenyan to speak three or more languages and to have a basic understanding of three or four others. Along with this, they are able to recognise other Africans by nationality and tribe before speaking to them and also to recognise that, with each recognition, there are specific ways of greeting and interaction. An awareness of this is placed in terms of politeness and respect of the individual's group. Nairobi provides a melting-pot, where there is an amalgamation of varying languages and cultures from all around the world. This provides for a greater awareness of cross-cultural dynamics and learning, if not the dynamics of language. This is not to say that this does not happen anywhere else in the world. Rather, this is being used as a focal point in that I have become more and more aware that those who are not sure about working in a transcultural setting are perhaps 'lacking' an understanding of 'another language'. This is founded in the following example. I have lived in three vastly different countries: Kenya, America and England. This provides a definite shift in perception and thinking. Having been exposed to and lived with several different languages and cultures, my inner dynamics are more finely tuned to different cultural-'ism'. This would be the same for any one who has experienced and lived with other cultures. There is the honing of cultural awareness. One learns a different 'language' and, when this becomes the 'natural', there is the 'forgetting' that this perception had to be learned. In Nairobi I have heard many a person start a conversation in English, for example, unconsciously slip into Kiswahili, break off into Punjabi, Kikamba, Kikuyu or Luo, divert into French, German or Russian and then finish in English, without consciously being aware of this shift in language. At the same time, the person/s who are being addressed, will listen as if they are hearing it in one language. This is the spoken dynamics. The inner dynamics is the recognition of the similarities within the cultures of the language spoken, whether it is one or more than one, spoken at different times or all in one sentence. In an environment like Nairobi, there is the need to be aware of the concept of communication in more than three languages in order to converse or keep up with the thought process and communication. In this manner, in counselling, I now have the tools to interact transculturally on differing levels through this learning process. In bringing this to a cultural surrounding that has not experienced the dynamics of interaction, with this closeness, and which is somewhat transculturally fragmented, the introduction of a learning process would be a progressive step. The 'learning of the language and eating patterns' has to be put into perspective. This is the area that is problematic, especially if the only 'language' that is spoken has been by the founders and pillars of modern-day western counselling formats.

On one of my journeys, while studying in San Diego, as well as being able to speak in English, I remember that we had a language qualification in Spanish. San Diego has a large Hispanic population and a notable feature is the Mexican culture. There was an understanding that if you are going to interact with the local population, you have to get to know something about their language and lifestyles. In turn, if the local population are going to interact, they must be in a position to feel comfortable in 'working' with counsellors and be able to establish some forms of communication and understanding. Invariably I sat down and ate with them, lived with them and 'learned their language'. That was some twenty years ago. In the twenty-first-century transcultural setting, there has to be a shift from the present-day eurocentric model, to one that encompasses a wider scope. The process of counselling and psychology has been in existence for centuries before it was 'founded by Freud'. Communities used to work together and resolve problems in groups. They would work on problems that affected either the community or the family, which would then be part of the group dynamics of the tribe. When this form of counselling became 'specialised' and was brought into the academic perimeters, the ideology of the person functioning as a smaller part of the group and therefore, in order to treat the person, the functions of the group should be looked into, was lost. Outside of the western individual context, the group orientation is still a strong focal point, for they still 'eat together' as a group and not as individuals: the shadow of an ancient past that is deeply rooted in the person and in their culture.

Further along, on the journeys through different western cultures, another item that makes itself prominent is that a person strives for a part of self-recognition, a part that says 'I am'. The individual strives for an identity. There is also the search for being and existence, a 'meaning to life'. To the African, this search ceases when the boy becomes a man or the girl becomes a woman, for the group mind has already embued the individual with enough presence that they do not need to seek a meaning outside of themselves. The individual, although an individual in their own right, gives a greater meaning to the group. Culture takes this to another level, but in some settings this is forgotten or not made clear and therefore, to clarify this, it must be stated that although pigmentation may give some clues as to ancestral origins, the culture of an individual comes from a deeper source. I have an awareness of different African cultures and different peoples of Africa. This is so much so that when walking towards another African, I have the presence of knowledge of where they are from, possible languages that they speak, background, reference point and what language to greet them in before I open my mouth. This is not an uncommon knowledge in the African setting. In the eurocentric counselling model this is not displayed, and in its place is the idea that 'everybody understands the same language and eats the same food'. Nothing can be further from the truth. In this, it is worth noting that the term 'cross-cultural counselling' is becoming the political correctness for a counselling process that takes place between white and black client/counsellor. Therefore there is the hidden agenda that, when counselling processes take place between peoples of the same racial backgrounds but of different cultural backgrounds, that this is not a process of cross-cultural counselling. In essence, cross-cultural counselling is not a 'black thing' as it is made out to be. The only process that makes this form of counselling subliminal among peoples of the same racial background is that they share an 'illusion of a commonality' and will encase themselves in this. The illusion is the 'security blanket' or banner with which peoples of 'sameness', whatever that 'sameness' may apply to, agree to cover themselves. As an example, the 'security blanket' may have the words 'British' written across it, and all peoples who think that they fit under this banner will incorporate it. However, there may be some people who think this would apply only to Caucasians, and others who may think it may apply only to peoples who have had family roots that go back tens of generations, and yet others may differ completely and define it differently. What is being brought to light here is that sameness is relative, and culture is tangible. The illusion of sameness can be perpetuated but never transcended. This would also apply in the reverse, whereby peoples of differing cultural backgrounds may be grouped as the same, because they 'look the same' or 'act the same'. The security blanket would apply to the individual who thought this because 'it made him/her feel safe'. This may seem quite obvious, but, seen in the light that a counsellor is not aware of the cultural background of his client, this poses a problem. Not only are the references missed out, but the whole 'language' is misinterpreted if not 'unheard'. The assumption is that the client/ counsellor has the same references and is therefore not engaged cross-culturally is a fallacy. When there is a shared commonality and an awareness of cultural background, communication is easier, although it does not mean that awareness of the dynamics of that cultural reference point is totally understood. However, this gives a reference point upon which to build, so much so that when the client says that 'he spoke to his dead mother and was told . . .' I will not immediately pull up the schizophrenia/psychosis card and obliterate all else. I will know that this is true and can focus on this point towards resolving a client's difficulty. When a client tells me that they have been bewitched, I know that this is also true and it is a reality. I am also aware that it is a reality that is not in the everyday confines of counselling of the western model. In order to understand this concept, a counsellor must have a prior knowledge of the culture that he or she will be counselling, working with in therapy or making psychological assessments about. In this manner, the client is not confined to the general classification of African. More importantly there is the recognition of national identity, cultural identity and tribal identity. This is where, in the African concept, the individual is more than the individual and carries with him or her the ancestral 'psyche'. To attempt to treat this person as an individual is to miss the whole idea of trying to help them. The 'psychic' fragmentation would only worsen. Is it any wonder that peoples from the 'ethnic minority' do not attend counselling as it is currently set up?

I met a prominent supervisor some time back and the topic of 'cross-cultural' came up. This inevitably led to the question of ethnic people not attending counselling sessions. As the conversation progressed, just about everything was mentioned: being different, cannot afford, drugs, commitment and so on. Before I left, I asked one question: 'What if the counselling process was changed and adapted to accommodate the ethnic minority within their cultures?' Needless to say, we went our separate ways and have not been in touch since.

I have dined with my western colleagues, heard their stories, shared their laughter and sorrow. I have been there to give comfort and marvel at their discoveries. I speak their language and tell their tales. Yet who has heard mine? Do they know the 'Song of Lawino' or any of my stories? Do they understand my sorrow and have they dined on Sukuma Wikii, let alone heard of it? Do they know anything about me apart from what they see? Do they understand any of my tribal heritage or even the language? Do they know what I know? No, they don't.

In order to understand African psychological approaches, it is important to be able to relate to living concepts of witchcraft, genes, ancestral spirits and death. It is important to comprehend the symbolic and metaphoric language.

Witchcraft; an understanding of life force

In order to give an overview understanding of the dynamics of why witchcraft is a central part of the African 'psyche', you must share a meal with me. I do not eat alone.

As a western subculture religion, witchcraft includes the acceptance of the belief in a supreme entity from which life comes and a spiral development of incarnations. Whether it be white witchcraft or black witchcraft, it concerns the development of an art that seeks oneness with nature. The western occult practices have five levels of membership, going from the apprentice to warlock or witch, to the wizard or enchantress, to the sorcerer or sorceress and finally to highest level of Magus, which is derived from Magi, supreme magician.

The term 'witchcraft' has had many guises throughout the world. From the days of old, it was central to the pagan mystery religions of Egypt, Greece and Rome. In the Americas it was termed 'Voodoo' and it was called, simply, tribal witchcraft in Africa. It is also known as Satanism in Europe.

Among the Romans and Greeks, witches were associated with darkness and death. Here the divine patron of witchcraft was a goddess, the moon, a goddess by the name of Diana, Selem or Hecate. She probably evolved from an Asia Minor deity. She had three heads and bodies linked by the three moon phases: full, new and old, and signified by Luna the moon and Diana the earth along with the underworld figure Proserpine, who ruled among night and darkness, blood and terror, tombs and dogs. In the belief of the Jews, the might riders (shadows personified) were identified with the cannibalistic vampires and ghosts. This belief was also held by the Romans and the Greeks. Cannibalism was sometimes ascribed to witches: rituals to gain power came from the weekly meetings of witches; these were called Sabbaths, although history writers have preferred the Latin and French spelling of 'Sabbat'. This was also to differentiate the term from the Jewish and Christian meanings of 'Sabbaths'.

There are countless other such incidences all taking the same basic course, and often with the 'Devil' portrayed as a man cloaked in animal skins or as half-man and half-animal. Most common among these is his portrayal as either a ram or a dog. One can note that this correlates with the Greek and the Roman depictions of gods of power, and through time how man projects the powers that he chooses to worship into forms he knows.

From the examples depicted above it would seem that the whole concept of this 'faith' is to fulfil a desire that is not fully allowed for in the modern technological world with its more astringent religious forms. The devil phenomenon, *per se*, is foreign to many peoples of Africa. Rather than the idea of the devil, there is the idea of possession, which is practised in religious ceremonies, and extends to some forms of witchcraft. The Azande of Central Nile/Congo believe that witchcraft is a psychic act. Distinction is made between the acts of witchcraft and sorcery in that the witches are mainly older women who dwell on the casting of spells in a continuous manner, at night, against unsuspecting individuals randomly. The other, the sorcerers, are persons whose actions are functional at ceremonies and do not dwell in the habitual casting of spells. On occasion their services are rented to inflict misfortune on one's enemies. Overall, they are the known conscious agents of their profession, as opposed to witches who are largely 'unknown', *per se*, and undesirable.

In the Transvaal area, the Lovedu witches are believed to use a slightly different technique to achieve their goals. With most witches, it is their souls that perform their evils. However, with the Lovedu the whole of their personality is involved. The physical appearances and capabilities of witches vary as well. The Yoruba in Nigeria have a belief that witches are women who fly at night and hold sabbats. They are associated with birds like the night jar.

The Akan of Ghana and the Ivory Coast hold the same belief, with the exception that the witches change into animals and emit a glowing light similar to that of fireflies. In this manner, one sees that the peoples of Africa often view a witch as a woman who has the ability to depart from her physical body and go to night congregations in the form of an animal or bird.

It must be made clear, however, that although Africans believe that the nocturnal activities of witchcraft are done in the spirit or soul form, this does not imply that they hold the opinion that witchcraft is illusionary. They have a deep-rooted belief to the contrary, for the spirit world in itself is a reality beyond any doubt, and thus witches perform the acts of which they are accused; a similarity to western thought, and yet removed in the sense that witchcraft is a 'reality'. Reality here refers to observable acts unexplained by western medical science. In this sense it is not an impersonal power, but personal 'spiritual' expressing itself.

Dreams also play an important role in witchcraft in the African setting, since it is from dreams that the powers of witches are sometimes derived. Bad dreams are associated with witches. Due to their nature and form, such dreams indicate that one may be bewitched. Nightmares are examples of bewitchment, since, in many cases, animal forms and bird forms are depicted, these being forms which are thought to be the forms that witches take on their nocturnal ventures. It would appear to follow that the encounter of these forms in one's dreams leads to being bewitched. It may also be that the witch is in search of the dreamer's soul. Sleep-walkers and persons who cry out in their sleep are assumed to be bewitched. There are two concepts that relate to the practice of magical beliefs. These are the concepts of animism and totemism. Animism refers to the soul or spirit in everything that is living and inanimate. An example of this would be found among the Abron peoples of the Ivory Coast in Africa, who offer sacrificial ceremonies to the earth god, to river deities and to their ancestors.

Among the tribes that practise totemism one is likely to find groups within the tribe embound to specific totems, such as an animal or a tree. These constitute their symbols of worship, and taboos spring up about the totems as a conveyance of their sacred powers, and in this way they are linked to the members of the group. It is to be noted that among the tribal peoples, spiritual phenomena are evidence of a spiritual world, and thus belief in the soul constitutes belief in spirits. The source is apparent and it manifests itself in dreams, visions and psychic distributions. Within the occult philosophy one should note two processes: (1) the co-existence of the hierarchy through which the tangible world acquires its ordering, and (2) the potential co-existence of personal experiences. The combination of these two functions of consciousness gives way to creative activity, which further allows the mind to encompass the universe. This idea of complexities gives awareness to man of being a spiritual entity. This concept of idealism functions as the acquittal of intellectual validity in their stagnant manifestation.

In some of its forms the occult caters to the dimensionally distended involvement between one level and another towards the fellowship that exists between man and spirits, or plant and animal life. This is the striving in an effort to attain oneness with the universe. The entire emphasis is upon the concept of the unity of consciousness, which in turn strives towards space and time.

In another example, the concept of 'being' goes further than the physical plane. The factor of the use of pronouns such as 'him' and 'her' are transcended through the reference of 'that one', followed by the revealing of the identity of the person being referred to. Him and Her are the definite terms as opposed to 'that one'. Here is where the element of 'space' is brought in. In transcending definite terms, one creates or allows for the 'person' to be a 'non-person' and takes on the element of undefined being, an existence that is quantified only through the defining identity. Identity in this case may be extended to being an 'it'. That is, the being can be seen in the form of male or female, but because they are more than this, for example, a spirit being in human form, they would fit the category of being an 'it'. This also allows for those who have been 'possessed', or rather those who can only be seen and defined in western terms as spirits, ghouls and so on, to be defined as entities that live with the human species. They become 'that one' or 'it' until defined by name. Even at this stage, the consciousness of 'him' and 'her' are not used. This unrestricted reference gives way to being able to refer to those who have died as though they were still present in the life form as is presently perceived. This model of thought also allows for existence of 'life' on different planes and thus different forms of life.

What can be manifested in western terms as 'multiple personalities' does not exist in a non-western environment. It takes the form of possession, but a 'possession' that is very different from the western mould. In order to begin to get to grips with this, one must abandon the current definitions of multiple personality, and embrace a more basic principle that there is no such thing as 'multiple personality'. In its place is the display of various traits of a single personality. Personality here pertains to the person and not the socialised mask, or the role that one adopts. An individual acting differently to the 'social mask' from time to time does not render that person to have a 'multiple personality'. The person or personality can only be one and in this one, it is true to itself. However, it is the masks that are in flux and therefore are interchangeable. It is the mask that society defines and judges and herein lies the dilemma. When one indulges the social mask, then current western social structures can relate to and absorb this. As soon as this stops being the case and a 'non-normative being' is 'created', then the structures find a label they can relate to and give some form of definition, for otherwise they are unable to accept this 'true being', as it does not fit into the normative. Normative as defined by society in a way that they can understand, cope and apply treatment.

In non-western societies and outside the eurocentric societies these labels do not exist, and possession is viewed as a behaviour mode. Possession here is taken to mean one 'psyche' enacting upon another. This then relates to the conflict with the being. The term witchcraft is a western term that does not equate to the African setting of what the daily process of 'witchcraft' is. The mindset would be more appropriate to be defined as 'one who is in touch with the universal force, a physis, an entity that not only gives life and existence, but is also in itself a life and an existence'. It is the very understanding of a life force, a power, a Ntu. This is what makes it real, for it is ever present, ever recognised and ever seen in different forms and shapes. So, I am not only by myself as I walk on my journeys, but I also walk with my family spirits, my clansmen and those who may protect me. They may make themselves visible or audible to me from time to time in any shape or form, and it is this that is hard to understand in a western structure. Therefore the process of 'witchcraft' as not understood by western culture is that it is a deep-rooted energy force outside of the self, that may be called on from time to time as part of a natural existence. It is in the lack of understanding of this concept that there exist labels such as paranoia, delusion and schizophrenia, before a process is fully understood. As of this time there has not been any tangible literature that examines this field in this light, in terms of cross-cultural understanding, despite the fact that peoples of colour have been in Britain for almost 500 years.

This section has been entitled 'Witchcraft; an understanding of life force' for the very reason that it is beyond 'that which is known'. Yet why should it be understood? The colonising process had taken hold and the 'master/slave' relationship was at its best. Those enslaved by 'easy riches' had now begun to look like their 'master', so why not treat them in the same way. The choice had been tantalisingly given and made. From there it would be a natural process of 'those who wore their master's shoes also wore his psychological clothing'. If one took on an identity, a social mask, then it would not be wrong to say that they would be governed by the same set of rules as the identities they bore. Therefore, should this not also apply to the psychological perspective that they are also judged by? In linear thought, this would be logical, as so too would the linear time process. However, when there are dualities and co-existence, linear thought and time become dysfunctional. Language is a good example of this. Those who speak more than one language may intermix a language structure within a sentence. Grammatically it may not be correct, but the essence would have been understood. If it is not understood then the process of communication becomes stunted, unclear and totally misunderstood in the translation. Like culture, and those who co-exist in more than one culture, or those who journey from one country to another, there may be a period of 'jetlag', but gradually there are the beginnings of understanding the rhythm of that culture. Along with this is the clarity of definition that 'the traveller' may never be recognised as part of that culture. In the same manner, the 'traveller' is also very clear of their cultural background and that their rhythm is different. It is in these differences that a recognition is made and striven for. Time ceases to be linear in the internal dynamics and cultural differences, and, due to the adaptation process and because there are two or more time lines in co-existence, time is governed by another force outside of the three-dimensional world of the 'foreign linear existence'.

Stepping into the world of duality

I would now like to step into worlds of dualities and attempt to explain the merging of the African psychological perspective with the western psychological perspective. There are standard symbols that are rudimentary in form but complex in interpretation. The forms may alter; for example, instead of the elephant there is the firebird, bear or hippopotamus, or instead of the old lady there is the old man or young girl, wicked witch, sorcerer; instead of the lizard there is the snake, fish, fox or ant. However, overall the symbolic figures are the same depending upon what the figures/representations stand for.

Let me take you into stories that illustrate this. This is a typical East African children's story.

> Many years ago, when animals could talk and man did not roam the face of the world, the rabbit was indeed a curious fellow. He went about his daily duties visiting the animals and telling stories of his daily events if not his weekly escapades. He would make sure that he visited during meal times and in between these he would sleep under a breezy tree. It was not too long before the other animals got wind of this and decided to hold a meeting to discuss what they were going to do. And so it came that a meeting was called to be chaired by Mr Lion. Now, Mr Lion had no quarrel with Mr Rabbit; after all, if the other animals had decided to feed him, then it was their fault. They should have known better. On the day of the meeting, there was much grunting and pointing of fingers. There were also old disagreements that had not been resolved. Mr Ant stood on a platform and complained of how Mr Rabbit had eaten his last grains and he had to go back and replant some more. Mr Elephant, who did not have a trunk at that time, complained that he could no longer feed on the plains as Mr Rabbit had uprooted most of the tasty greens and left him with the stale parched leaves. Mr Hippo, who had a full set of teeth, just smiled and looked on, while Mr Hyena laughed at the other animals and ridiculed them, before deciding to go to sleep. Mr Owl kept a sharp eye on Mr Snake; the two never did get along. Mr Crane thought that

Mr Rabbit should be kicked out of the animal kingdom, he still remembered his invitation to Mr Rabbit's house. While all this was going on, unbeknown to the rest of the animals at the meeting, Mr Rabbit had been napping under a small bush and had been woken up by the commotion. He listened intently and heard all the mutterings and plotting. He had not thought that his liberal ways would stir up such a commotion and was somewhat amused by this. Anyway, he listened and came up with a plot of his own.

The next day, Mr Elephant set out to search for Mr Rabbit, who he found whistling merrily in the woods next to a river. On seeing Mr Elephant approaching, Mr Rabbit sensed something was wrong.

'What is it then?' asked Mr Rabbit. After Mr Elephant had finished, Mr Rabbit jumped up in the air, proclaimed the ridiculousness of it all and challenged Mr Elephant to a strength competition. Mr Elephant was puzzled and somewhat amused. How could Mr Rabbit challenge him to such a competition? At this time, Mr Rabbit was really in a state of rage and he told Mr Elephant to go gather all the animals one side of the river and have them wait by the riverbank. In the meantime, Mr Rabbit said he would prepare himself on the other side. Not really seeing any sense in all this Mr Elephant left, to gather the animals at one side of the river. Mr Rabbit had gone across the river to see Mr Hippo and enacted out his rage once more and challenged him to a competition, asking again for Mr Hippo to gather the animals on another side of the river. Mr Rabbit had been busy preparing a rope for the tug-of-war. But more than just preparing the rope, Mr Rabbit had prepared something else. At just after midday, by an enclosed bank on Mr Elephant's side of the river, Mr Rabbit said, 'Here Mr Elephant, I will show you my strength so that all the animals do not see me as lazy and eating off them. I work hard in distant places, so when I am asleep I am resting from a long journey.' He then gave Mr Elephant one end of the rope and told him that whoever gets pulled into the river first is the loser. Mr Rabbit explained that he would have to go across the river to the other side. So off he went and explained the same thing to Mr Hippo. Not seeing how Mr Rabbit could possibly win such a competition Mr Hippo agreed, at which Mr Rabbit once again said he had to go across the river to the other side. And off he went. After a short while Mr Hippo heard Mr Rabbit say, 'When I count to three, pull'. Unbeknown to Mr Hippo, Mr Elephant also heard what Mr Rabbit had said and so counted to three and pulled, gently. Feeling the tension in the rope, Mr Elephant pulled harder and then harder still. Nothing moved. 'Is that all you have?' shouted Mr Rabbit. Mr Hippo was not amused. He pulled harder than before, holding the rope in his jaws. In the meantime, Mr Elephant had tied the rope to his stumpy trunk and was using that in this ridiculous competition. They pulled for three days and three nights, with neither giving in or moving. Mr Rabbit taunted them for three days. On the fourth day, both animals collapsed on either side of the riverbank with exhaustion. On seeing this Mr Rabbit first ran to Mr Elephant and claimed his victory, to which Mr Elephant, exhausted, bewildered, and confused, agreed. 'Well then,' said Mr Rabbit, 'I do not need to stay around here.' Then off he went. No sooner had he disappeared from Mr Elephant's sight, than he raced across the river to Mr Hippo to claim his victory. Unbelieving, Mr Hippo agreed, and Mr Rabbit raced away to sleep off the effects of such a strenuous three days.

Now a strange thing happened. When Mr Elephant was able to speak and move about, he found that his nose, although sore, was rather long and dropped from his face. On the other bank, having made a few strides to an open clearing, Mr Hippo could now see Mr Elephant, and he burst into laughter as only Hippos can. Strange, thought Mr Elephant: what has happened to Mr Hippo's teeth? Apart from the front two all the others were worn away. On seeing this Mr Elephant let out a trumpet-like cry and ran away. To this day, both the elephant and the hippo do not walk together and that is how the hippo lost his teeth and the elephant gained his trunk. The hidden truth of this is that Mr Rabbit had tied both ends of the two ropes to two big trees, neither of which could be moved.

Sit for a while and think. Please do not analyse the figures and their representations. This is just a story, a children's story. However, whether or not you like the story, or even do not understand its relevance, or even think that it is too long, there is a relationship with the story at some level. This story is the same in any other language, in any other culture, in any other surroundings, to any other group of people. There is no analysis, no representation, just interaction. In this way the whole world interacts, the story being the focal point of existence and the light to meaning, some a little more close than others.

The same stories are repeated whether it be in the aboriginal plains or the Ghats. It is the story-teller who is different, and he can use the process of the story either to his advantage or disadvantage, depending on the circumstances. Just as I have presented you with the story, I chose it for a purpose; it is colourful, imaginative and intriguing. It also holds a special place in the hearts of those who 'hear' it. This is a cultural process, and since the dynamics of an individual are dependent on how that individual relates to that culture, then the method chosen to 'hear' or 'not hear' is an individual one. Therefore, the process in which this story is received is an individual process: yours.

In the same line, here is a case study, my first as a young counsellor, straight out of an American university and plunged into the East Coast of Africa.

Case study 1

A young woman came to see me because she had been having trouble sleeping over the past few weeks. She was also very anxious about meeting her brother, whom she had not seen for several years. The reason why they had not seen each other was because of his wife. She had bewitched him and he acted differently.

As children they had been very close and they shared many moments playing together. They had grown up in a typical African family, with aunts and uncles doubling up as mothers and fathers. Their parents were farmers and they had a reasonable sized farm. How she loved that farm as a child. Then something changed. There had been a death in the family, her uncle on her father's side. The conditions of this were dubious, but that was not her concern. It is what happened to her brother after that. He had frequent bouts of convulsions and spasms, and when this happened he would mutter strange phrases. The local hospital had no explanation for this, for medically there was no explanation for his condition. She was frightened by this and very concerned. Her parents tried different forms of treatment but they did not work. Rumours spread quickly and soon neighbours distanced themselves from her parents. There was talk of bewitchment, possession and sorcery. This soon took a toll on the family and they moved away, leaving a cousin to attend to the farm. In time, her brother's condition lessened but she never got over what he was like when he experienced these convulsions. It scared her. Now, as a young adult working in the city, she was once again in fear of meeting her brother after a long period apart and facing her sister-in-law, who she knew had turned her brother against her. But that was not her main focus. She was once again afraid that here was a situation where she had some power over her brother and this was similar to the feeling of helplessness she experienced when as a child she saw him having convulsions and spasms. She blamed her brother's wife for many things that had changed about him. She said he had been bewitched and that there was little she could do without incurring the wrath of the 'muganga', the local witch doctor/medicine man. For this reason she had come to me, the psychologist.

Being my first case and full of Jung, Freud, Maslow, Millinowsky, Rogers and so on, I started to explore the symbolic representations and Electra complexes. It soon occurred to me that I was so full of my own learning that I had missed everything she had said. I had stacked nice little boxes with all the jargon of western learning, but I had not given consideration to the factor that perhaps this was not what was needed here. I had come to share a meal after filling myself up with chocolate and ice-cream, a setting for a stomach ache. I vomited. Vomited all my theories and implanted concepts of counselling. I vomited western models of self-identity, need and existence. Retched at the model of the western nuclear family and the need to perpetuate this existence, the importance of finding oneself and self-identity. Shuddered at the frivolity of the concept of I, the individual, and the thinking that one is 'an individual'. When I had finished all this, I washed myself and looked long and hard at the face in the mirror. That is when I knew that my education had just begun and my client had come to 'teach' me. From then on I took a different course. I had studied long and hard in the western world only to come back to my own soil, to be taught that which I had spent five years attempting to perfect. Life's little jokes. From then on, I only ate 'local food', the ever-filling 'Ugali and Sukuma Wiiki', and I learned more and more. I grew to appreciate that which I never appreciated before, eating with my hands and how this adds flavour to the texture of a 'meal'. I now know what it was to share a meal with my client. I then set about and got rid of all my neat academic boxes and labels, and began to experience my existence. In my rebirth the process of Skiatism was born. A counselling format, this is neither western nor African in its existence and yet incorporates each of these formats in its being without embellishing either. In going back to the story about Mr Rabbit and using that as an African experience, I can also say that it is the same story as my first case study. The two are parallel and yet remain different in their identities. Each is separate and yet interlinked: just as the elephant and the hippo got new appearances, it was the same in my client study. Initially I was ill equipped to comprehend what I was encountering. In my studies there were no references on what to do with cultures that have a deeply imbedded background in witchcraft and sorcery. Jung and Freud did not design an 'appropriate' model for this setting. For them it was either the likes of 'Oedipal regression' or 'Projection transference', both deeply disturbing if a whole continent is labelled in this manner. There needed to be a re-education. This process of Skiatism needs to be understood, this has been the predominant focus of this chapter. The process of Skia is elusive but must be understood in its own right. It is a Greek word meaning shadow or silhouette and just as the shadow or silhouette gives a definition of what is moving in front of a light, it also has the capacity to expand or shorten the image, depending on the distance from the light. In the case study the woman had presented with a very unfamiliar situation to that ascribed to in the eurocentric setting. It cannot be examined within the eurocentric model or definitions. This is what I had attempted to do. All of this must be put aside and the case heard in the 'language' in which it is being presented. This means that there must be some understanding of the 'language', and the concept that, when the individual appears in the counselling room, he or she brings with them their entire family, either live or 'belonging to another plane'. The individual is never 'alone', but rather a fractile of a much bigger piece. Therefore, when the young woman went on to present her brother, his wife, the bewitchment process and his strange affliction, these must not be distorted or interpreted. They must be seen in their own light. The only way to understand this is to 'share a meal' with peoples of differing cultural backgrounds and not attempt to 'learn from the client' as the counselling process goes on. This would defeat the whole process of hearing what is being said. At this juncture one may question my 'learning' from the client. I will make this very clear. My client brought in a realisation that was already inherent in myself. Therefore, although I may imply that there is the concept of 'client/teacher', I imply it in this case to demonstrate that our clients can be instruments of learning from which counsellors can benefit. In order to go through the whole process counsellors would have to do that in their own time and not during the time they have with their clients. In the African setting, a counsellor would have to acknowledge different realities and that witchcraft is not a pagan illusion. It is a way of life and therefore needs to be understood in this manner. The existence of a society that is formulated upon basic beliefs will have a structure that is basic to its needs and functional to its purpose. Here bewitchment is the reality, a reality seen on a different plane from the west. Here time and space are one and there is continuity. Life is known on different levels in a 'fourth' dimension; that is, 'life' does not cease when one 'dies', and death becomes an ever-present 'companion'. When the 'reality' of 'live witchcraft' is applied to the western mould of reference, it loses translation. Its context loses translation, and because this is a format that the west has 'departed from' and therefore seen as unacceptable, it loses its value. The cultural aspect cannot be communicated in its true context. The cultural aspect is then lost and whatever dialogue that was to take place is meaningless.

Possession then becomes incomprehensible and is found in labels of schizophrenia, catatonia, or delusions of grandeur. This is rational to the 'complex mind'. A rationale formulated by a perspective that could not comprehend the symbolism of simple cultures that exist on a basis of belief and communication. The western interpretation of incomprehensible behaviour reverts to a form of madness, madness being the operative word for 'I cannot translate/relate', a transposition of chaos within a mental process. Take simple sentence structures of communication; for example, 'I will see you tomorrow'. This is a sentence of pure speculation, where one party has already drawn a conclusion that either party will be alive and well in order to comply with the meeting. Here is a sentence structure where time is definite, causality is defined and space is restricted. The symbolism has turned to signs in that the phrase 'I will' is definite, but becomes hypothetical when tomorrow is added. Tomorrow is an illusion, and into the illusion urban man has added the structure of a linear system of existence called time, to give illusion a sense of 'reality'. Due to factors of this nature those in the western world have difficulty in communication with non-western peoples when it comes to time.

Causality then is the outcome of the interplay of psychic elements. One being in time and space is directly related to the effort of psychic interaction. The process of life is to keep these psychic interactions in a balance where one force does not weigh too heavily on to others. In the case where one force gets the upper hand, the results are usually negative (i.e. one may experience an accident of some sort or death may ensue, or a loss of opportunity). This is standard belief in non-western cultures. A happening is never of its own volition, but rather it is aided by another entity.

The concept of Skiatism rests not on the language of interpretation but on the affiliation of recognition of 'things as they are' from one culture to another. This invariably means that there needs to be an understanding of the culture to which one is relating. In the western world, the African exists because he or she can adapt, and with this adaptation comes the deeper understanding that they do not forget their own heritage. The western model does not as yet cater to this for, in attempting to understand the cultural differences, it misses out on the rudimentary factor that it is based upon a code according to the western perspective. In another light, the western model works because of its heritage, catering to a western perspective; however, outside of this, who understands the stories of 'Abunuasi', who reads the concepts of Menaseh's dream or ventures into the realm of the firebird, Prince Amilec or the Queen of Quok? Does anyone really contemplate that as an 'outsider', for that is what we are; outside of the western model.

I would like to make this point again. In reading this chapter, if at this stage you still do not understand the concept of Skia and the process, the question must be asked if the right tools are being used. If not, then perhaps a relearning has to occur, and this can only take place within one's perception. I will give an example, a case study.

Case study 2

An elderly man came to my practice many years ago and revealed that his household had been bewitched and that they could no longer sleep there. He had been away on the day of the bewitchment and on his return found his wife and children all turned out of the house. He went on to describe what had happened while he had been away and that he had to give his eldest daughter away in marriage in order for the spell to be broken. The old man had great difficulty with this, especially as he had to give his daughter away to a gene. The village elders saw no other way out of his difficulty and did not want to anger the gene further. The local witch doctor did not want any involvement in the matter, as this form of spell casting was beyond him. On this basis the old man approached me.

Although I had heard of genes, I had never experienced people being turned out of their house by a gene, let alone seen one. I apprehensively offered whatever assistance I could. However, first I had to come to terms with his 'truth'. It was after much self-questioning that I began to prepare for this strange situation. I am a counsellor and not an exorcist, I remember telling myself, as I pondered on what I was going to do. I had no training in these matters. Explain Jung, Maslow and Freud to me and I will understand. Explain genes to me and nothing within the psychological realm that I had been taught makes sense.

In my re-education I had to think like my client, with my Africanness and everything that was culturally binding to me. In this way, we began working towards a solution. We no longer spoke and thought in English. Instead we communicated in Kiswahili and thought within the bindings of our cultural similarities.

I sat down to eat a meal one day, and I was alone, in a foreign place, eating a foreign dish, not fully comprehending the flavour of the meal. In time I learned and appreciated the meal and others came to join me. In this, they all brought their own meals and, although we ate together, we did not eat from the same bowl, so I sat and ate my own meal 'alone'. In another setting, I sat and began to eat. Soon some children joined me and I shared what I had. One of them brought a 'mandazi' and we shared that. Then some adults from different parts soon joined in and more food was brought in and shared. Eating different foods was not strange, but became a feature. To this day, I do not dine alone. Share experience and learn, the pillars of being and, in it, that which was strange becomes familiar, the very concept of Skiatism. Out of a gathering came one thought: people enjoy food because it is the common denominator. We eat to appreciate and exist. And so it should be in the twenty-first century counselling world. In the present counselling world, counsellors eat 'separately together', with the thought 'I' and the 'projection of authority' thinking we are one. One wonders . . . for how long? I have invited you to my table. Come eat with me, for I do not eat alone, and in the sharing of this meal we may exchange our stories and realise that when you look at me, you look at yourself, and everything about yourself as you are, you see in me.

Synchronicity is not a philosophical view, but an empirical concept which postulates an intellectually necessary principle.

Bibliography

Besant, A. (1959) *Study in Consciousness*. Madras, Theosophical Publishing House.

Bollas, C. (1987) *The Shadow of the Object: Psychoanalysis of the Unthought Known*. London, Free Association Books.

Bryson, L. and Finkelstein, L. (1954) *Symbols and Values*. New York and London, Harper.

Buhrmann, V.M. (1984) *Living in Two Worlds*. Cape Town, Human & Rousseau (Pty).

Campbell, J. (1953) *The Hero with a Thousand Faces*. New York, Bollingen Foundation.

Campbell, J. (1973) *Myths to Live By*. London, Souvenir Press (Educational and Academic).

Campbell, J. (1989) *The Power of Myth*. New York, Doubleday.

Cavendish, R. (1976) *The Black Arts*. New York, G. P. Putnam and Sons.

Cooper, J.C. (1983) *Fairy Tales – Allegories of the Inner Life*. London, The Aquarian Press.

Douglas, M. (1970) *Natural Symbols: Exploration in Cosmology*. London, Barry Rockliffe.

Douglas, M. (1985) *Cultural Difference and Cultural Deprivation; A Theoretical Framework for Differential Intervention*. Basingstoke, Macmillan.

Ellemberger, H.F. (1970) *The Discovery of the Unconscious*. New York, Basic Books.

Fair, C. (1971) *The Physical Foundation of the Psychic*. Middleton, Wesley B. Press.

Fordham, M. (1956) 'Active Imagination and Imaginative Activity'. *Journal of Analytical Psychology* 1(2).

Fordham, M. (1960) 'The Emergence of a Symbol in a Five-Year-Old Child'. *Journal of Analytical Psychology* 5(1).

Fox, D.J. (1969) *The Research Process In Education*. New York, Holt, Rinehart and Wilson.

Hanh, T.N. (1974) *Zen Keys*. New York, Anchor Press

Hazer, H. (1969) *Truth about Witchcraft*. New York, Doubleday.

Hillman, J. (1979) *The Dream and the Underworld*. New York, Harper & Row.

Jahn, J. (1961) *Muntu: An Outline of Neo-African Culture*. Faber and Faber.

Jones, M.E. (1948) *Occult Philosophy*. Philadelphia, PA, David McKay.

Jung, C.G. and Kerenyi, C. (1951) *Introduction to a Science of Mythology*. London, Routledge & Kegan Paul.

Karno, M. and Egerton, R.B. (1979) 'Perceptions of Mental Illness in a Mexican American Community'. *Archives of General Psychiatry* 20: 233–8.

Lindzey, G. (1957) *Theories of Personality*. New York, John Wiley and Sons.

Maduro, R.J. and Wheelwrite, J.B. (1977) *Analytical Psychology*. Itasca, IL, F. Peacock Publishers.

Makinde, M.A. (1990) *African Philosophic Culture and Traditional Medicine*. African Series no. 53, Centre of International Studies, Burson House, Ohio University.

Obeyeaekere, G. (1990) *The Work of Culture: Symbolic Transformation in Analysis and Anthropology*. London, University of Chicago Press.

Ogden, C.K. and Richards, I.A. (1949) *The Meaning of Meaning: A Study of the Influence of Language Upon Thought and of the Science of Symbolism*. London, Routledge & Kegan Paul.

Ornstein, R.E. (1971) *The Psychology of Consciousness*. New York, Freeman.

Soyinka, W. (1990) *Myth, Literature and the African World*. Cambridge, Cambridge University Press.

Spence, L. (1994) *Introduction to Mythology*. London, George G. Harrap & Co.

Stein, L. (1957) 'What is a Symbol Supposed to be'. *Journal of Analytical Pychology* 2(1).

Chapter 4

Assumptions and expectations

Adapting to diverse cultural settings

Sally Wolfe and Piers Vitebsky

Introduction

What are a client's expectations of a therapeutic encounter? Much depends on the assumptions which they bring with them, and on how these meet with the assumptions of the therapist. But much also depends on the setting within which these assumptions and expectations are played out. Where there are differences of understanding, it is the setting which may determine whether or not a working compromise can be reached.

The idea of a 'setting' is a complex one. Every counselling or therapeutic encounter takes place within a setting which is potentially inter-cultural. But we will also argue that even the rooms and institutions where therapist and client meet are themselves heavily laden with inter-cultural meaning.

To see every encounter as potentially inter-cultural means that we are faced with a wide, perhaps infinite, range of possible assumptions and expectations among both therapists and clients. How can one deal with all this? Obviously, one cannot be an expert in all the cultural situations which may arise. In fact, we shall argue that 'cultures' are not separate, discrete, bounded entities at all. Our aim is to lay out a range of variables about which one might at least wonder when one encounters a new client. This range comes from our own experience, and readers may wish to draw on their own cultural background and professional experience to produce a picture which may well be rather different.

We look at this issue from two different but complementary perspectives. Sally Wolfe is a counsellor and inter-cultural therapist, initially trained psychodynamically but now using a number of models. Her origins are Irish and Scottish. Piers Vitebsky is a social anthropologist who has worked with shamans and spirit healers around the world, but particularly in Siberia and India (Vitebsky 1993, 1995), where he speaks local languages and has worked for the past twenty-five and twelve years respectively. His origins are Welsh and Russian-Jewish. We are a married couple who have travelled together and been influenced by each other's work for many years.

We shall quote a case history from our recent work in Siberia, where we have recently been involved with local colleagues in setting up therapy services for young people under conditions of rapid social change. In this location, various indigenous (East Asian) peoples live in a complex relationship with Russians, Ukrainians and other (European) peoples who came to their land as colonists from the seventeenth century onward. Although the location will be unfamiliar to many readers, we believe that it will throw up import-ant issues which are central to the work of therapists in inter-cultural settings elsewhere. Part of this will be to throw into relief some difficulties associated with the globalisation of therapy.

First, we should like to argue that it is misleading to imply that there can be such a thing as separate 'cultures', each of which is a hermetically sealed box, as when people are categorised in huge homogenised blocks, such as 'white', 'black' or 'Asian'. According to such a view, the 'inter-cultural' must somehow take place when one reaches out from one of these boxes to another.

But this view ignores the huge variation at a micro level, a vari-ation which is often more important for the person concerned. Instead, we see 'culture' as a flow of ideas, feelings and patterns of behaviour, and as the totality of the ways in which these are shared with other people. In this more fluid vision, the inter-cultural is not just where billiard balls bounce against each other, but a complex interaction of threads and patterns of behaviour, values and senses of self and identity. Yet at the same time, many different kinds of people share the same overall total social space, a shared cultural domain which allows us to meet and interact at all. An analogy might be the concept of ecological niche among a community of plants or animals, which between them occupy a total ecological space. In our example from Siberia, we shall see how the European Russians and Ukrainians are associated with mining and engineering while various indigenous, Asian people are associated with the herding of specific species of animals such as horses or reindeer.

It is from this that our claim arises that every therapeutic encounter is at least potentially an inter-cultural one. 'Culture' should be understood, not only in the more obvious sense of association with a conspicuous ethnic identity, but also in terms of fine gradations of region, class and generation – all the variables, in fact, that people often use to talk about their own lives and social relations but which the official discourse of therapy sometimes finds uncomfortable. These may have a great influence on the process and outcome of therapy, but are often hidden, ignored or even denied. These differences entail a great diversity of expectations, implicit assumptions and explicit demands. Finally, we will suggest that the accepted rules of the profession may need to be modified to meet the setting of the encounter and the cultural background of the client – and in some cases even question whether a model of therapy is appropriate at all.

This inter-cultural dimension may be present in virtually every encounter between persons. Even two individuals bring their own internalised world to every encounter. They cannot be sure at first of shared assumptions and have to spend time finding out, reading coded signals and making errors of judgement.

In the same way, every family may have its own 'subculture'. Many of our clients' problems come from contradictory expectations and sensibilities between, say, the families behind two partners in a marriage. This is most obvious if one family is 'white' and the other 'Asian' or 'black'. But there may be differences between client and therapist even when they seem to be of the 'same' culture, gender, race or class. Even so-called white British clients are not homogeneous.

These differences are often hard to perceive because of the stereotypes we all live with about various groups being shy, bold, aggressive, oppressed, powerful and so on. Perhaps we need these stereotypes as a kind of shorthand, but we should recognise how much of reality they can mask. When we move to Siberia we shall encounter people whose consciousness has been formed under a completely different political system, with possibly very different ideas, goals, values and understandings of what is good and bad in social life. Some of them may have been members of the Communist Party. Some may have been gaoled as dissidents. Sometimes these are the same people at different stages of their lives. They live today in the post-colonial setting of a former superpower, a setting in which they are struggling with a very complex racial, ethnic and cultural identity.

The diversity of settings

Before turning to Siberia, we should like to explore the idea and implications of settings in the more familiar space of the UK.

However much we may strive to make it so, there is no such thing as a neutral setting. A good therapist has to transcend more boundaries than we are perhaps aware of. Even without taking into account the personality of the therapist, each one of these settings has cultural implications, for example, in terms of intimacy versus formality, or cosiness versus intimidation, or of differences of articulacy or kinds of narrative.

Each of these settings also has implications for the kinds of client who may feel comfortable, uncomfortable, empowered, intimidated or supported on coming into that setting, and thus about how far they may thrive or fail in the therapeutic work. The furnishings, the therapist's clothes, the path and the door: all of these convey meanings to the client and go beyond mere style, to the heart of what we call culture. A smart solicitor may work well only in a room which proclaims professional distance and control, even coolness; a young unemployed person may prefer a more casually arranged space with cushions and maybe even some personal mementoes. Even the most discreet and soothing works of art in a well-heeled therapist's room (to say nothing of the precious statuettes of ancient gods on Freud's desk) can seem intimidating to a person of low income, while the simplest objects from foreign cultures can intimidate a client with a monocultural outlook.

When we talk later about Russia, we shall see that the informality of the kitchen table (Ries 1997) provides the culturally ideal model setting for intimate, safe conversations. This is starkly opposed, with little or no middle ground, to institutional settings which almost always carry implications of a state interference in private affairs which is frightening and disempowering and can easily lead to psychiatric hospital or gaol. One important problem for people who are currently trying to introduce therapy in the post-Communist era is how to set up a space which conveys the feeling of being both professional and yet at the same time safe and non-intrusive. Similar issues must face any therapist who has to deal with victims of torture or state violence – though as with any other form of trauma, one may not be immediately aware of the nature or extent of this.

Settings in the UK can also carry a surprisingly strong message in terms of intimidation or reassurance. But these qualities are not absolute, and settings may be experienced differently by different clients. For example, Sally Wolfe has worked as a therapist in the following settings, among others, and it was these experiences which first drew her attention so forcibly to the importance of diverse settings.

A voluntary agency providing free counselling and information for young people under 25

This agency is set in a Victorian house in a side street in the centre of a small city. A friendly reception area in the front room provides seating, a computer with Internet connection for clients' use, information in files for reference and numerous leaflets to take away, and access to consultants for special problems such as housing and advocacy. Many clients come just for these facilities, while those who have booked counselling sessions go to counselling rooms in the interior. The place is managed with a light touch, and every effort is made to avoid an institutional feeling and to appear youth-friendly.

Since all services are free, there are no anxieties about payment (though the waiting list can sometimes be lengthy). Counsellors also give their time on an unpaid, voluntary basis. Paid supervision is provided by the organisation, and the counsellor feels supported by a team-based roster and protected by the presence of other workers on the same shift.

Although it is larger and more complex than local conditions there can support, we offered this service as the basic model to our colleagues in Siberia – not least in order to counteract ideas of interference by state and parents (see our case study, pp. 77–80).

Private paying therapy in a garden room

Clients reach this room by walking down a passageway and through a side gate. Here, they step straight into a 'secret garden', with bowers and cascades of climbing plants, in summer covered with scented flowers and full of birds. Though it is only a short way off a main road, many clients comment on how they look forward to each visit as a haven of peace. The furnishings and style suggest a bohemian, artistic, middle-class woman's taste. The tranquillity of the setting contrasts with the tough work which sometimes has to take place here.

Questions of boundaries can come out very differently here. There is no toilet, even though this may be a physical or psychological need of the client. For this, they are led through the garden and into the house, where the presence of family photos and the debris of family life may create boundary problems or open up an intimate, non-professional world which may relate to some clients' own needs.

Here there is no institutional back-up, no roster team as in the previous setting or 'multidisciplinary team', as in the GP's practice or the hospital below. There is also no protection for the therapist if the client becomes physically aggressive.

Using premises in the formal setting of a GP's practice

Here, the consulting room is fully professional and impersonal to the point of being clinical. In this busy practice, with receptionists and waiting room, a client's entrance is very public. Some people did not want to be seen going into the room used by counsellors, and found this more embarrassing than to be seen going in to consult a doctor for what people would presume was a 'medical' reason. Though clients' consultations were confidential there was supposed to be some degree of team spirit among medical and paramedical staff, but owing to a lack of understanding by some doctors of the therapeutic processes this did not work well in practice (though it does in many other practices).

In a small inter-cultural therapy group

This group was founded by Sally Wolfe and a colleague, Joan Harcourt, for people who have a close involvement with other cultures or who move between cultures, for example, through having made an inter-cultural marriage.

People in these situations often have no place to talk about their inter-cultural experience. When Sally and Joan have been in this situation themselves when living abroad, they have noticed how they sometimes missed their own culture, however dedicated they were to their new setting. Sometimes they had no opportunity to speak their own language, and hence to express their innermost thoughts and feelings. They were sometimes bewildered by all the unspoken, but deeply felt, rules of etiquette, by all the non-verbal gestures which go far beyond spoken language. They felt de-skilled, as their own ordinary skills became unusable, like children who had to be taught the most elementary skills of daily life. This experience provides a useful reminder of how our clients may feel, for all sorts of reasons which we cannot necessarily know, as they walk in through the door of our consulting room.

In a large Victorian mental hospital in the process of being closed down

The 'contract' which is set up in a mental health setting is very different from the contract which is set up in a private therapy room, or even from that in a GP's practice. Confidentiality is maintained within a team and the hospital is answerable to the local Health Authority. Unlike private work, you can check up how your client's work with you affected them afterwards, for example, by finding out how they behaved when they returned to the wards (even though you hear of this only at second hand).

Before the first meeting with the 'patient', the therapist has already been told, in medical terminology, what their condition is. I was thus faced with a diagnosis much earlier than I would have been in my garden room, and one cast within a medical narrative which tends to be limited in its scope and self-reinforcing (cf. Sinclair 2000).

One very important factor affecting the setting is that therapist and patient are not always given continuity or security of space. Even in the middle of a session one may be moved on from room to room if a doctor needs the space. There is clearly a clash of models, in which the medical model seems to incorporate or accept constant interruptions in the name of a higher good (though these interruptions may also occur because the patients are too dangerous for you to be left alone with them for too long).

So overall, in that setting I did not feel that I was able to set up the secure, confidential space which is the cornerstone of individual work in other settings: I found it difficult to make my client feel safe if I did not feel safe myself. The atmosphere was sometimes tense, with alarm bells, suicide attempts and searches for escaped patients in the grounds with heat-seeking helicopters. The buildings were being progressively abandoned and the institution and its funding run down. Much of our work consisted of creating and managing endings because patients were being prepared for a move to 'care in the community'. There was broken glass everywhere around the grounds and both of my clients have scars on their wrists from using this glass. Some of the patients (like some of the staff) had been there for most of their lives. They were institutionalised persons (cf. Goffman 1968) and formed a captive client group. This was very different from my work with other clients who are voluntary and seek to function better in the outside world.

Establishing a counselling service in Siberia

When representatives of indigenous communities in Yakutsk, a town in the remote northeast of Siberia, approached Piers Vitebsky for help and foreign contacts in their attempts to set up therapy services locally, which of these many variants should get carried over into the establishment of their therapy programme, and why and with what modifications?

Flying over the tiny patchwork fields of western Europe, where people put up fences to preserve privacy, you start to cross the thinly populated forests of eastern Europe. To understand working with people from the former Soviet Union, you first have to appreciate the feeling about land. Even staying with them in their little home-made country cottages (*dacha*), you learn how much people need those summer breaks from cramped community apartments in tower blocks in the city, and the importance of growing vegetables there to sustain them through winter shortages.

But nothing prepares you for the land that lies beneath you after crossing the Urals. The tundra, treeless and flat, is covered with a network of pools and tiny waterways branching out like leaf mosaics or fossilised ferns on a landscape that looks devoid of any human habitation. Rivers like the Ob, several miles wide, stretch across the land like huge, shining seas. Then there are forests, hundreds of miles of them, and mountains with pockets of ice that stay there all through the year. One might imagine that no humans could live down there. But indigenous people have lived here for thousands of years, and Russians for hundreds, in tents, wooden huts, and the occasional modern town or city. This place is not just the country of Gulag prisoners.

Yakutsk is six hours' flying time northeast of Moscow (or two weeks overland) and with its population of some 300,000 has the air of a booming frontier town. At the same time it is still very remote, lying nearly a thousand miles north of the Trans-Siberian railway. It is the main town in the Sakha Republic, previously known as Yakutia, which is part of the Russian Federation and occupies an area almost the size of India. The Republic's population of just over one million belongs to a mosaic of ethnic groups, both indigenous and European. Each people is traditionally associated with a different ecological niche and sector of the region's economy. Thus, the main indigenous group the Sakha (Yakut) are horse- and cattle-herders, while Russian, Ukrainian and other European immigrants are associated with trade and mining. In addition, there are semi-nomadic indigenous minority peoples such as the Evén who number only a few thousand each and are scattered in small communities across a vast landsape of forest, swamp and mountain ranges, where they live mainly by hunting and reindeer herding (Vitebsky 1992, 1996).

Ethnic identity is fluid, so that we have heard people say, 'I was born an Evén in a reindeer-herding community. But then I got a job as a horse herder and became Sakha for a while.' Statements like these remind us that we canot take ethnic labels too literally, and that the inter-cultural dimension of encounters between persons is as much likely to be in terms of lifestyle as of ethnicity.

Like the rest of Russia, this region has been undergoing rapid social change since the mid-1980s. This has led to some severe social problems, particularly in the area of family life. This can be measured by various criteria, but it is perhaps sufficient to point to the rapid increase in the number of children being taken or given into institutional care, or the huge escalation of the rates of divorce and one-parent families (Barashkova 2000).

Family stress is related to the local variant of the widespread crisis in the Russian economy, which has depressed every part of this region except the capital Yakutsk. In response, many Russians and Ukrainians are returning to the western end of Russia, from where they originally came. This is a retreat from a frontier back to their heartland, a retreat from their former empire. For indigenous peoples, migration has quite another dynamic which sometimes gives rise to serious psychological and social problems. Sakha teenagers and young adults from the villages migrate from the collapsing rural economy to the boom town of Yakutsk. Most of the other, minority indigenous peoples are too remote and disheartened to migrate any-where, but stay in their villages suffering from the highest of all local rates of depression, alcoholism and suicide. If they come to the city they are often unable to adjust and soon go home again.

Local government departments, social workers and others are deeply concerned about these tendencies. Many respond by issuing statements deploring these changes and exhorting young people to live a healthy lifestyle. Others adopt a more practical attitude, and some have begun to establish telephone hotlines and counselling or therapy services.

However, the attitude of society towards these attempts is ambiguous. We have worked for several years with a local voluntary organisation concerned with the growing problems of teenagers and young adults in the city and its surrounding rural areas. The organisation had been struggling since the mid-1990s for official recognition of its work. For a long time, it seems that the need for such work was widely denied and organisation was unable to raise support for even so much as a telephone line. However, in 2000 its two leaders were both allocated a regular salary from a government department, and this now allows them to devote themselves full time to this work.

What kind of setting do these people work in, and what kind of setting do they offer prospective clients?

Their office is a small, long, narrow, windowless room in the basement of a block of flats. The walls are covered with rotas, appointments and memos, and there is now a computer giving Internet access. The basement is approached by passing a heap of abandoned lumps of concrete and ducking under a massive, heavily lagged pipe which brings in heating from a boiler in another building. At the foot of the stairs inside the entrance is an old sofa with the foam rubber of the cushions showing through the frayed cover. This sofa serves as a waiting room for both the therapy service and the ladies' hairdressers in the next room. Clients are received for consultation in the office after working hours as well as in a corner of a large assembly hall upstairs at any time, whenever it is vacant.

How can we understand the cultural significance of this setting? We will look first at what we came to understand about local professional assumptions and working conditions for therapists, before moving on to how this seems to work for their clients.

We learned about their working conditions during a three-day workshop we organised in 1999, at which we brought together some twenty medical psychiatrists, social workers, spiritual healers and others, followed in 2000 by an intensive two-week workshop for a small closed group of people engaged more narrowly in what would be called in English psychotherapy (*psikhoterapia*: there is no additional separate word in Russian for 'counselling' or 'counsellor').

We believe that the issues which arose are likely to be paralleled in many parts of the world such as India or Africa, where counselling and therapy are only just beginning to make their appearance, often against a background of previous traditional healing practices (in this case shamanism: Vitebsky 1995, in press).

Some of the procedures which in the 'west' are considered basic, such as assessment, referral and supervision, turn out to be largely unknown. It is worth looking at the cultural and practical implications of this.

Assessment

Assessment at the first meeting with a potential client is intended to help the therapist work out what the client really needs and to assess whether they can or should work together. The therapist may review the client's history of attachment and loss, their openness to a psychologically oriented approach and motivation for coming, the degree and nature of their vulnerability, their medical history, their economic and ethnic background, and their expectations of the therapeutic encounter. But as the case below will show, many of these assumptions about attachment or the usefulness of a psychological approach may not be valid outside a certain 'western' cultural domain.

Our local colleagues were extremely sensitive by nature and cultural background to many of these points, since local indigenous cultures place great stress on intuiting another person's moods through non-verbal communication (Vitebsky 1997; Wolfe 1997). However, the absence of a concept of assessment means that local therapists tend to believe that they can and should handle any cases which come along, however difficult or dangerous they may be.

Referral

The lack of emphasis on referral is linked to the lack of a support network of parallel specialist services. Assessment presupposes the possibility of referring a client to a range of other therapists or agencies. This brings us up against the limits of assessment, since there are few such facilities in a Siberian town, any more than there are the training workshops, refresher courses and weekend retreats which give professional support and are taken for granted in the west. This is one of the major practical (as opposed to theoretical) points on which 'western' models would need substantial adaptation. Almost the only limit to which client a therapist takes on is that of the threshold beyond which a therapist should refer a seriously mentally disturbed client to the psychiatric system. At any point below this very high threshold, a therapist seems to be vulnerable to taking on more than they can handle.

Supervision

The absence of a concept of supervision places a great strain on local therapists. In the "west" the regular supervision of therapists by a senior colleague is considered essential to protect both therapist and client. Everything we hear convinces us that this is particularly necessary under local conditions of high stress levels and politicisation, in order to avoid overload and burnout. There seems a danger that in exchange for a modest level of public support, a small organisation like that of our colleagues may be expected to make a significant impact on some huge social problems with the wave of a therapeutic wand – a potential recipe for failure and ultimately for loss of that same public support. Given the shortage of senior therapists and the absence of any trained supervisors, we encouraged our colleagues to explore the concept of co-supervision (suitably modified for differences in seniority and experience within the group). This has the added advantage of allowing a small community of therapists to build up a collective history and archive of experience in the absence of available literature or a professional association.

We initiated a supervision group which developed into an applied exercise in co-supervision. It became clear that the occasional fragmented conversations which busy therapists generally snatched with each other were no substitute for this kind of sustained discussion and analysis of difficulties in their ongoing work with clients, set within the focus and boundaries of a formal, timed meeting.

Although Piers Vitebsky speaks Russian, he could not function as interpreter in addition to his other roles in the workshop. Earlier experience had shown us the importance of having a translator who also understands the subject matter and is sympathetic to what we are trying to do. We were lucky enough to find a perfect translator who became almost transparent in the work. We spent evenings with her, debriefing and checking her understandings of the hidden implications of much that had been said (and left unsaid) during the day.

Cases presented

In this ongoing supervision group, we discussed a number of current and recent cases from the UK and Siberia. The cases presented by our local colleagues revealed a range of local issues and conditions, but most of them have a familiar ring in multi-cultural settings in the UK, though with a distinctive local tone. However, we will single out one case (cited with appropriate permission) as raising some issues which are also of fundamental importance for working inter-culturally in the 'west'.

Case study

This case was inter-cultural in a number of ways. It was inter-ethnic in the obvious sense that the therapist was Russian (i.e. European) and the client Sakha (i.e. Northeast Asian). But it also stretched across the gulf between urban and rural. In addition, the generational difference between the middle-aged urban therapist and the 20-year-old rural client (both of them women) likewise stretched across an important gap. It turned out that in many ways the case was about exactly these distinctions, and about the client's changing position within them.

The client came from a remote village to the city to ask the therapist for help in dealing with her mother, who expected her to do exhaustive housework even after a day's work outside. In further sessions the girl was accompanied, sometimes by her boyfriend (also rural Sakha) and sometimes by the mother about whom she had initially come to complain. The mother had not wanted to come at first, insisting that the family would sort things out together without any outside intervention. When she finally did come, however, she seized the initiative and took over the session with a tirade against her daughter's ingratitude.

The mother was a middle-aged schoolteacher. As the therapist put it wryly, this in itself was a problem. She was not used to negotiation since 'she assumes she knows everything'. She had decided long ago that her first task was to bring up her children and do everything for them. Later they would be forever in her debt and would repay her accordingly. However, she had not negotiated this understanding with her children (to the extent that one ever could), even while they were growing up. So when the daughter wanted to move out and live with her boyfriend (still a novel kind of arrangement in a Sakha village community), the mother objected by pointing out that the girl was in her debt. The girl acknowledged this debt (*ya obyazana*), even to the point of feeling guilt (*vina*), but at the same time resented it and actually made a move to get away from it.

This feeling of indebtedness came to replicate itself in all the girl's other important relationships. Her boyfriend helped her in difficult moments and she now felt indebted to him too. She also had feelings of indebtedness surrounding her job and her colleagues at work.

The father of the family was conspicuously absent, as in so many families here. He had walked out (or been thrown out or driven away by the mother). He had also became an alcoholic, though it was not clear if this had happened before or after he left the home. Whenever the girl tried to get away or to become more independent, the mother would remind her (and the rest of the family) of how he had deserted her.

There was also a small boy in the family, the son of the teacher and the brother of the presenting client. When the mother and daughter quarrelled, this boy (who played only a small part in the narrative) would get upset and be unable to sleep. The therapist feared that as the daughter moved away from her mother's control, the son might be unable to separate or find his own masculinity.

This was the therapist's first experience of dealing with more than one client, and without previous exposure to any model of family therapy she found herself caught in a dilemma, unsure at any given moment of whom to side with. As in an artfully constructed novel, the therapist first heard about the other characters as figures in someone else's narrative, but then came to meet the characters one by one and gradually build up a picture of her own.

At first, everyone in the supervision group shared the therapist's initial reaction and felt that the mother was behaving outrageously. But as the discussion went on, some people started to sympathise with the mother. Women in the group said that they understood how she felt, abandoned by an alcoholic husband and suffering in so many ways just to keep her family alive, having her house used by a grown-up daughter who was not willing to do housework.

The therapist had also moved during her consultations with the client's family towards a fuller understanding of the mother's position, though for different reasons. She had realised early on that the mother was completely intransigent and closed to negotiation. So she had concentrated instead on helping the rest of the family to understand the mother better, to see that the mother's history was different from theirs, and even to try to find out what it was.

But as the discussion continued it gradually became clear that there were other things going on:

- A series of repetitions to do with senses of obligation and the trauma of being abandoned, in which the mother drives other members of the family away and then blames them for leaving. We wondered whether the daughter was having to replace her father as husband and companion to the mother, and whether even the therapist was becoming the absent father in the transference.

- Though it was the daughter who was the initial client, in the overall scenario it appears that the children serve as projections of the mother. What the mother is looking for involves denying other people's agendas and perceived needs, or co-opting them to her own. This makes the daughter's separation (and perhaps the son's, in the future) extremely difficult.

- The mother's assumption was that any resolution of the situation would not involve any structural or attitudinal changes. This is a way of saying that she will not change, so everyone else has to do so. It seems as if she is still stuck in the loss of those hard years.

- The therapist's dilemma in a situation in which she cannot keep control of just which of the family members is her client. Will each of them have fantasies about what the others are saying in the room? Can she support the mother and the daughter at the same time, or support only one? If only one, should this be the daughter, and if so, is this because she was the initial client, or because she found it easier to sympathise with the daughter's position and regarded the mother as selfish, demanding and unreasonable? If so, is this because she is an urban Russian woman whose expectations of a daughter might be less old-fashioned and 'Asian' than those of a middle-aged Sakha mother?

We see how many of these questions do not simply concern individuals, but have an inter-cultural dimension. Apart from their own personal narratives, the family were caught up in a wider process of cultural change, and their case reads almost like a microcosm of change among indigenous Asian peoples in post-Soviet society. Traditional Sakha culture was based on the values of the extended

family, and in addition, Soviet ideology ensured that the older generation did indeed labour long and hard and with a strong sense of duty
and self-sacrifice.

Yet now they are left high and dry. Like many girls of her generation, the daughter wanted her freedom to come and go and to earn
money, but not to be forced to set up a separate household since
neither she nor her husband had the resources to do this. At first
sight, one might feel that the mother has a narrow, calculating, almost
accounting view of a child's debt to its parents. But on reflection, it
seems she is merely putting very bluntly a concept of duty which is
widely understood and accepted within Sakha culture – or at least,
has been until the present generation of young Sakha in the city. The
family's problem is one of cultural change, in which the concept
of duty itself is fading. At the same time, caring for older parents is
becoming even more of a problem because – actually unlike this girl –
many young adults are migrating away from the village to the city in
quest of fortune. Staying behind to look after aged parents is completely incompatible with this tendency.

One therapist in the supervision group who is herself a Sakha
from a rural area felt that she recognised something of her own
mother and family in this case. As the youngest child in her family,
she could not imagine leaving or marrying until after her parents had
both died. Another Sakha therapist remembered that as a small
child, whenever her mother was ill she would cry into her pillow as
she imagined all her sisters dying off in turn and leaving her with the
sole responsibility of looking after her mother. She said that this is
why she does this work now. We believe that these responses provide
valuable clues to local women's psyche and feelings of responsibility,
and thus to the kinds of conflicts which are likely to arise.

It may also be significant that this client came for support to a
Russian therapist, who could well have been associated in her mind
with a more narrowly defined nuclear family pattern rather than
the traditional Sakha extended family. What the client did not know
was that this Russian woman was married to a Sakha man. After
the workshop, the therapist said that it had raised many issues of
inter-cultural awareness which had not even occurred to her before,
including her relationship with her own children.

Implications of the case

Like other cases which were presented to us or which we know from
our own previous fieldwork in this region over the past twelve years,
this case gives a strong picture of assumptions and expecations
among clients. These are related to their cultural or ethnic background as Russians, Sakha, or members of the minorities, but this
relationship is not always direct and clear-cut. The therapist in turn,
like her colleagues in supervision, is still uncertain about how to
respond to this. Living in a shared cultural domain, they share many
of these assumptions, yet are working within the idiom of a profession which is based on assumptions that are sometimes quite
different.

We saw how the therapists' own supervision group was divided
over their response to the demands of the mother, with an older
woman therapist from a similar Sakha village experiencing some
sympathy for her position. At the same time, however, the urban
Sakha women in the group grew impatient with the mother's expectations. The gulf between rural and urban lifestyles is now becoming
greater than that between the different ethnic groups and their
supposed 'cultures'. Many young Sakha in the city are fairly
'Russianised', and consider the ethnic and racial issues which are so
prominent in local politics to be a concern only of older generations.

The notions of separation and individuation which underpin
much of the theory and practice of therapy do not necessarily apply
in other cultural settings (and even among white British outside certain middle-class subcultures). Like many young clients in the UK,
for example, those of Indian or Chinese extraction, young indigenous people in Siberia are torn between two incompatible sets of
assumptions about what is right in terms of family relaions and
responsibilities, and of expectations about how they should behave.
One major area of discussion with our local colleagues arose from
our choice of a young person's counselling and information service
in the UK as an initial model.

Young people's organisations in the UK tend to reflect and foster
an ideology of the young adult who is independent and strongly
separated from their family. Many youth workers are themselves
young. They do not have children of their own and have never
experienced the process from the other side. In Yakutsk, youth issues
are dealt with largely by mature women who are themselves mothers.
They tend to work with both parents and young people, trying to

bring them together rather then to assist with 'individuation and separation'.

When we talked about the UK's numerous and highly elaborated services to support young people (almost none of which exist in Siberia), therapists and journalists there repeatedly asked us how we support parents and what we did to keep parents and their grown-up children closer together. We had to acknowledge that the cultural assumptions of the west were fundamentally ageist; and that they could be seen as encouraging what they saw as the breakup of the family through a weakening or severing of relations between the generations which often leaves old people lonely and uncared for (when living in India, we have never been able to defend this against very strong criticism and incomprehension). They were even more struck by the realisation that this is considered culturally desirable, and that therapists could regard an inadequate 'separation' as pathological – although we pointed out that a therapist can ideally work towards encouraging a good transgenerational relationship within a model of separation.

Many of the cases in Siberia concerned issues which therapists consider to be very common and basic. The cases presented in Siberia included people with homosexual and bisexual tendencies; ex-soldiers from the Chechen war suffering from the trauma of what they had seen and been forced to do but who received no support from the military; and village girls coming to town who suffer from a high rate of sexual abuse.

As in many societies around the world, especially where 'traditional' values are still strong, public discourse in provincial Russia is more conformist and censorious than in the UK, and more unforgiving of any perceived deviance. These secrets thus become much more difficult for clients to speak about and more dangerous to reveal. For example, while alcoholism is widely discussed and the focus of many official campaigns, sexual abuse receives no public discourse whatever but rather a deafening silence, with corresponding difficulties for victims in finding help. A particular barrier in this case is a culturally perpetuated self-image of being a society in which such things could not happen.

This changes the nature of talking as a way of dealing with problems. There is a big gulf in Russia between the private and public domains, with very little in between. There is thus a strong defensive barrier around the community of family and friends. The growth of therapy as an idea and practice suggests that this community is

breaking down and that there is a growing need for a more profes-
sionalised confidential kind of space. However, there is still a strong
cultural attitude, especially among men, that it is weak and shameful
to seek professional help and that one should endure whatever comes
one's way in silence (perhaps with the aid of alcohol).

If therapy is to be useful in 'non-western' societies (and there is
no reason to assume this), its practitioners will have to build a suitable range of settings and find a middle line between the informal,
unstructured and unprofessionalised kind of talk which takes place
between friends around the kitchen table (Ries 1997), and the various forms of official encounter which are still considered intimidating and coercive. These take, or took, various forms. Until recently
there was the Soviet confessional meeting, in which one publicly
acknowledged one's sins in front of colleagues and neighbours
(Kharkhordin 1999). However, this concerned political misdemeanour or incorrect thoughts and left many other areas of one's personal life untouched. Otherwise if one's personal problems become
too difficult to bear, one still tends to fall very quickly into the hands
of the psychiatric hospital (which was itself also used as a political
tool: Voikhanskaya 1977).

The idea of a single confession session may be linked to the pre-
dominance of clients in Yakutsk who come for a single consultation
only. The nature of a single-session client in the UK (e.g. a young
person who wants to discuss a problem which they see as finite and
then move on quickly) is not the same as in Yakutsk, where a client
with the most complicated problem may have an expectation of an
instant solution. With such an expectation, there is a risk that when
this is not met they may become disappointed and angry with the
therapist. We found that culturally, long-term work is generally
not even seen as a possibility, and that in our terms many clients
use therapists to 'dump and run', rather than seeing their first
meeting as the beginning of a process of thinking and gradual
self-understanding.

Both clients and therapists were puzzled by the idea of long-term
work altogether, and in public perception it seems to be considered
as an indulgence with scarce resources. Clients tend to regard
therapy like a doctor's prescription. Rather than begin a long process
of self-evaluation, they want to bring an identified 'problem' and
have it 'solved' by an expert. This is surprisingly like the expectation
of shamanic or spiritual healing in many parts of the world such
as tribal India (Vitebsky 1993), where one animal sacrifice to the

attacking spirit may either be acceped or rejected, but people have difficulty understanding the concept of going to hospital for a long course of treatment.

It can also be seen as a residue of Soviet helplessness in the face of authority figures such as parents, teachers and government. Soviet society was one of certainty rather than of individual initiative ('Tell me what to do, come and rescue me!'). Even after the disaster of the Kursk submarine in the summer of 2000, a woman was heard on television saying that Putin should have protected them, because he was their father.

As was shown by the case of the mother as teacher, the authority, respect and power of the teacher role remain intense, even though teachers tend to be conservative and are little exposed to the diversity of life paths which their juniors now have to face. The mother in the above case study was not prepared to negotiate because she felt she had nothing to learn, only something to impart. This is an attitude which may be widespread in communities around the world where becoming a teacher is one of the main avenues of upward mobility and respect.

Implications for practice at home

How could this kind of experience sensitise us to things which we may be missing when we meet clients from various backgrounds at home? This hinges on another question: What are we to make of the differences between the assumptions of local therapists and their clients, and those which we brought with us from the UK?

Much of the culture and etiquette of Siberian Native peoples is to do with guarding against intrusion into personal space. People feel very uncomfortable looking each other straight in the eye. Pointing a finger at someone is also bad and is associated with witchcraft. These actions imply aggression through a trespassing across very import-ant boundaries of the person. It could be said that local cultures in this region of Siberia have elevated discretion, non-exposure and non-intrusion into key values. Though there are many variations, it seems reasonable to suggest that this forms part of a wider general pattern of East Asian cultures which extends into neighbouring Japan and Korea.

We can draw out certain implications for our view of counselling on a global scale. Seen from this perspective, even the 'talking cure' which is the absolute foundation of counselling also emerges as based on a cultural assumption. Might it not be damaging if the counsellor assumes that it will automatically be right for the client to open up? This is implied by the kind of approach, common in some circles in the 'west', which insists that people who do not talk freely are repressed, bottled up and not 'in touch with themselves'. Among Siberian Natives, as in many other parts of the world, it is the Native cultures which are more reticent, while their European conquerors are seen by comparison as brash.

We might even ask: Is it imperialist to foster counselling in a region like this? Is it therefore wrong, or right, to impose it or make it available in all other cultures? Could the dedicated, well-meaning counsellor end up becoming a missionary, in the bad sense of the word?

One way of responding to these questions is to acknowledge that counselling too has its own culture, in the sense of a more or less shared set of values and understandings about the world. A basic cultural assumption of counselling is that you can talk about problems, and that it is good to do so because this talking can change a client's situation for the better. Built into this view are certain ways of talking about taking responsibility for one's own life. The problem may be that these assumptions are not shared by much of humanity, for whom the unfolding of a person's life is also affected by spirits, or who value long-term dependency relationships which are often judged here as pathological. The arrival of counselling in such people's lives can now be seen as part of a wider process of culture change. It now becomes an option, in an increasingly plural society, to see one's life and destiny in these terms as well as in various other, more traditional ways. The task becomes to work out which kinds of people, if any, could benefit from which kind of counselling.

The fact that counselling is starting to appear in the town of Yakutsk despite all these difficulties and misunderstandings may be taken as a demonstration of this. A culture is more than a shared set of values. It also has a basis in institutions which exist to formulate, support and develop those values. When you turn to your supervisor for advice on how to handle a situation which has arisen with a client, you are consulting an elder of your tribe. (Of course, this is not a tribe in the sense of a community you are born into and are tied to by genetics; it is a community you have chosen to join and which has agreed to accept you.)

The Code of Ethics of a professional association of counsellors or therapists functions partly as a tribal law code. Their professional journals announce publicly that the high priests have tried wrong-doers and expelled them into the desert for breach of professional rules. But misunderstandings are always possible because your client may not share your professional or institutional culture. In Siberia, this is most striking in the field of self-revelation through talk. In the UK it emerges in different forms. One sometimes hears counsellors saying that one should not give a client a cup of tea (what a strange idea if you come from India, Siberia, Japan . . . !). Or that clients do not understand or observe the 'rules' about boundaries, time-keeping, contracts, dependency, and so on. Of course they do not – this is not part of their own culture, and we also know that they sometimes see it as coldness in the counsellor.

So what kind of compromise should you make? Are there any absolute truths, is there an unchallengeable way of doing things?

The study of life in other parts of the world shows how important it is to think about the niche which counselling may occupy in the client's own mind. What might this counselling be a substitute for? Who is the person you represent – not just in the sense of trans-ference, but in the sense of who might have been there to help in their own culture? What are the equivalents (if any) in the other person's cultural background? Was it family and friends? Was it healing rituals? If it was rituals, were these low-key and conver-sational rituals like the Sora (Vitebsky 1993), or were they dramatic and violent involving possession and exorcism like the Siberian Native peoples in the pre-communist era, and much of the rest of the world today? Were they private, so that counselling can realistically step in as a substitute; or communal, in which case one-to-one counselling may be almost impossible without an enormous adjust-ment? What are the concentric circles of support – and of under-mining, since family and social relationships can do this too – which surround this person? This can be especially important for refugees, recent migrants, and people spread out far from their own kind, away from any ghettos.

If we try to distinguish what is cultural from what is part of a universal human psychodynamic process, we shall come to see more clearly the strengths and limitations of the models and terms we all work with.

Acknowledgements

We are grateful to Oktyabrina Tutprina and other colleagues and collaborators in Siberia for their courage and determination, as well as to the many people over the years who have been Sally's clients and supervisors and Piers' anthropological informants. Thanks also to our translators Tanya Argounova, Masha Pol'skaya, Tanya Kornilova, Yaroslava Pol'skaya and especially Tanya Gounko who worked without payment for the whole of the two-week workshop in 1999. We are also grateful for funding which has come at various times from various sources including especially the British Academy, the Gilchrist Educational Trust and the Economic and Social Research Council.

Bibliography

Barashkova, A.S. (2000) The genesis of incomplete families in the Republic of Sakha (Yakutia). *Anthropology and Archaeology of Eurasia* 38(4): 67–78 (Russian original in *Sotsiologicheskiye Issledovaniya* 12 (1998): 72–8).

Freud, S. (1953) *The Standard Edition of the Complete Psychological Works of Sigmund Freud*, Volume 2. London: Hogarth Press.

Goffman, E. (1968) *Asylums: Essays on the Social Situation of Mental Patients and Other Inmates*. Harmondsworth: Penguin.

Kharkhordin, O. (1999) *The Collective and the Individual in Russia: A Study of Practices*. Berkeley: University of California Press.

Ries, N. (1997) *Russian Talk: Culture and Conversations During Perestroika.* Ithaca, NY, and London: Cornell University Press.

Sinclair, S. (2000) Disease narratives: constituting doctors. *Anthropology and Medicine* 7(1): 115–34.

Vitebsky, P. (1992) Landscape and self-determination among the Eveny: the political environment of Siberia reindeer herders today, in E. Croll and D. Parkin (eds) Bush Base Forest Farm: Culture, Environment and Development. London: Routledge, pp. 223–46.

Vitebsky, P. (1993) *Dialogues with the Dead: The Discussion of Mortality Among the Sora of Eastern India.* Cambridge: Cambridge University Press, and Delhi: Foundation Books.

Vitebsky, P. (1995) *The Shaman.* London: Macmillan, and Boston, MA: Little Brown.

Vitebsky, P. (1996) The northern minorities, in G. Smith (ed.) *The Nationalities Question in the Post-Soviet States.* London: Longman, pp. 94–112.

Vitebsky, P. (1997) Counselling and therapy around the world: is it good to talk? *RACE (Race and Cultural Education) Journal* 13: 8–12.

Vitebsky, P. (in press) Dreams and omens in Siberia. *Transactions of the American Museum of Natural History.*

Voikhanskaya, M. (1977) Life in an ordinary mental hospital: the view of a Soviet psychiatrist, in S. Bloch and P. Reddaway *Russia's Political Hospitals.* London: Futura, pp. 458–62.

Wolfe, S. (1997) Healing, landscape and experience in Sibertia. *RACE (Race and Cultural Education) Journal* 13: 13–16.

Chapter 5

Working with the effects of divorce on Asian women in Northampton

Wajiha K. Mohammad

Introduction

I am a 36-year-old British-born woman of Indian origin. I lived the first twenty-one years of my life in London and Northampton. At 21, I got married to the man I always knew I was going to marry. It had been arranged by both our mothers when I was a year old. For the next nine years I lived in Bombay, India with my husband. I was seen as a happily married, comfortably well-off, middle-class housewife. As I grew older and more dispirited with my lifestyle, I began to feel that I did not have an identity of my own. I lived in the shadow of my 'Professor/Scientist' husband. I was not allowed to pursue higher education or a career as this was seen as an insult by my father-in-law. My father-in-law is a very wealthy landowner and proprietor of many businesses. My pursuing a career would have been seen as an insult to his status and too trivial to be acceptable. He once offered me a 'salary' to look after my husband! We, the women in the family, were seen as emotionally weak and therefore unable to make rational decisions. We were told what to do and were seen as 'the shoes of our husbands'. This phrase is used by some Indian men to mean 'women are of no value'. Women are similar to shoes; 'you wear them on your feet and step on them as you wish'. By the age of 30 I became very restless. I decided my happiness and my future lay elsewhere so I 'walked out' of my marriage with my then 3-year-old daughter and returned home to Northampton where I felt I belonged. The pain, the fear, the grief and the family pressure to go back to my husband were traumatic. I felt at the time that I did not get any understanding or support from my community. However, the counselling I had from the mainstream voluntary sector was helpful but did not fulfil my need to be culturally understood. I felt my English counsellors could not empathise with my confusion over the mixture of my values, which are a combination of both the Eastern and Western cultures. During this unstable time I had a 'rebound marriage' with another Muslim man. The complete lack of support in all areas prompted a more devastating second divorce. This research was undertaken to achieve the resolution of feelings surrounding my divorces. I have chosen to explore the particular needs of other divorced Asian women living in Northampton as I feel we are an exclusive and under-researched group.

Aims

1   To investigate the outcome of divorce for my sample of women.
2   To identify the impact of isolation among the above women.
3   To provide recommendations for white counsellors for counselling ethnic minority women.

Local statistics

In 1991 the resident population of Northamptonshire was 578,807. Of these residents, 3.5 per cent (20,316) were from ethnic minority groups. The total number of Indians in Northamptonshire was 6580 or 1.1 per cent of the total population. Thirty-eight per cent of these Indians were born in the UK and 62 per cent were born outside the UK. It is important to note that the majority of Indians in the UK are of the Hindu religion and many are the children that have grown up in Britain since the 1973 Asian migration from Kenya and Uganda (Figure 5.1).

In general about 15 per cent of ethnic minority families are lone-parent families, compared to about 12 per cent of white families. As a whole 91 per cent of lone parents are female. Some lone parents may live with elderly relatives, and therefore these figures are most probably an underestimate of the actual number of lone parents in Northamptonshire.

A national Asian paper reported that a survey carried out in 1989 found that there were 21,000 Asians who were single parents out of a total of almost two million in Great Britain (Sarkar 1997: 29). Sociologists believe that the figure is much higher today. Asian women often face greater stigma if they are not part of the traditional family

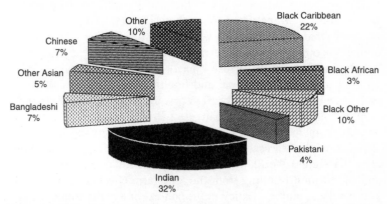

Figure 5.1 The ethnic minority groups in Northamptonshire, 1991 (expressed as a percentage of the total minority population)

unit, and the value of the extended family becomes a double-edged sword as they add to existing pressure.

Literature review

The term 'Asian' is used here to describe people of South-east Asia who are mainly from India, Pakistan and Bangladesh. There is very little material produced that identifies in particular Asian women's experience of divorce. As there is a lack of data on this issue even Asian researchers such as myself are limited in what work can be carried out. This kind of research is usually done in concentrated Asian population areas such as London, Bradford and Birmingham. The small ethnic minority population of Northampton is usually ignored, making the Asian women living there even more isolated.

The official system and men classify British women by marital status which divides them into the single, the married, the widowed, the separated and the divorced. Presently in Britain 16 per cent of all households with dependent children are headed by a lone parent, 90 per cent of whom are women (Chandler 1991). The same official system which classifies women in this patriarchal manner traps them as lone parents in the benefit system. This supports the argument that women from the poorer sections of society and from ethnic minorities are even more disadvantaged.

Culture is a complex word. There are over 160 different definitions of culture in social science literature. Lago and Thompson (1996:

3–33) argue that culture is not a 'biologically transmitted complex but a socially transmitted one'. Considerable confusion exists between what is 'racial' and what is 'cultural'. The term 'multi-ethnic' encompasses both the racial and cultural identities of the people who constitute British societies. However, Britain is also referred to as 'multi-cultural' and 'multi-racial' if either culture or race is being emphasised. These terms are discussed by Fernando (1995); 'multi-culturalism' means that British society has within it strands from various cultural traditions mixed up together. This stems from the waves of immigration over many years, especially after the Second World War, the subsequent collapse of British rule and the turmoil resulting from the long-term effects of colonialism and slavery. A major question in the context of a multi-ethnic society is whether mainstream organisations can deliver appropriate services to members of the minority ethnic communities or whether the problems and needs of these communities may best be served by organisations representing these communities. Service planners may make assumptions in service provision based on 'cultural need'; for example, family stress from male domination of the household, taking precedence over the individual needs such as housing or childcare. Both the 'image' problem and 'culturalisation of need' problem relate to the issue of stereotyping. Stereotypes are assumptions which may apply vaguely or not at all to a number of people, but which do not fit the situation of any one person.

Scholarship concerning itself with Eastern and Western approaches to how women may deal with divorce is scarce. However Fernando (1995: 17–44) is a rewarding source. He argues that generally speaking in Eastern thinking, integration, balance and harmony, both within oneself and within the community, are important aspects of what may be considered as mental health, while in the West, self-sufficiency, efficiency and individual autonomy seem to be important. The Eastern and Western approaches to mental health are different:

Eastern	*Western*
Acceptance	Control
Harmony	Personal autonomy
Understanding by awareness	Understanding by analysis
Contemplation	Problem solving
Body–mind–spirit unity	Body–mind separate

I use this dichotomy to analyse, in the context of the trauma of divorce, the six testimonies of my sample women.

Methodology

I chose to investigate qualitatively the experience of six divorced Asian women living in Northampton. The women were of a variety of ages, social class, linguistic and cultural backgrounds. Three had been born in the UK and three had been born in Asia. Their identities are disguised:

Name	Details
Fatima, 31	British born. Middle class. Urdu speaker.
Yasmin, 23	Bangladeshi born. Agricultural background. Bengali speaker.
Noorjahan, 35	Pakistani born. Business background. Urdu speaker.
Farida, 38	Indian born. Agricultural background. Urdu speaker.
Sukhi, 42	British born. Middle class. Punjabi speaker.
Jamila, 27	British born. Working class. Muslim. Punjabi speaker.

Semi-structured interviews provide a flexible means of questioning which allowed the women to elaborate what was important to them. By choosing women from diverse social backgrounds I aim to highlight the similarities and differences of their experience and also, when a marriage breaks down, how perhaps sexism and racism have a double impact on their lives. I located the six divorced Asian women through friends and family. Each woman was separately recommended. They did not know each other. Every woman whom I contacted the first time agreed to be interviewed. They all wanted to talk and perhaps 'unburden' their personal experiences in a confidential environment with another Indian woman who had experienced divorce. This in itself is significant, as it highlights acute isolation and possibly the lack of community support for Asian women in Northampton.

I asked where and when it would be convenient to see them. The three British-born women decided to come to my house to be interviewed and the three Asian-born women welcomed me to theirs. This may be due to the fact that I am acquainted with the first three. The

Asian-born women whom I had never met before may have felt safe in their own home environment for the interview. I wrote a short brief of the questions and areas I wished to explore with these women. I then showed the women the set questions at the beginning of the interview so they would be aware of what I would be asking. My aim was to make them feel as safe and comfortable as possible. This I felt would allow the women to discuss their personal and private thoughts with me in a spontaneous manner. I was overwhelmed and grateful that they all trusted me with such honest personal information and it is this rich disclosure of material that is the basis of my research. I am aware that as I knew three of the interviewees, this may have limited them in disclosing certain issues, as I did not have the anonymity of an unknown person who after the interview would not be seen again. However, they used phrases such as 'you know what I mean' and 'you understand', suggesting that empathy was present between us. The three Asian-born women's interviews were carried out in Urdu, and as I am bilingual I had no problem in understanding these women, who wanted to and felt more comfortable in speaking their own language. I feel I 'matched up' with my interviewees and that there was no obvious power imbalance, as they knew they were helping me in my research and in return I was asked to do them favours. For example, Farida asked me to contact the Council to repair damp in the ceiling of her flat and Noorjahan asked me to counsel her teenage daughter.

The reasons why divorce was instigated

> Historically, women have been oppressed and beaten with the approval of societies dominated by men.
>
> (Brinegar 1992: 2)

One ancient law decreed that a woman who was verbally abusive to her husband was to have her name engraved on a brick, which would then be used to knock out her teeth. In the Roman Empire, a woman could be stoned to death if her husband accused her of not being a virgin on their wedding night. She had no recourse. Her husband could also divorce her by taking a piece of parchment and writing on it his declaration of divorce. Wife beating was expected when a woman stepped out of line. It may be argued that not much has changed. Domestic violence is a common pattern of behaviour mostly associated with men, and transcends all social classes in both the East and West. Noorjahan, Sukhi, and Jamila were all victims of violence. Noorjahan's husband was a businessman, Sukhi's husband was from a wealthy family, and Jamila's husband was a factory worker.

For every two marriages in the United Kingdom there is one divorce. On average each year more than 350,000 people get divorced. Since the early 1970s, the number of marriages registered has fallen by over 15 per cent, while the number of divorces has more than doubled. Remarriage rates fall dramatically for women over forty and are presently declining among all the divorced (Bieber 1995: 27). It may be argued that the reason why more than half of remarriages fail is because women are now more able to support themselves and less willing to live in a 'bad marriage'. As Sukhi a well-paid professional argues, 'I'm happy on my own. I am financially self-sufficient and independent.' In households without resident men, women gain wider control and freedom to run their homes and lives and to rear their children more as they please.

Along with the highest marriage rate, Britain now also has the highest divorce rate in Europe, with each year thirteen divorces for every thousand existing marriages. Chandler (1991: 63) compares divorce with death: 'whoever initiates a divorce describes the process as harrowing.' The divorced woman attracts less sympathy than the widow and divorce, unlike death by natural causes, is seen as somebody's fault. Whatever the commitment to a clean break, divorce does not have the finality of death and, where children are involved, women have ex-husbands rather than no husband at all. Again, as with bereavement, divorce undermines health and women are more likely to consult their doctors. Noorjahan was in psychoanalysis for three years and on anti-depressants for eight years before she ended her marriage. It was easier to label herself as a victim of pressure and emotional abuse rather than acknowledge the possibility of divorce. Most of the women were aware of the stigma divorce has in the Asian community and that racism in Western society has a double impact on limiting their choice, so they felt there was more support within their family home and accommodated a lot of stress before getting out of a detrimental marriage.

Cohabitation appears to have grown and has an important transitional status as a popular prelude to marriage and aftermath to divorce. In my sample, Fatima is the only woman who lived with her husband prior to marriage. She firmly believes in cohabiting. Fatima argues that their whole relationship changed once she got married: 'the day we were married he changed.' Her husband did not allow her to go out or drink but to 'behave as a Muslim'. Fatima is now living with her new boyfriend and has no plans for marriage in the near future. It is significant to note that the husbands after having been married for between nine and fifteen years have all remarried, or began cohabiting fairly quickly after divorce. Out of all the women in my sample only Jamila, who was in the most violent relationship, has remarried.

All the women in my sample did most of the housework. However, it seemed it was less of an issue to them then it would perhaps be to Western women. Housework was a cultural practice more acceptable to all the Asian women. Money was the issue in the arguments between the married couples. Fatima and Noorjahan both state that this was the major reason for divorce. Sukhi and Yasmin financially supported their husbands, causing a lot of dissatisfaction. Only Jamila was lavished with presents but had to endure violent beatings from her husband: 'he used to buy me nice things but would hit me if I did something wrong.'

It seems that the main reasons for divorce were similar to the Western pattern: incompatibility, abuse and money management; causes consistent with Fernando's identification of self-sufficiency, efficiency and individual autonomy as Western characteristics. The only trace of integration, balance and harmony (the Eastern characteristics) were in the validity given to housework.

The influence of Islam on divorce

> It is He who has created man from water, and made him kindred of blood and marriage. Your Lord is All Powerful.
>
> (The Quran 25: 54)

Islam regards marriage not as a 'sacrament' but as a contract for life, which may, as a last resort, be dissolved by divorce. Marriage is intended not to be an arena for the battle of the sexes nor the imprisoning of women but as an institution which will offer security and stability to both partners and the children they may have. In Islam, divorced or widowed women are allowed to manage their own affairs when it comes to arranging a marriage.

A Muslim man is allowed to marry a Jewish or Christian woman but a Muslim woman can only marry a Muslim man. This is because

Islam recognises that a woman carries on the lineage of her husband. Providing for all the living needs of housing, clothing, food and so on is the responsibility of the husband, and in exchange for this the Quran (30: 21) says:

> And among His signs is that He created for you, of yourselves, spouses that you may live in joy with them, and He has set love and mercy between you; surely in that are signs for those who reflect.

Polygamy although allowed is not encouraged. A prospective bride is entitled to know about any other wife and a first wife should also know about any second wife. The Hadith (the teachings of the Prophet Mohammed) makes it clear that marrying more than one wife is to help widows and orphans in times of war, and not to satisfy one's lust. The Quran (5: 5) specifically forbids sexual relations for 'fornicating and receiving paramours in secret', as this does not impart dignity to women and leads to greater exploitation. Marriage safeguards women and men; as the Quran (2: 187) says, 'husband and wife are each other's garment'. It may be argued that it is better to marry a second woman and give her the 'status' of marriage than have a secret affair. Islam allows polygamy but British law does not. A second wife married only according to Islamic law would have no rights as far as the British law is concerned. Family has a crucial place in the Islamic way of life; the Quran and the Hadith are explicit about living an ethically and socially responsible life.

When a woman is married it is an essential part of the marriage for the bridegroom to give her a dowry. It is a gift and it becomes her exclusive property, even after divorce. In the case of 'khul' (divorce at the wife's request) she may be required to pay back part of it. However, if divorce is decided on, the Quran says: 'Then keep them in all decency or part from them decently. It is not lawful for you to take anything you have given them.' Yet all the six women in my study were left with nothing by their ex-husbands.

Noorjahan states that her husband only wanted a 'cook and cleaner' and how they 'were not suited'. She further adds about her long-term psychotherapist, 'I could tell him anything, however things remained the same at home with my husband'. As Noorjahan was born and brought up in Pakistan, the patriarchal culture and pressure to remain with the husband is doubly strong. However,

Islamic law allows her to divorce if she is dissatisfied but this is rarely taught to women in Asian families.

Divorce is taken to be the last resort in Islam. The Prophet Mohammed said, 'of all the things God has permitted, the one he most dislikes is divorce'. The procedure of divorce in Islam is such that it encourages reconciliation where possible. After divorce the woman should wait three menstrual cycles during which her husband remains responsible for her welfare and maintenance. The main purpose is to clarify whether the wife is pregnant. The second use is as a cooling-off period, where relatives or the community try to help towards a reconciliation and better understanding between the partners. The Quran (4: 35) says:

> If you fear a breach between a man and his wife, send for an arbiter from his family and an arbiter from her family. If both want to be reconciled, God will adjust things between them.

The 'arbiter' is a counsellor. If divorce is decided on, the wife is free to marry another man. The first husband is not permitted to remarry her unless she has in the meantime married another man and been divorced. It may be observed that recent developments in Western society are tending towards the Islamic pattern, namely the stressing of guidance and counselling before divorce, privacy of divorce proceedings and speeding up of the process of divorce.

Unfaithfulness, real or feared, on the part of the wife is the only instance in which beating the wife is allowed in Islam. This is misinterpreted and used as an excuse by many men. But how far this may have contributed to the violence in my sample of case histories is not apparent, and therefore cannot be explored in this research.

British Muslim women sometimes become prey to 'visa hunters'. These are men who are interested in acquiring British nationality rather than settling into marriage. This is what happened to Yasmin. It is the two younger British-born women, Fatima and Jamila, who have settled down with English men. Jamila quotes her mother as saying, 'no one in the Asian community will marry you'. This is a strong statement yet true. Most single or divorced Asian men will 'date' other women, both Asian and white, but will usually marry much younger 'virgins'. As Sukhi says, 'I was bitter about the age gap. She [the new wife] is just a couple of years older than my first daughter!' This may be why most of the Indian-born women in my sample have resigned themselves against the possibility of remarriage. They rationalise their situation by saying they 'don't trust men' and have accepted 'God's will' and found support in religion.

Fatima says her husband brought religion into their marriage and that is the reason she will not become involved with another Muslim man. This mistrust expands to cover Northampton's community leaders and priests. Farida uses religion to justify her husband's affair. She argues, 'Islam allows up to four wives. I know the Islamic laws. I can bear them.' The word 'bear' connotes pressure; it seems she is unquestionably waiting for all to be right again. For Noorjahan religion is her solace, it is her 'protection' and her way of accepting divorce. Yasmin and Jamila, the two youngest women in the sample, make no strong reference to religion as their reasons for divorce. Although all the sample women identify themselves with religion it does not influence their day-to-day activities which is similar to Western culture. Yet, despite the expectation of harmony and acceptance which is evident in Quranic teaching, these women are being influenced by the Western culture they live in.

The effect of divorce on children

> Children begin by loving their parents: after a time they judge them: rarely, if ever, do they forgive them.
>
> (Oscar Wilde, *A Woman of No Importance*)

The family is the place where one's world is formed. Single-parenting can be preferable to being raised by parents in a dysfunctional marriage. All children have a fundamental need for security. Divorce is an emotional uprooting for a child. It takes sensitivity and skill to avoid causing them lasting damage. One in five dependent children will be raised in a lone-parent home. Lone mothers are specialist mothers, as children are typically the only other members of their household. In these houses there are fewer divided loyalties. Children may become the woman's main or only source of personal meaning as they are all that is left of 'the family'. In this context women may feel that their children are owed emotional compensation for living in an incomplete family. Within this there is ambiguity, as mothers feel they should be more available to their children, while also feeling they have to give so much that the children tie them to the home. Chandler (1991: 142) argues that single-parent families appear more democratic and more permissive as they are inevitably less hierarchical. Children are encouraged to become more self-sufficient and responsible. Discipline may become a difficult area; as lone mothers become more emotionally and practically dependent on their children, they become enmeshed in negotiation, rather than parenting in an authoritarian manner.

My sample of case studies provided similar patterns of parenting. Sukhi states: 'I always talk to my daughters. We always sit down and debate everything.' Sukhi now finds herself in the position of not being able to remarry, as her daughters have threatened to move out and leave her if she does. It seems Sukhi actually fears this, and is emotionally compensating her need for a partner in order to stay close to her daughters. Her boundaries have blurred.

Both Sukhi and Noorjahan state that their children understood why they divorced, implying that divorce was discussed prior to separation. Noorjahan says: 'They suffered more when we were living together. They have witnessed him beating me several times. I still feel guilty that they had to go through all this.' However, Noorjahan, Sukhi and Farida state that their children are still 'close' to their fathers. All the women say their husbands have always been 'good fathers'. The children have regular access, and are happy with the relationship with their fathers. Farida's 14-year-old daughter's resentment towards her father's new white family is extended to cover the whole white population; as Farida says, 'my daughter doesn't like whites. She has nothing to do with the other family.' This prejudice which originates from Farida ('that white woman') filters through to the children and highlights how intolerance begins at home. This emphasises the complexity of racial antagonism and demonstrates that prejudice exists in all cultures. Yasmin's suffering for her 3-year-old daughter is very apparent when she says:

> He gives no maintenance for my child. He never showed affection for my child either. My daughter does not know her father. When she grows up she will ask about her father and this worries me. When she sees the ice-cream van and the other children with their fathers, then she asks me, 'where is my father?' But he wants no contact with us. He phoned me nearly two and a half years ago to say that. He has completely disappeared. There has been no contact since.

This case highlights the abandonment a mother and child feel when they are betrayed by the father, who takes no responsibility for his family. Yasmin is very keen to find employment as soon as her daughter starts school. This may well be for reasons of using her time to earn extra income and also to remove herself from the terrible helplessness she feels in her present situation.

Jamila's case is an example of the other extreme, where the ex-husband has taken custody of almost all the children through the court system. The term custody emphasises 'control' rather than care. The courts have tried to develop procedures and post-divorce arrangements that minimise disturbance for the child. They increasingly favour joint custody. However, in Jamila's case the courts have failed to protect her children as they are being 'shipped' between the parents. Jamila accuses the father of using the children to 'spy' on her and her marriage:

> It's not good for the children. It gives them hatred. The children don't know where they belong. I feel the children should all be together in one environment. He feels I'm not fit to be a mother. I keep quiet. I still suffer depression. But I long for my children. I want them to know that I do love them.

This is the painful testimony of a mother who has had her children taken away by the father and the legal system. The parents get so caught up in anger and vengeance that they sometimes fail to see how the aftermath of divorce can damage their children. Harmony is destroyed. It is these children who 'rarely forgive' their parents.

The effect of divorce on the family

> All happy families are alike but an unhappy family is unhappy after its own fashion.
>
> (Tolstoy, *Anna Karenin*)

After divorce mother, father and children may all have a different conception of who is in their immediate family. Cherlin (1981: 85) argues 'one can no longer define "the family" or "the immediate family" except in relation to a particular person'. The family has a high profile in popular culture. Television and newspapers thrive on the image of the family as a metaphor for everything that is homely and secure. This stands in stark contrast to the public images of the 'broken home' and the loneliness of life without a partner. Marriage is an important transition point for young women as they move towards adulthood. Securing a job or embarking on a career is the major transition for men. Patriarchy influences the lives of all women (and is especially strong over Asian women) and the lack or absence of a husband may give women control of the household but without escaping from any of the wider patriarchal structures. Without a male breadwinner they may be more economically vulnerable. State policies are caught in the dilemma of seeking to give no financial advantage to single parenthood while simultaneously trying to prevent child poverty. Yasmin and Noorjahan are the most affected by these policies within my sample. They both have young children and cannot afford the 'child-minding costs' to enable them to work. They do not get any maintenance from their ex-husbands and live alone in very low-quality housing with their children. These families are in poverty.

The establishment of a new sexual relationship may not be easy or attractive for women who are no longer married. There is a wariness and fear that a new person would be too similar or too different from former partners. Many busy single parents postpone developing a new relationship because they feel burdened enough. Double standards persist, where men presume the availability and willingness of lone women, but simultaneously despise those who easily succumb (Chandler 1991: 72). Yasmin and Noorjahan, both very attractive women, keep themselves 'covered' as they fear being labelled with a 'bad reputation' in the Asian community. The issue of reputation pushes back many women into a safer, all-female world. As Yasmin says, 'I do not trust any man now'; this is a very poignant statement for a 23-year-old to make.

For women who feel an obligation to control the sexuality of their children and set a moral example, there are difficulties in how open to be about new sexual partners. Correspondingly, children who are jealous of the new relationships may strive to undermine them. Likewise, Sukhi has avoided open contact with men to shelter her daughters, and now, as adults, the daughters will not 'allow' her to even think of remarriage.

Other women sometimes become suspicious of lone women, seeing them as a threat to their own relationships and thus keep them at a distance. Noorjahan and Jamila both said they lost many close friends after divorce; this is the price they pay for being attractive. The sheer busyness of many women, especially those with children, reduces their ability to reciprocate, whatever their personal need for support themselves. Chandler (1991: 84) states, 'the majority of married women in their twenties and thirties spend most of their time at home'. They are kept there by housework and childcare. Lone mothers have an even less active leisure life.

Fatima is the only woman in my sample who had cohabited and then married her husband, and is now cohabiting with her new boyfriend. A report in the *Independent on Sunday* states, 'Living in sin is the norm now. Yet new research shows that those who cohabit first are even more likely to divorce than those who don't' (Cook 1997). Research by psychologists at the University of California, who carried out a survey of 45,000 marriages, found that 50 per cent of cohabiting couples who subsequently married were divorced within five years, while less than 40 per cent of those who married without living together first, split up during the same period. It appears to be the same story in Britain. According to a Population Trends report from 1992, couples who married in the 1980s after cohabiting were also 50 per cent more likely to divorce within five years of marriage compared to those who marry immediately. After eight years the figure rose to 60 per cent. However, the 'allure of marriage' is still strong for the majority of women. What has changed is that they are more willing and economically able to escape when it goes wrong. Family-values campaigners are already 'gloating over the latest findings', hoping that couples will marry rather than cohabit first. However, this is unlikely, as more than one-third of unmarried men and women in their mid-twenties to early thirties live together. It is worth noting that relationships which tend to fail are those which were unsatisfactory to start off with. It would be interesting to analyse the cohabitation patterns of Asian women in Northampton, but this may not be possible as most of the community know each other and may be reluctant to admit to living together. However, it must be noted that Asian families are as diverse as white families and thus generalisations are not possible.

Most Asian households are now nuclear families but kinship ties remain strong. Economic and material assistance as well as emotional support are found in these links and are shared across generations and households. Asians will travel long distances for family events. All the women in my sample were emotionally close to their families of origin, and especially to their mothers. They all consulted with their mothers before divorcing; even Jamila was allowed, by her very abusive and controlling husband, to see her mother when she became physically ill under the strain of her marriage. In Indian culture the family is emphasised, and that is why perhaps loyalty to kin is more important than personal fulfilment in marriage. Pressure from the family may keep many couples together. Marriage is seen more in practical rather than emotional terms, so lack of affection between spouses may not be seen as a problem. This may explain why Indian marriages in Western society are fragile; they too are held together only by emotional ties. Taylor (1995: 268) states 'three-quarters of divorce petitions are by women'. This reflects the higher expectations (Western) women have of marriage due to greater equality and increased opportunities to escape from unhappy marriages. Taylor (1995: 259) also argues that:

> As life expectancy is increasing most women marry relatively young, have a small family and often return to paid employment in their middle years. Childbearing and child-rearing now occupy a smaller portion of women's lives. Greater geographical mobility has also meant that traditional extended family net-works have become weakened and therefore wives rely more on husbands for support.

Similarly, it is this constant need for support and mutual satisfaction that, if deprived, becomes a reason for Asians divorcing in Western society.

Societal expectations for women to slot into a caring role as daughters, sisters, mothers and wives is even more strong in the Asian community. All the women I interviewed made references to the impact their decisions to divorce had on their families. Fatima took her mother's support as she 'needed back-up'. Yasmin's family feel guilty as they arranged her marriage. Noorjahan's husband's family and then his illness pressured her to stay. Eventually Noorjahan's mother supported her decision to divorce. Farida's whole family are in India but her situation pains them and they are upset. Sukhi's family reconciled with her many times, yet after the divorce the family were relieved as she had made a final decision. Jamila's family were originally worried as they felt a single woman would be taken advantage of. Likewise, Jamila's mother supported her decision to remarry.

It is an assumption that Asians live in large joint families; my sample of women all belonged to 'the nuclear family' structure and were in contact with their extended family mostly by telephone. This may be the reason why harmony (the Eastern value) is frag-mented and the Western value of personal autonomy strengthens and becomes absorbed within the Indian family unit. This may account for the similar causes and effects of family breakdown within Indian families living in the West.

The effect of divorce on finances

> The most detrimental aspect of the absence of fathers from one-parent families headed by women is not the lack of a male presence but the lack of a male income.
>
> (Cherlin 1981: 81)

It is often difficult for single parents to function effectively. Saddled with sole or primary responsibility for supporting themselves and their children, single parents frequently have little time and few resources to manage effectively. Divorced and separated women who are raising children often find that their economic position has deteriorated sharply. If satisfactory childcare was available many women would be able to look for work. It is due to these factors that lone mothers and single parents have become the focus of debate about the feminisation of poverty.

Yasmin and Noorjahan retain prime responsibility for childcare and this responsibility is a hidden cost to employment. Without extensive childcare support it is hard to sustain full-time employment that is necessary to raise lone mothers' income beyond state benefits and make any employment worthwhile. As there are limited state-run nurseries, these women will have to earn a considerable income to pay for childcare to stay gainfully employed.

Our welfare system tends to treat women as primarily mothers and dependants and not as workers. Lone mothers are permitted to be long-term claimants, receive an additional child benefit allowance and can earn small amounts before this is removed pound for pound from their benefits. But there is ambiguity as, on one hand, they are encouraged to engage in part-time work, and on the other hand the benefit system assumes that people are 'in full-time work or out of work'. The need for part-time work is virtually ignored. Thus, the system forces women to choose between employment and state support, and presently women are opting for state support. Chandler (1991) argues that similar principles differentiate the treatment of different types of women. Widows receive more favourable financial treatment than the separated or divorced. They receive benefits that are taxed but not means tested. Widowhood is seen as involuntary and a legitimate misfortune. In policy terms, there is greater encouragement for them to participate in paid employment. Furthermore, an ageing population is seen in government circles as an economic burden and the state wants to limit its financial responsibility in this direction. As pensions are more devolved to private organisations, so a woman must imitate the career pattern of a man to become eligible, or remain married to a man with a pension to inherit.

From my sample of six women, three women get no maintenance from their ex-husbands. Yasmin's husband is in hiding from the authorities. Noorjahan's and Sukhi's husbands are on state benefits and so do not pay maintenance. Jamila's ex-husband has custody of three of her children, so he pays no maintenance; thus Jamila's new husband supports her and her youngest daughter. Only Farida receives maintenance. This may be linked to her still being sexually active with her husband, and therefore may have an influence on his being responsible in providing financial support. Farida seemed 'comfortable' and enjoyed her 'freedom'. After the interview I drove her into town where she wanted 'to do some shopping'. Farida obviously enjoys shopping and does it regularly, as her home is well decorated and she wears expensive clothes and jewellery. However, this may be her way of compensating for not having a 'live-in husband'.

Sukhi is financially better off without her husband. This is due to her not having to support him or his drinking habit any longer. Fatima is financially better-off also; she used to earn more than her husband and this caused problems. Fatima says:

> Things are much better than before. We are now in the process of buying this house. I have got a brand new car. My boyfriend's got his own car. Before I had to share a car with my husband. But I keep thinking my bubble is going to burst.

However, she confesses her husband has left her with many emotional insecurities which are slowly getting better, but she finds it difficult to believe she can live happily. It seems even emotionally 'strong' women can be intimidated by their husbands into believing they are of 'no importance.'

Yasmin and Noorjahan are classic examples of 'the feminisation of poverty'. Both are living with young children in very low-quality housing, on minimum benefits and no maintenance from their ex-husbands. Both Eastern and Western societies unfairly 'trap' women with children. Men usually 'move on' without the day-to-day responsibility of children.

It seems that Sukhi, Fatima, Jamila and to an extent Farida, are 'managing' financially after divorce. Yasmin is keen to find work as soon as possible to get out of poverty. Noorjahan feels her emotional relief after divorce is of greater value compared to her present poverty. Noorjahan is a model for Eastern culture. This elegant and poised woman seems to be in harmony with herself and calmly accepts her present circumstances.

The effect of divorce on housing

One year after divorce, the standard of living for men had risen by 42 percent, whereas the standard of living for divorced women had fallen by 73 percent.

(Weitzman 1985: 374)

Asians very quickly reached levels of owner-occupation which were greater than or equal to those of the white population, observed Jones (1993: 148–55). Owner-occupation was actually higher among the lower socio-economic groups; the reverse situation to that in the white population, where owner-occupation was associated with affluence. This was because for Asians owner-occupation was a way of obtaining poor-quality housing at low cost. 'Discrimination in both the private rented sector and the council sector was a key factor behind this development.' This discrimination continues. Ethnic minorities remain in lower status jobs, still suffer higher rates of unemployment compared to whites and live in lower standard housing.

Lone mothers are often concentrated in cheap public housing, where unsafe neighbourhoods confine them and their children to hours cooped up in their flats. In order to buy or privately rent better accommodation women need financial resources which many do not have. Out of the six women in my sample, five had lived in private homes with their husbands prior to divorce. Only Fatima has lived in the same council house for the past fifteen years; her husband moved out leaving her with arrears to pay. Fatima is now intending to buy her house. Sukhi paid the mortgage on her marital home and now also pays it on her 'new' home. She is the only woman in my sample who lives in an 'affluent' suburb of Northampton. Yasmin,

Noorjahan, Farida and Jamila all live in areas that may be described as 'rough neighbourhoods'. These women live in the 'less desirable' housing areas of Northampton. I feel it is discriminatory to place lone Asian women with young children in high 'racial incidence areas' (categorised by Northamptonshire Victim Support's 'Referral Policy' 1995: 2). I had great difficulty in locating Noorjahan and Farida's flats. I felt very uncomfortable on their housing estates, thinking that either my car would be vandalised or that I would be attacked. These women were unaware that, for example, their GP could be the 'doorway' to helping them access appropriate housing through the housing department. However, there are limitations, as Jacobs (1988: 111–13) considers what minority housing organisations have drawn attention to:

> The inequalities in the systems used by the local authorities in making allocations and how procedures have been conducted in a way that discriminates against minorities. This has been alleged in Labour as well as Conservative administrations.

The evident fear of unsuitable or low-quality housing emphasises the isolation many Asian women feel. They do not have a 'choice' in moving out of their marital homes. Noorjahan verbalises this fear as 'where would I go with my children?' and then substantiates her isolation with 'now I live in council accommodation. It has been a struggle.'

Refuges are limited to offering shelter only, and the high probability of getting poor housing may keep many women struggling on in bad marriages for a long period. In my sample of women, each stayed on for ten years or more. There may be many unhappy Asian women in Northampton 'struggling' in bad marriages and fearing the outcome of divorce. Yet, although Noorjahan is living in very poor housing compared with the other women I interviewed, she still finds it better than living with her husband. The condition of these women's housing is appalling and needs intervention; no woman with children should live in such poverty, be it in Eastern or Western society.

Social support in the context of divorce

> To be empowered is to be an encouraged and encouraging human being.
>
> (Brinegar 1992: 135)

The reactions to divorce says Bieber (1995: 31) are shock, denial, anger, sadness, frustration, bitterness, fear, insecurity, jealousy, guilt, hatred, despair, loneliness, anxiety, self-pity, desperation, rejection, loss of control and grief. To slowly and surely rebuild life after divorce the individual needs to accept these feelings as normal. Chiriboga (1991: 92) clarifies that first and foremost, stress-resilient individuals perceive themselves as exercising control over the situation. A second characteristic of effective copers was being involved in meaningful and pleasurable activities. A third ingredient was a more developed social network. Using Fernando's (1995) classification, these are very Western characteristics. Chiriboga (1991: 105) further argues: 'Divorce was a relief from the chronic duress of an unhappy marriage, for some it was a crisis, but for all it posed a challenge: to forge for themselves a new life.'

Chiriboga (1991) concludes that 75 per cent of divorcing persons experience continued attachment to their spouse. Many individuals seem to retain strong attachments to their former spouse, while simultaneously pursuing new relationships and accepting their single status. This was also observed in my sample of women.

About five out of six men and about three out of four women remarry after divorce, states Cherlin (1981: 29–89), and about half of all remarriages take place within three years after divorce. However, the divorce rate for remarried persons is modestly but consistently higher than for persons in first marriages. This stems from the lack of institutionalised support. The absence of accepted guidelines means that these often complex families must resolve perplexing issues by themselves. Remarriage is more likely to connect individuals who are at different points in their life courses and this can strain relationships. The ambiguity of remarriage and the difficulties of blending families create the potential for rifts and undercurrents of stress in the relationship. In the past the remarried population was dominated by widows, whereas today it is largely the province of the divorced. Class is also influential. Analysis of divorce in terms of the husband's socio-economic position shows an inverse relationship. The divorce rate rises with the fall in socio-economic status. Conversely it may be argued that some women are afraid to leave a comfortable lifestyle for an uncertain financial future and thus stay in unhappy but wealthy marriages. However, if women are in well-paid jobs, they are the least likely to remarry. These are women in command of adequate resources to remain unmarried and the least comfortable with traditional male dominance; these are women most able to resist remarriage. Fatima and Sukhi may be identified in this group; they are financially independent and thus can challenge the Indian cultural norm of male dominance by living their lives as 'single women'. Fatima argues that community leaders 'are mostly male. So I don't trust them. I wouldn't go to them or that kind of environment for help or advice because they actually judge.'

It may be argued here that some community leaders misinterpret religious teachings to keep women 'under control' and, by maintaining their male dominance, create an environment of mistrust. However, Sukhi goes beyond male dominance and verbalises her frustration with the local Asian centres as a whole:

> The local Asian services are not safe. They operate at a different level. Their views are different. They don't have respect and I don't trust them. It's not a healthy environment. They are immature. They don't know their own values so how can they help others?

Northampton has a service for Asian women, yet it seems it does not provide appropriate support to some individuals in the community who may need it most. Through the testimonies of some of my sample women, the women appear to be at the discretion of staff, who can help or refuse services, depending on who they are, or who they know within the organisation. Nepotism has a strong influence in Asian culture and filters into all areas. Other research has also touched on this controversy; for example, Watson (1977: 6), who argues:

> With a few exceptions, the self-proclaimed 'immigrant spokesmen' or 'community leaders' are highly educated, middle-class migrants from larger cities; the mass of ordinary workers are preoccupied with their own affairs and usually have little in common with these leaders.

He argues that anthropologists have demonstrated repeatedly that people tend to create alliances and change loyalties according to their own best interest. It is important here to highlight that within the Indian community in Northampton, there are many different languages and cultures present, as is shown by my sample of Asian women. To stereotype means to label people or attribute characteristics to a whole group. Duijker and Frijda (1960) define stereotypes as a relatively stable option of 'generalising and evaluating people'. A stereotype refers to a national population, race, a professional group and so on, and suggests that they are all alike. It is therefore an undifferentiated judgement which contains implicitly and explicitly an evaluation. It is this stereotypical evaluation of all Asian women being the same held by the statutory and voluntary sector that is so alarming and that many women have to deal with the crises of divorce in isolation so appalling.

Out of the six women, only Yasmin, Noorjahan and Jamila received help from outside of their family and friends. Yasmin speaks highly of Women's Aid and their Asian worker: 'Women's Aid helped me a lot. Their Asian worker helped me tremendously. I felt she understood me. I could communicate very well with her. She understood what is in my heart.' It is this kind of matching of ethnic backgrounds and another woman outside of the family who listens which is so important. This is the beginning of recovery and support for the divorced woman and needs to be available to the wider Indian community.

Noorjahan received support from doctors and psychotherapy, but after three years she voluntarily ended therapy. However, in talking to me in the interview, I felt she saw me as her counterpart, another divorced Indian woman who really understood what she was saying and empathised with her feelings. This may explain why she told me (a complete stranger) such painful and private thoughts in our first meeting via the interview. Jamila's experience of social services and the refuge was good but again limited. The almost three hours she talked to me highlighted her need for appropriate counselling also.

Fatima, Sukhi and Farida have had their mothers or close friends as supports. Although Fatima and Sukhi are not keen on counselling, the disclosure of such detailed information about their private lives is an indication that if they did have an appropriate and non-judgemental counsellor listening they may well find it therapeutic. Farida's suspicion of outside services is perhaps more to do with the authorities 'discovering' her ambiguous financial link with her husband. Yet again, her trust in me indicated her need for professional support.

In Northampton the barriers for Asian women in accessing the major institutional and organisational public services are summarised as follows.

1   Lack of knowledge and confidence in using public services.

2   Lack of awareness of rights and entitlements.
3   Lack of choice in services which can be used.
4   Inaccessible information, i.e. language, style, format.
5   Lack of interpretation and translation services.
6   Staff attitudes/racism.
7   Physical environment which is not welcoming.

At present there is no conciliation work or family therapy and no ongoing counselling for Asian women in Northampton. However, Relate is training two Asian women counsellors, one being myself, which in the near future will be of benefit to the Asian community. This is an encouraging step forward in social support for Asian women in Northampton.

Conclusion

> Despite all its misery and hurt, divorce is ultimately a process of self-renewal
>
> (Bieber 1995: 154)

As was the case in my sample of women and in many other marriages, it is the lack of communication, the not hearing what the other partner is saying or feeling, that leads to reasons for divorce, as Brinegar (1992: 108) says:

> Talking keeps the lines open for intimacy. When you encourage your mate to talk you are encouraging your marriage to work. Without the intimacy of talking and sharing, marriages break down.

In 1993, according to Dunn (1996: 30), of all the divorcing couples, 95,000 (58 per cent) had children under the age of 16. This represents 176,000 children whose families were broken up by divorce, 5 per cent more than in 1992. However, in a more positive analysis the issue may be seen as not that one-third of first marriages fail but that two-thirds survive. There is also another perspective to take, as all around us there are positive examples of lone-parent families who, against all odds, achieve and succeed. The achievement of these families goes largely unrecognised. Research and public debate tends to focus on the problems; it would be of benefit to focus on the positives of these families.

Similarly, it should be remembered that the vast majority of Asian marriages work as positively and as well as marriage is intended to work. I have focused only on the small proportion of Asian marriages that have detrimental effects on women. This study has highlighted the negative outcome of divorce on these Asian women, their children, their family, their finances, their housing and how most women had to deal with the crises of divorce in isolation or with very limited social support. In many ways the distinctions made by Fernando (1995) leave Asians with particular mental health deficits as they live in Western society. Therefore, all the pressures towards divorce with the kin support, which might normally mitigate these, were either felt as pressure or were dispersed with the political emergence of the nuclear family.

Isolation was a prominent feature, as none of the six interviewees knew each other. Three women felt they were 'the only' divorced Asian woman in Northampton. All were 'shocked' by the estimated number of Asian lone-parent families. Many Asian women feel isolated in Western society because of the 'double discrimination' of being 'black' and a 'woman'. Although many of my interviewees thought they did not require counselling, they did benefit and acknowledge the relief they felt in 'off-loading' their emotions during the interviews. There is a need for more education in making Asian women aware of the benefits of counselling. Local authorities need to implement specific policies for Asian counselling services. As most counsellors in Northampton are white and have limited experience with Asian cultures, they are unable to make the 'therapeutic alliance' with ethnic minority clients. White counsellors see the employment of Asian counsellors as good practice, and this practice should be encouraged further.

Recommendations for making a therapeutic alliance with ethnic minority women

It is strongly suggested that when white counsellors work with ethnic minority women the following issues are taken into serious consideration.

1 Understand the needs of the client. Are they strongly rooted to their culture or do they identify more with their white peers?

Never make assumptions about your client. They may be very 'British' in every sense; for example; they may eat, dress, socialise in a Western style or live with a white partner. Their views on life may be the same as yours. A few years ago I had a 17-year-old Pakistani girl come for counselling. She wore the traditional 'Shalwaar-Kameez' and appeared very shy and timid. She had childhood sexual abuse issues to deal with. I remember counselling her in both English and Urdu and 'assumed' I had a good therapeutic alliance with her. I felt empathy for her feelings around her mistrust of men. However, after a few sessions of counselling I was informed of her 'arrest' by my organisation. She had been involved in a 'sexual' incident in a local bar. That was the first time I learned that what a client says and the way she presents herself may not be the whole picture. She had previous warnings from the police of 'lewd behaviour'. It was because of her dress sense that I categorised her as very 'shy' or 'timid', yet she was very complex in character.

2 Explore how they interact with their family and extended family

Check out how close they are to their family when making decisions or whether they are autonomous and make their own life choices. Living in a joint family or living in a nuclear family may have different repercussions on individual choices. There may still be a colonial heritage in the first generation of immigrants who may still want to behave in a manner where they 'mind their own business and get on with their life'. Younger generations are now more vocal and demonstrative in wanting 'better conditions and equality'. For example, my parents are very easy-going and gave into their neighbour's bullying tactics over parking space. Recently, having had enough of my parents moving their cars and suffering much inconvenience, I challenged the neighbours. After what I would call a heated and assertive exchange of words on my part, the matter has been resolved. My parents no longer move their cars if they have arrived first in the 'shared' carport. Younger generations are becoming more vocal, and justifiably defending their own rights and those of their families.

3 Recognise that religion and spirituality is a strong part of their identity

Explore this with them in detail. Many women keep up religious practices as a way of socialising within their community. Ask them which religious or spiritual practice is special to them and what its significance means to them. There are ceremonies to celebrate brother-and-sister relationships, husband-and-wife relationships, festivals of light, thanksgiving and so on. Check out with your client how they interact in these family gatherings. Are they positive occasions or are they challenging? The family may influence and instil such strong values and customs that the children may feel obligated to carry out these ceremonies so as not to 'let their parents or other family members down' and not so much because of the religious implications.

4 Recognise the importance of interpreting correctly what your client is saying. Check out your understanding. Words may be interpreted with different meanings by you or your client

Keep reflecting back to the client what you understand by their use of words. This clarifies meaning for you both. Use 'precise language' and ask what the client means literally. For example, a woman may say, 'the family will ostracise me if I do that!' Ask 'who exactly would ostracise you?' This will enable the counsellor to pinpoint whom the client is most fearful of, the mother, father, brother or sister, and thus begin the task of untangling and enabling the client to communicate and negotiate their feelings effectively.

5 Don't try to over-identify with your client if they talk about prejudice or racism: you may come across as patronising

Treat the client as an individual. Keep a balance in your response, as power relationships between therapist and client may reflect the imbalance of power between the indigenous population and ethnic minority communities. Again keep the focus on the client's problem and explore options to resolve the issues at hand. Do not get tempted to involve yourself, or be drawn into a general political discussion over racism. You are there to enable and empower the client, not to resolve current affairs. The recent tragic loss of life in New York's World Trade Center may, for example, create a situation where an Asian client comes in fear of reprisal or other related effects on them. As a counsellor, focus on this fear and do not lead the client to justify or clarify your own curiosity about where the client stands politically on this issue.

6 Ethnic minorities generally have a strong value placed on respect: respect for elders and respect for authority. So problem-solving approaches may be more useful; for example, The Egan Model or behavioural approaches

As most ethnic minority women have been conditioned from child-hood to respect authority and to listen to what elders want, the counsellor has to encourage clients to have confidence in themselves and to trust their own judgement and to renegotiate a 'win-win' situation with elders. What does the client want to happen and what is the best way to achieve this? This needs to be explored in great depth with an agreed *action plan* at the end. I had a young female client who said she always did what she was told, as she was aware 'her parents wanted the best for her'. However, her brother's freedom to do as he pleased caused her much resentment. I focused on her need to be the 'perfect daughter' and what the pay-off for her was. After working on this issue for a while we explored her concept of 'responsibility'. In the end she chose to accept and appreciate her need to be the 'obedient daughter' because in the long run she did not have to take responsibility for her life. She felt safe in the know-ledge that she could blame her parents if 'things didn't work out for her in the future'.

7 Be aware that values and behaviour are influenced by cultural traditions, which tend to be malleable and resilient. Clients may be active participants in both their own and also British culture, i.e. bicultural or multicultural

Again your client is an individual and will have her own personal values and principles. Respect her individuality and explore where she feels she fits in or does not. People behave in certain ways because there is a 'pay-off' for them. They will adjust and adapt their behaviour to suit their needs. For example, I may be strong and capable of making independent decisions in my academic workplace as a 'course leader' that will affect the outcome of student learning. Yet I may go home and become the obedient daughter and not do or say something that will affect the 'honour' of my parents, even though it may mean that I have to sacrifice something I want or desire. At the moment my mother feels a third marriage is out of the question for me! I should deny any further needs of love and companionship and concentrate on the moral upbringing of my daughter. Thus I can be living in two different worlds on the same day.

8 Have specific cultural awareness training to recognise and understand the issues faced by the various communities in Britain

This has proven to be very helpful for white counsellors and should be encouraged further. Training and interaction with other communities encourages trust. Trust encourages commitment to better understanding and equal opportunities for all. I have found that generally, white counsellors fear that they may say something out of ignorance and not malice and that this may be interpreted as racism. Very recently an acquaintance of mine, who is a white upper-middle-class woman in a very powerful role within her organisation was saying how she was talking to an Asian woman counsellor 'in simple terms about a loop-hole' in the law regarding advertising. The Asian counsellor took offence, and in an accusatory tone said she understood technicalities as she had a Masters Degree in Law. The white woman said she was genuinely taken by surprise, as it is not very common to come across lawyers who were practising counsellors also. She explained that she was trying to use simple language and not jargon for a clearer understanding of the law, not because she was trying to 'patronise' a fellow counsellor. Therefore, be very aware of your tone of voice and verbal expression. Match your language with your client.

9 Show respect, empathy and genuineness to your client

Treat ethnic minorities with sensitivity to their specific culture. Show respect and understanding by greeting and acknowledging clients appropriately. For example, bowing the head or nodding to welcome an Asian or Chinese woman is more appropriate than shaking her hand, especially if the counsellor is male. You must put the client at ease straight away to enable a trusting working alliance. Understandably, this is harder to achieve when the client is under stress or grief. However, a genuine interest and wish to support your client will come across.

10 Finally, be honest and ask if you do not understand something your client says

Discuss any issue to clarify understanding and meaning for you both. Your client will appreciate this, as it shows you are really listening to them and are interested in what they say and who they are. You must enable clients to believe in themselves, to be true to themselves and who they are, even when they are fighting their conscience in going against their family, culture or traditions. Are they willing to betray others to be true to themselves? A hard decision, but crucial in the development of the individual 'self' living in a family where harmony and the collective 'us' is given more significance. For example, the case where a daughter-in-law wants to create a nuclear family set-up, where she is responsible for her own life choices. Will she be able to 'betray' her loving and caring in-laws who provide emotional and/or financial security in return for a more autonomous life? Also, another scenario is where it is the son who wants financial freedom from 'looking after' his parents, yet it is the daughter-in-law who gets blamed for causing a rift in the family set-up.

Thus, always try your best to *understand* the culture and the issues a client may or may not be aware of in implementing the above suggestions. This will enable good practice, and create a successful therapeutic alliance between a white counsellor and an ethnic minority client.

Bibliography

Ali, A.Y. (1983) *The Holy Quran*. New York: Amana Corporation.

Bieber, J.D. (1995) *If Divorce is the Only Way*. London: Alma House.

Brinegar, J. (1992) *Breaking Free from Domestic Violence*. Minneapolis: Comp Care Publishers.

Census Report (1991) *County Report; Northamptonshire (Part 1)*. A publication of the Government Statistical Service. London: HMSO.

Chandler, J. (1991) *Women without Husbands. An Exploration of the Margins of Marriage*. Basingstoke: Macmillan.

Cherlin, A.J. (1981) *Marriage Divorce Remarriage*. Cambridge, MA, and London: Harvard University Press.

Chiriboga, D.A. and associates (1991) *Divorce: Crisis, Challenge or Relief?* New York: New York University Press.

Cook, E. (1997) 'Can Living Together Damage your Marriage?' *Independent On Sunday*, 13 April.

Duijker, H.C.L. and Frijda, N.H. (1960) 'National Character and National Stereotypes', in V. Coombe and A. Little (eds) (1992) *Race and Social Work: A Guide To Training*. London: Routledge.

Dunn, M. (1996) *Community Care Fact File 1996/7*. Rochdale: RAP Limited.

Fernando, S. (1995) *Mental Health in a Multi-ethnic Society: A Multi-disciplinary Handbook*. London: Routledge.

Jacobs, B.D. (1988) *Racism in Britain*. London: Christopher Helm.

Khattab, H. (1994) *The Muslim Woman's Hand Book*. London: The Islamic Foundation.

Jones, T. (1993) *Britain's Ethnic Minorities: An Analysis of the Labour Force Survey*. London: Policy Studies Institute.

Lago, C. and Thompson, J. (1996) *Race, Culture and Counselling*. Buckingham: Open University Press.

Lemu, B.A. and Heeren, F. (1993) *Woman in Islam*. London: The Islamic Foundation.

Northamptonshire County Council. (1995) *Ethnic Groups in Northamptonshire. 1991 Census Topic Report*. Policy Division, Northampton.

Northamptonshire Victim Support Scheme. (1995) *Referral Policy*, 1 July.

Sarkar, P. (1997) 'Young, Free and Single'. *East: The Asian Newspaper*, 10 January.

Taylor, P., Richardson, J., Yeo, A., Marsh, I., Trobe, K. and Pilkington, A. (1995) *Sociology in Focus*. Ormskirk: Causeway Press

Watson, J.L. (1977) *Between Two Cultures: Migrants and Minorities in Britain*. Oxford: Blackwell.

Weitzman, L.J. (1985) *The Divorce Revolution*. New York: Free Press.

Chapter 6

Racial and cultural issues in counselling training

Duncan Lawrence

Introduction and background

Counselling and psychotherapy as 'vocations' both have widely held premises that are based upon the 'western idea'. In the west, we focus on the 'individual' and the notion that a 'greater self-awareness' is generally seen as a 'good thing' to strive for. Our society actively encourages people into relationships between a client and their counsellor therapist, a one-to-one relationship thought to alleviate emotional distress, and various other human challenges associated with living and working in Europe.

However, counselling professionals, in what is often described as part of the 'caring professions', regularly do their non-white clients a disservice by not really understanding them, or having a real appreciation of the role of race and culture in the 'formation of identity' within their clients' lives, their families, and their clients' entire 'way of being'. I completed a Masters in counselling back in the early 1980s, and when questions of race and/or culture were introduced, the trainer's regular line was something like 'we should treat everyone the same': a nice wish but I never witnessed any substantial training on race and/or cultural awareness back then, and for a long time never actually had any real hope of my profession ever being able to carry off this lofty dream.

> You have what we Eskimo call 'white man's disease'
> ('Fred' 1984)

The above statement was made to me about a month after I began a split post of alcohol treatment coordinator and village volunteer trainer with the Inupiaq peoples of Kotzebue, Alaska. As a counsellor it was an 'eye-opener' for me because I had recently completed my MA in counselling in addition to completing a two-year stint as a drug and alcohol counsellor, and so I started my job in this region of the world in a very 'confident' position. As an African-American who grew up in the heart of the civil rights movements and riots of the 1960s, I experienced racism first hand on a daily basis, so being thought of as having the 'white man's disease' was something I never thought I would hear in my lifetime. In that region of the world, if you were not an Alaskan Native you were considered a 'white' American – an 'outsider', regardless of your heritage. But 'Fred', one of the local villagers who soon became a good friend was one hundred per cent correct because, although I had lived in Alaska for almost twenty years, I lived in the city and had never really ventured into any Native towns and villages before, and therefore missed the world of experiences all around me. If I am really honest my very intensive counselling training never once looked at, or encouraged me to look at issues associated with living and working with 'Native peoples'; I had to learn from my mistakes and from very gracious people like 'Fred'. An example of this was that early on in my prac-tice I made assumptions about when my native clients were showing me maximum respect by regularly avoiding direct eye contact in our initial sessions.[1] In my 'eurocentric' mindset, I regularly mis-understood this gesture and wrote in my case notes that my Native clients were 'avoiding' issues, were in constant denial and so on, when in reality 'my views' were all professional and personal reflec-tions of my own limitations at that time. When I asked 'Fred' what I needed to do or learn to move on, he simply said, 'get to know our people, they will show you who they are, who their family is and what is wrong or right about them . . . and finally . . . get to know who you are when you are around us'.[2] This statement, especially the last sentence, was to have a profound impact on me as a person and the part of me that was involved in counselling and development.

Over the seventeen years since the above statements were made to me, my involvement in developing fair and 'world-centric' training has been a very challenging struggle, where it seems as if, in my training and consultancy practice, I am constantly removing the same set of roadblocks and facing the same type of unhelpful assumptions and bias from one staff group to the next. The recent tragic deaths in America and related events worldwide can at least be indirectly linked to the unfortunate long-term impact of cultural misunderstandings, racism, discrimination, and xenophobic tendencies, so clearly there is still a real need to further develop opportunities for greater racial and cultural awareness. I have benefited from the teachings and patience of others from a wide range of races, cultures and religions, and have felt quite honoured to share my time and experiences in return.

Our society is one that was built upon and exists with diverse collections of peoples, colours, races, cultures, faiths, and any counselling training should at least reflect a true appreciation for the non-western viewpoints that may exist within it.[3] This chapter will look at some of the issues related to race and culture in counselling training:

- The challenges of introducing race and cutural dimensions into counselling training.
- Racism, internalised racism, zenophobic conditioning.
- Student views: some of the reasons for and against an integrated programme.
- Assumptions about racial and cultural minority clients.
- A discussion: practical ways forward.

Do race and culture really matter?

From my experiences of being involved at least indirectly with the training of at least one thousand counsellors in the UK and having been involved with at least a few hundred trainers, a large number from both of these groups appear to have limited insight as to the 'impact' of racial and cultural issues 'in their own lives generally and within the counselling training setting specifically'. For example, when asked 'what difference/impact, say, on a counselling course would having training staff that reflect the "images of modern society" have (even though a majority of their trainees may be white and women)?', the responses I got in the 1980s, 1990s and now in 2000 range from 'I do not know' to 'there would not be much difference at all'.

As part of my practice of regularly asking others what they think about working with issues of race, culture and human difference and diversity I administered a survey to 120 counselling students and their lecturers. The primary intention was to obtain their views about what difference do (or could) diversity issues make to their counselling course. The secondary aim was to compare and contrast some earlier 'informal' surveys carried out in the late 1980s and early

1990s (Lawrence unpublished manuscript) looking at myths, fantasies and assumptions that 'social care' sector trainees and trainers (which includes counselling trainees and trainers) had about each other and their training. The survey group consisted of fifty 'black'[4] respondents and seventy 'white'[5] respondents from training centres in London and Birmingham. They were asked to fill out a survey that contained twelve question areas that directly or indirectly related to race and cultural issues.[6]

For this particular group the survey highlighted that white students felt more comfortable on their courses than did their black counterparts, and this holds true for trainees and their trainers. All respondents felt that the race and/or culture of their tutor would affect their training experience, and although white respondents felt more confident in their tutors' use and knowledge of diversity issues than did their black counterparts, a significant number of the total respondent group did not. Both groups generally had little confidence in their peers' abilities to use/and knowledge of diversity issues and black respondents felt more confident in their own use of diversity issues and/or general knowledge of diversity issues than their white counterparts' use/and knowledge of the same areas. When asked if they had previously mentioned these levels of concerns and dissatisfaction regarding diversity issues, the trainers and trainees alike made comments like 'I wish you could have done this survey a long time ago, I feel really alone . . . as if fighting on my own', 'It's not safe to do what you did' (ask questions), 'I am always with other black students, certain [white] people never choose to work with me', 'I am not a racist, I really do not know about these issues. . . . If I am really honest none of us do', 'I want people to see me as a tutor first and a black person second. . . . If I push race and culture too much they think I have a chip on my shoulder . . . but if I do not it will not happen at all', and so on (Table 6.1).

To me, from these limited samples results, if they are only partly consistent with the counselling training course experience generally, then survey sample staff and students are saying that, yes, they are somewhat aware of the 'impact' that race and culture may have within the training setting, but these same respondents are consistently saying that there is a 'gap' in what could be an opportunity to work through and with the diversity area of race and culture within their counselling training.

Table 6.1 Comparison of the views of black and white counselling students and their trainers

Respondents	Black	White
Would your current course experience have been any different if your tutors were. . . . :		
Women ?	100% yes	80% yes 20% no
Non-white women?	100% yes	100% yes
White men?	30% yes 60% no 10% not sure	60% yes 40% no
Non-white men?	80% yes 10% no 10% not sure	20% yes 70% no 10% not sure
Trained primarily in 'non-western' methods?	100% yes	100% yes
Do you feel confident in your tutors' use/knowledge of diversity issues?	40% yes 60% no	60% yes 20% no 20% not sure
Do you feel confident in your peers' use/knowledge of diversity issues?	20% yes 80% no	40% yes 50% no 10% not sure
Do you feel confident in your own use/knowledge of diversity issues?	60% yes 40% no	40% yes 50% no 10% not sure
Is having an appreciation for diversity (within a 'non-western' perspective) important for yourself?	100% yes	100% yes
Is having an appreciation for diversity (within a 'non-western' perspective) important for your peers?	50% yes 10% no 40% not sure	80% yes 20% no
Is having an appreciation for diversity (within a 'non-western' perspective) important for your clients?	100% yes	100% yes
Should having an appreciation for diversity (within a 'non-western' perspective) be important for all counselling courses?	100% yes	100% yes

The impact of racism and internalised racism within counselling settings

Many people debate the position of racism, in terms of its capacity to damage individuals, and their human potential. As a black man, I have learned from my parents and their parents that in order to have a 'fulfilling life', while being able to provide for my family, I would need to work hard, harder than the average 'white person', but not to forget my 'blackness' and my heritage. From their real experiences of racism and prejudice one always had to be two or three times as good in order to get those in power to give you a job that you were more than capable of doing. To some readers this may seem an 'outdated' attitude, but, as many racial and cultural minority groups will tell you, the world has made some advances in the area of democracy and human rights, but, from their individual perspectives and/or 'political positions', racism is very much alive and continues to thrive today.

For the purposes of this chapter, the definition of racism is as follows: *Racism = Prejudice + the institutional power* to unfairly discriminate against or oppress others simply due to their race and or cultural heritage. This may manifest itself in covert and overt ways such as in attitudes, behaviours, racially motivated offending/race hate crimes, changing the 'rules' constantly to keep certain races, and cultures, 'in/out', operating in only one language and/or offering limited human perspectives in education, training, media and so on. The term 'discrimination' is often 'misused' in place of the term 'racism'. Racism as a 'concept' can be a very confusing and emotive topic, but giving members of society an equal chance to be heard can help all people to 'open up' and can also help them to begin to get past the 'literal wording discussion and debates' and on to the more important consideration of the real and devastating effects associated with being any particular minority race, colour and/or culture in certain societies around the world.

Over the years some of my counsellor trainees have described their experiences of racism as feeling like: 'You always have to fight daily, whether you want to or not', 'People automatically think we are victims or need special considerations', 'I have reached my age in life and have never seen people like me or my family in text books (including on my counselling training) . . . it is like we do not exist and have never made any contributions [to counselling and psychotherapy] . . . how would you feel if this was you?', 'We spend our whole lives learning how to move within their world as well our own, but yet we get no acknowledgement, nor do they even try to get to know our lives ... they seem to be only interested in the negative stereotypes of people like me'.

Internalised racism can be simply described as a situation in which some individuals, groups, and cultures, that have historically been victims of racism and other forms of oppression (directly and indirectly) begin to turn this same process of racism and discrimination against themselves and others who have experienced daily and historical racism and discrimination. On a counselling training course you may see students actively involved in internalised racism when they engage in *'negative self-talk'*[7] that could lead to the same negative and debilitating effects similar to those of racism.[8] This 'self-talk' is not usually conveyed in an 'overt manner'.

Internalised racism to some is just as damaging as racism. One of my white colleagues recently came to me in a very perplexed state. They were teaching counselling at a centre which had approximately 50 to 60 per cent non-white students at any given time. Their concern was the fact that like many people this particular trainer had assumed that all 'people of colour' got on better than the average general white population and he was having great difficulty in accepting that at times some non-white students and/or staff do some of the same things to each other that racist mainstreamed society does to them. The trainer's main worry was that he and his students were stunned and were possibly playing into their own negative assumptions by actually doing nothing to actively address the situation.

For many people from racial/cultural minority groups, we may feel that internalised racism is one area which is 'too culturally sensitive' and as such should be dealt with only 'behind closed doors' within 'our' support groups, 'our' families, 'our' churches, 'our' communities and so on. As a person who has possibly unwittingly perpetuated internalised racism, as well as at times being a victim of internalised racism, I fully understand those concerns but strongly feel that for some people, *internalised racism is a challenge for daily living and as such is an issue for trainee counsellors to consider*. If the subject is handled respectfully and timely, internalised racism should be put on the agenda of any counselling training programme.

When internalised racism is prevalent within the training environment I have found it best to 'name it' and work through it honestly. I have also found it useful to allow trainees and or staff to develop their own 'support groups'.[9]

Student views: Some reasons for/against an integrated programme

From my experience most trainees who are regularly introduced to race and cultural awareness from their first days of counselling training are better able to integrate anti-racism practices, and overall become better practitioners than those trainees who have 'race/culture days' only sporadically. In-depth appreciation for race and cultural considerations takes time.

John

'John' was a student who was taught by a white staff team during his first year of counsellor training. At 33 years old, John was a real student whom I taught over three years in the mid 1990s. He is currently a well-respected counselling psychologist practising in London. He has graciously given permission to be presented here. His story is similar to many of my past trainees.

John's past experience of exploring issues of race and culture: 'None: my primary and secondary school textbooks only had blacks and other minority groups as "stereotypes", never as people in charge or with any real power. I had one race awareness course on my residential social work programme . . . it really did not prepare me to be on a counselling course with others . . . before my new tutor spoke I had already sized him up . . . big . . . black and "out to get his own back" on white students . . . boy was I wrong.'

John's past experiences of tolerance: 'I did not really mix much growing up . . . I played football with other cultures on a Sunday league, but not much involvement with diversity prior to beginning my counsellor training.'

Year 1: John was a counsellor trainee and also a residential social worker. He self-describes his race/culture as 'white British'. When beginning the counselling programme, most of the black students and some of the white students as well found John 'very stand-offish' to them. I initially found him that way as well.[10]

John always did enough to meet all the course requirements. The first 'challenge' to our relationship arose during any exercise or other classroom experience connected to human difference and diversity, similar to those discussed within this chapter. In the group he would consistently come out with comments such as: 'I feel that it was only the "politically correct movement" that made you [his tutor] say that people should have the right to "self-define" themselves rather than have counsellors, social workers, society, etc. put them into "ethnic monitoring categories" . . ., I feel that black people specifically (and black trainees indirectly) had always sought the sympathy from others and I feel that they have already been given too much,' etc.

Needless to say, John was not popular with his peers, especially those from racial and cultural minority groups. Even though his course included working with human difference and diversity in all areas, John still carried on with this narrow path for the remainder of his first year.

Year 2: John began the year rather like an amateur stage performer. He tried desperately not to upset anyone, so he never gave his opinions about anything whatsoever, especially anything connected to race and culture. He 'blew his top' however a few weeks into the first term.

A black student accused him of not knowing enough about his own culture and therefore should not be working with any clients yet, especially those from racial and/or cultural minority groups. John's very angry response was that if the group did not have me as a black tutor, then 'race' would not be an issue in the first place.

He expected to be kicked off the course and had asked to meet with me privately, to speed up his departure I presumed. When we met, John was clearly amazed and taken aback, first when I did not kick him off the course and second, when I added that his main statement was unfortunately too often true. I continued to tell him that I genuinely believed that he could make a real difference if he would stop fighting what my colour represented to him and instead use the energy to explore what his own race and his own culture meant to him. It is important to explain that for me at least, these 'learning moments' do not follow any 'pre-scripted rules of engagement'; I simply take a deep breath and lead in with respect for and commitment to the students and their potential clients. John explained that his father was passed over for some jobs in the 1980s due to the 'positive action' plan.[11] In this case racial minority groups and women, that also happened to be under-represented in the workplace were given 'set places' based on merit so that his father was always the 'odd man out'. John said he could understand positive action 'intellectually', but 'emotionally' he had conflicting feelings, such as not knowing much about his own culture, having seen confusing internalised racist situations both in and out of the course room which left him very confused and, in addition, John had conflicting views about his own racism and culture. I honestly felt that I met the 'real John' that day, the John who temporarily looked past his bias, stereotyping and fantasy and who caught a glimpse of 'me' that day as well.

Because placement visits were part of this year, I had to ask John to explore issues about his own culture, racism, etc. within personal therapy, before allowing him to go on to a placement. He agreed, and had his second-year work extended into the summer.

Year 3: John returned to the counselling training in great spirits. As part of his welcoming statement to the group, he said something like this:

> 'Hi, I am John . . . I am a rediscovered "Scot" and I am very proud of it. . . . At first I was very, very angry with my tutor for extending my second year . . . no one ever made me stop and think about me. . . . I wish he'd done it a year earlier . . . this letting us find who we are by ourselves is bloody difficult . . . I've learned warts and all about my culture, my parents and my grandparents . . . some of it was crap and some of it makes me and my family what we are today . . . I now know how I became a racist and what I need to do to work through it.'

John's peers stood up and warmly applauded him. It is successes like John's that honestly give me hope and inspiration to continue with counselling training and development.

Assumptions about our racial and cultural minority clients

During most of my professional training in education, counselling and mental health there was usually a limited session-module(s) on working with 'discrimination'.[12] Regardless of the subject area, there was usually a 'list of characteristics' to explain how people who were discriminated against usually feel. This list generally had highly emotive and value-based words and phrases such as 'low self-esteem', 'victims' of racism and discrimination, which leads to limited prospects for the future, language challenges and related communication difficulties and so on. I used to get anxious during these sessions because, regardless of whether I was on an undergraduate-level course or a masters-level course, in each case my white peers would usually be actively scribbling down the lecturer's notes and verbally agreeing with what was being stated as if what they were hearing were actually 'truths' that were 'written in stone'. In my head however I was usually bursting inside to say things like 'we are not just products of racism, what about our core self, our personalities ... I can do racism in my sleep ... for those for whom English is not their first language who are so much further ahead than us, they can process what we say into their mother tongue and then process it back into English for us ... to me the inferior one is us'.

I felt this urge continue inside of me, a need to explain to other white counsellors and white tutors that it is simply not ethical to use a list or a 'hand-out' to explain the characteristics, attributes and/or areas for consideration when working with black and other cultural minority individuals, families and communities, but equally I did not wish to be considered to 'have a chip on my shoulder'. After a supportive push from one of my early supervisors I began to organise my thoughts and ideas on paper. Over several years these ideas were used in diverse education, social work and mental health settings. An example of such a model to illustrate how others may see their own lives is one I call the *human diversity model of self*[13]. It begins with two basic assumptions: first that everyone has what I call various 'life tracks' or paths that they will have to be concerned with over their own lifetime (e.g. race, culture, gender, sexuality preference), and, second, that regardless of one's race, culture, colour, class, gender or sexual orientation, every single person on the planet is a combination of mind, body and spirit/heart. All of us strive for some type of 'balance' between the mind, body and spirit/heart. For example, some of us put a lot of time and energy into our spiritual/emotional development and expend less energy, say, on our minds and bodies. Some of us may put time and energy into the development of our bodies and perhaps not as much into the development of the mind and spiritual/heart aspect. Either way, we are all striving for some kind of balance (Figure 6.1).

Second (some would say most importantly), it assumes that individuals have various paths ('life tracks') that they follow just trying to live their own lives. For example, I as a black man have what I would describe as a 'two-tracked life'. The first life tracks are the *'everyday things'* that 'impact 'on me daily (see Figure 6.2).

These same impactors, or things I have to consider daily, are generally associated with *most* people's lives, regardless of race, culture,

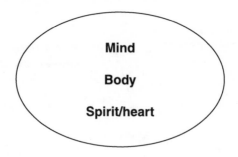

Figure 6.1

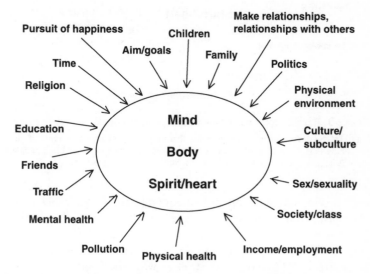

Figure 6.2 Track 1: Daily stressors and impactors for everyone

gender, sexual orientation, and so on. Most of us would say that any one of these areas can at times prove quite difficult to deal with or manage!

My second life track consists of the impactors on my daily life that are directly and/or indirectly associated with my *racial and/or cultural heritage* (see Figure 6.3). For me personally I find racism easier to deal with on a daily basis, say, than compared to if I had to experience internalised racism daily. Part of this can be directly related to how my parents and grandparents had prepared me to live as an individual within a racist world. Some black people see racism

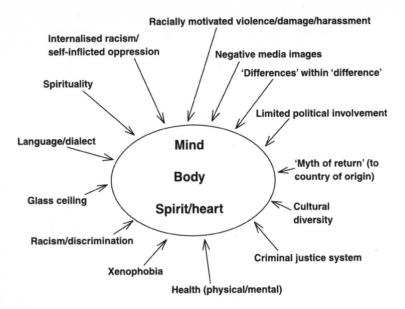

Figure 6.3 Track 2: Stressors and impactors for black people

Note: The bold items/arrows refer to areas that most people have to deal with at times. However, these areas are compounded, usually on a daily basis, for black people in Britain, due to the power of racism, discrimination and oppression.

and discrimination as an insurmountable challenge, while others may have similar thoughts to mine, or other, different variations altogether.

If I was, say, a woman from an Asian heritage, I would have a 'three tracked life', the first dealing with the everyday stressors (Figure 6.2), the second dealing with daily stressors/impactors related to 'race' and/or 'culture' (Figure 6.3), and the third specifically related to being a 'woman' (see Figure 6.4).

If we follow the simple logic of this 'life tracks' theory which looks at the various paths and tracks that people follow in their daily lives we can see that my first illustrated life track (Figure 6.2) might represent 'an average blue-eyed, blond-haired white male' in the UK, although quite clearly all of us have some of the same daily stressors/ impactors. But if I am, say, a black man living in the UK, I not only have to deal with the everyday stressors/impactors, I also have to take on the daily stressors/impactors associated with being black in Britain, hence I would be 'living a two-track life'. If I am, say, a black

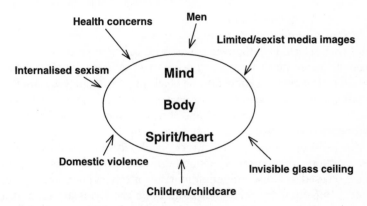

Figure 6.4 Stressors and impactors for women

woman living in the UK, I would be living a 'three-track life'. So you can see that a black woman's life in the UK is potentially more stressful than that of, say, a white or black male living in the UK.

Hopefully the thinking behind this theory is becoming clearer: No two people are ever the same, not even those with some of the same attributes such as race, culture, class and so on. Similarly, a person's 'self' is developed and influenced by how they perceive, respond to and/or may be influenced by their own unique life challenges (e.g. life stressors/impactors).

A discussion: practical ways forward

- Honestly identifying some of the issues and challenges for counselling training;
- Achievable action plans.

In my experience, trainees like John are not the exception, and from my observations most counsellor trainees begin their counsellor training with little or no exploration of the impact of race and culture for themselves or their families, and trainees usually have even less experience of exploring the impact of race and/or culture for others around them. In saying that, John posed some interesting points to consider, such as how training could be impacted by having black training staff and the problems with any training programmes that show bias for one culture to another, one theory or approach to another and so on.

Some of my past action research project results showed many white professionals stating that it was mainly 'non-white peoples' who came to mind when considering issues of race and culture, and not themselves. The opposite is true with my experience of any personally aware black trainers who see themselves as 'black trainers' and/or 'trainers who happen to be black'. Unfortunately, because of their commitment to anti-discriminatory practice, most believe they were sometimes marginalised and were never in a position of real influence within their counselling curriculum.

To a lot of people, the term race[14] and culture is used as a 'self-description' to state one's belonging to a 'centre' or 'home', or it may be used as a discrimination marker for others in separating out one group from the other, but more often the terms are used as a category separating others away from the main societal resources and the basic components of equal human rights such as respect of difference, right to exist without oppression, right to goods and services that reflect an understanding of you and your culture, and the right to be treated as a citizen of humanity, especially when in environments such as the counselling training setting.

Because of my work interests I often travel to diverse communities, locally, regionally and internationally. Through these journeys I have learned from trial and error that I can have a 'easier time/life' if I try to live like a 'local' wherever I go. This does not mean that I pretend to be something I am not; it means that I now walk quietly into other communities, and respectfully watch, learn and share from within their perspectives. I may not always get what I want when and how I am used to 'back home',[15] but I usually get information about some of the ideas and issues that may be 'universally' important, but from a 'local perspective', sooner rather than later.

Counselling may be a western phrase, but the idea of a personal development process that may be experienced through a relationship with a 'central person/other people' (e.g. sage, guru, teacher, elder, mentor, clergy, parent) has been around from the beginning of time and within all cultures. *No one person or any one particular school of thought owns this experience.* If one wonders why counselling and psychotherapy training has not been too quick to embrace the clear benefits of better integration of racial and cultural issues one has only to look at the rest of the world for the answers. The quest for power it seems is generally accepted as the root of most exclusion, oppression, war, greed, murder, exploitation and the like. For those promoting and perpetuating the idea that 'counselling' as a relationship concept comes from a limited area, a limited time and from certain individuals of the world keep certain 'schools of thinking' as 'absolute truths' and the 'great and the good' in lofty positions where they are often afforded all respect, all value and all consideration or power. A 'new spirit' of revisiting the definition and scope of the counselling relationship does not mean that one has to throw out or disregard 'European thinking', the basis for most counselling courses and textbooks; on the contrary, modern counselling should be about embracing human differences and diversity, as 'messy' and complicated as that may be at times, especially with the inherent but 'natural contradictions' that are bound to present themselves. The training setting could be a good venue to actively promote ideas from around the globe, even if it means that those who originally made the 'rules' have to give up some of their power positions in order to share with others and develop as interdependent movements: people and communities dedicated to developing inner peace and unlocking human potential together.

Centres may also find through trial and error as I have that counselling models and curricula which show an understanding and appreciation of one's trainees as 'human beings' and have a general awareness of and respect for the 'worlds' they may reside in, will make trainees feel more welcome which hopefully in turn will create the desired learning foundations that the centre can build upon.

To some, the above sentence may sound like 'social work rhetoric', but I will take the risk to say further that from my experience of being a guest speaker, trainer or consultant, most of the trainees and staff who were from racial and cultural minority groups were generally 'glad to see me', but some often held their breath until I began to talk about my commitment to the integration of diversity issues in every area of counselling, and furthermore how I would run their particular training event as a 'learning model'. Usually by the first coffee break, trainees and their staff came to me and said things like 'it's nice to feel welcomed . . . I wish we could do this all the time.' I am under no illusions here to think that complete strangers would share these things with me because they may think I wanted to hear them. I have often heard similar accounts from other trainers who have declared their commitment 'up front'. Minority students are first glad to see other racial and cultural minority trainers, but most are more than pleased when their trainers clearly demonstrate an appreciation for issues of race and culture rather than avoiding them. The key here is to make people feel welcomed and not alienated.

Adding 'personal development' components to any counselling training should be done very carefully. Some 'non-western' societies see 'self-reflection' and 'self-exploration' as the primary reason for living. This involves work on yourself, for yourself, through yourself – through religions and cultural systems of development, and through regularly speaking to or following the 'teachings' of elders, clergy and so on. Centres, trainers and trainees should be encouraged to take advantage of human diversity in terms of the possible range and scope for self-expression, and not to get stuck by just using 'talking' in training groups as the 'preferred model' for personal development. Centres which continue to do the opposite are possibly putting potential students and clients at a 'distinct disadvantage' in terms of the range and scope of personal development and personal expression opportunities that are offered within training settings.

Related to both the personal development and the counselling process is the 'western notion' of congruence, one of the 'planks of western thinking', and one that may not fit neatly into some of the frameworks presented within this chapter. Carl Rogers, considered the 'founder of humanistic counselling', refers to the idea of 'congruence' often within his written work, where the aim is 'be yourself' without what Rogers calls a 'facade' (Kirschenbaum and Henderson 1990). Since we all make assumptions about other people, cultures and so on, being congruent may often prove quite embarrassing and possibly hinder development of healthy relationships if being 'real' to us means showing our racism, our discrimination, our oppression, our xenophobia, our intolerance.

A counselling training setting operates on several levels. On one hand, most counselling centres have rules stating that racism and oppression will not be tolerated, but on the other hand those same centres want all their participants to 'risk being themselves' so that they can 'benefit from group feedback and mutual support'. For a classroom setting this is a somewhat reasonable expectation, but on a more practical level, a more realistic standard might be to not expect too much from participants, say, on certificate-level course work, and to increase expectations for participants on a diploma-level course; for example, having participants demonstrate appropriate levels of personal development work, with evidence of an appreciation for issues of human difference and diversity in themselves and others.

Where the above reasoning can come 'unstuck' is when you consider working with clients or through other interpersonal moments with others who may not 'readily' have an 'unconditional positive regard' for their counsellor. Most of us either 'warm to people' when we first meet them or we don't; our potential clients and those with whom we would like to have a relationship are no different. Some of these same people with whom we hope to make new relationships may read 'auras', or 'vibes' at conscious or unconscious levels, so they may see 'us' whether or not we want them to, so being 'real' may prove as difficult as trying not to be.

Another challenge here is to consider alternative ways of 'making sense' of new relationships, rather than considering only 'western ways' of interpreting them (e.g. 'Freudian transference' and counter-transference), or choosing only western models as a way of explaining how our racial or cultural minority clients may or may not see 'us' (CPCAB 2000; Murday 1999; Paniagua 1998).

Even though I have attempted to present 'accessible' suggestions and developmental frameworks, some centres and trainers may still find some (or all) of the areas daunting and will possibly still not know where to start. As a suggestion, centres may find it useful to (1) ask current staff and trainees to identify what they feel in terms of challenges, roadblocks and solutions and ask potential trainees/ trainers to identify what would make them feel more welcome or unwelcome by their counselling training centre and obtain their thoughts about how the situation may be improved. (2) Have regular staff team days to explore your model of counselling, whether it is still relevant within a multiracial, multicultural and diverse society, and explore what may be done to better integrate issues of human difference and diversity. Finally (3) regularly monitor and evaluate the effectiveness and relevance of your 'model'. This can be integrated easily into your course by asking trainees to provide surveys to their clients, staff at their placements, to their supervisors, to relevant outside agencies and so on. The results can be compiled, with any 'learnings' incorporated into existing course programmes without too much difficulty. This can be completed two or three times per academic year and may easily become a regular part of the course curriculum.

Notes

1 At least until we officially got to know each other.

2 In this region of the world, Inupiat peoples have cultural values based around love and respect for elders, love and respect for culture, love of children, love of nature, love of man, and so on.

3 In this instance the term 'non-western' refers to human value structures that originate 'outside' of Ancient Greece/Europe such as Asia, Africa, the southern hemisphere, polar regions, and so on.

4 This designation was a category for respondents that 'self-described' themselves as 'Black', 'Black British', 'Jamaican', 'Mixed Race', 'Turkish', 'Irish', 'Asian', 'Indian' and 'Japanese'.

5 This designation was a category for respondents who 'self-described' themselves as 'White', 'White British', 'European', 'Welsh', 'Scottish' and 'French'.

6 The entire survey format is not presented within this illustration. Taken from CPCAB (unpublished) *Integrating Issues of Difference and Diversity into your Counselling Training.* © *CPCAB 2000.*

7 Inner thoughts (and actions) similar to those of racists and xenophobes who are 'internalised' (e.g. black people are inferior, etc.).

8 This could include trainees not taking certain training and/or training staff seriously, not taking certain theories seriously, some trainees over-working in order to meet self-imposed/unreasonable demands, some trainees visibly disregarding constructive peer feedback, some 'put-down' of thoughts, feelings and expressions of own and/or other racial and/or cultural minority groups, some trainees who may 'distance' them-selves from any 'outward signs' of belonging to a cultural heritage, and so on.

9 Support groups in this instance are meant as an 'opportunity' for indi-viduals with similar experiences of 'oppression' (e.g. racism, internalised oppressions, discrimination, sexism, etc.) to meet, discuss and share positive strategies and attitudes, which in turn may help them to make better use of their training. Others who are not directly part of these groups such as staff/students may have all sorts of fantasies about what these groups may or may not be discussing, (e.g. 'anti-white attitudes', etc.) but if these groups are allowed to develop respectfully and not just allowed to exist when classroom difficulties arise, they can empower individuals as well as the entire training group. In addition these groups are good models/frameworks that all counsellors may consider when supporting their non-white clients and families that may be experiencing internalised racism.

10 John was not an unusual trainee. I have worked with trainees with vari-ous levels of racism, sexism, mental distress, etc., ones who often 'pro-jected' their issues on to myself and/or on to other trainees. In saying that, over a three-year course I have seen trainees make enormous per-sonal growth. The amount of growth varies, and seems to be directly related to the amount of appreciation and understanding of 'self'; in this instance I am referring to understanding of uniqueness and of the impact of one's own difference and diversity as it might relate to self and others.

11 Positive action in this instance relates to all strategies designed to re-address imbalances within the workplace. For example, if there were, say, 10% local citizens from Turkish descent then a good employer would commit themselves to strategies to make sure their workforce represents the community in which it exists, hence they would be implementing 'positive (employment) action'.

12 In this case the term 'discrimination' usually equated with the terms *racism*, *black* and *oppression*.

13 This model has been developed by D.E. Lawrence, who holds joint copyright with the CPCAB (Counselling and Psychotherapy Central Award Body, United Kingdom). Used by permission. For some, 'self' relates to the 'I' position, for some this relates to the vantage point of one's family/family consideration, for some to the vantage point of one's culture/culture considerations. All these vantage points should be taken seriously from the outset of any 'counselling relationship'.

14 This chapter's usage of the term 'black' refers to those individuals, families, groups and cultures that suffer daily oppression and discrimination (directly and indirectly) within western societies that can be directly traced to racism, skin colour and culture.

15 Place where my 'spiritual' home resides, where my parents are etc. To others this may be where they were born, where personal ideas and assumptions they may hold as 'familiar' reside or originate from.

Bibliography

Alleyne, A. (1998) 'Which Women? What Feminism?' in *Feminism and Psychotherapy*. London: Sage.

Amen, R.U.N. (1990) *Metu Neter, Volume 1. The Great Oracle of Tebuti and the Egyptian System of Spiritual Cultivation*. USA: Khamit.

BIIP (1997) *New Controversial Discussions; Experiences of Differences*. British Institute of Integrative Psychotherapy.

Bowlby, J. (1971) *Attachment and Loss*: Volume 1. *Separation Anxiety and Anger*. Harmondsworth: Penguin.

Bowlby, J. (1973) *Attachment and Loss*: Volume 2. *Separation Anxiety and Anger*. Harmondsworth: Penguin.

Casemore, R. (2000) 'Should We Challenge a Client's prejudices?', *Counselling Journal*, British Association for Counselling February, 11 (1).

Cavlen, P. (1983) *Women's Imprisonment*. London: Routledge and Kegan Paul.

Cheetham, J. (1981) *Social and Community Work in a Multi-racial Society*. New York: Harper & Row.

Claes, T. (1996) 'Theorizing the West: A Second Look at Francis L.K. Hsu,' in *Cultural Dynamics*, 8, March. London: Sage.

CPCAB (1998) *A Tutor Guide to Integrating Working with Difference (and Diversity) into your CPCAB Programmes* (Version 1.1: July).

CPCAB (2000) *Integrating Issues of Difference and Diversity into your Counselling Training*. Unpublished.

D'Ardenne, P. (1989) *Transcultural Counselling in Action*. London: Sage.

Donnellan, C. (1991) *How Racist are We? Issues for the 90's*. Volume 6: *Independence*. PO Box 295, Cambridge, CB2 2EN.

Dryden, J. (1982) 'A Social Services Department and the Bengali Community: A New Response', in J. Cheetham (ed.) *Social Work and Ethnicity*. London: Allen & Unwin.

Epstein, M. (1995) *Thoughts Without a Thinker: Psychotherapy from a Buddhist Perspective*. New York: Basic Books.

Fernando, S. (1996) 'Black People Working in White Institutions: Lessons from a Personal Experience', *Human Systems: The Journal of Systematic Consultation and Management*, 7 (2–3), pp. 143–154.

Field, A. (1990) *'We're Here Too!'* Research Project into the Needs of the Bangladeshi Community in Sunderland.

Fleming, C.M. (1992) 'American Indians and Alaskan Natives: Changing Societies Past and Present', in M. Orlandi and R. Weston (eds) *Cultural Competence for Evaluators*. Rockville, MD: US Department of Health and Human Services.

Fraser Wychu, K. and Crosby, F. (eds) (1996) *Women's Ethnicities: Journeys through Psychology*. Boulder, CO: Westview Press.

Geertz, C. (1993) *The Interpretation of Cultures: Selected Essays*. London: Fontana.

Gilbert, M. (1986) *The Holocaust*. London: Collins.

Gurnah, A. (1984) 'The Politics of Racism Awareness Training', *Social Policy*, 11, pp. 6–20.

Humm, M. (1995) *The Dictionary of Feminist Theory*. London: Prentice Hall/Harvester Wheatsheaf.

Jackson, R. and Nesbitt, E. (1993) *Hindu Children in Britain*. London: Trentham Books.

Jandt, F. and Pederson, P. (ed.) (1996) *Constructive Conflict Management: Asia Pacific Cases*. London: Sage.

Katz, J. (1978) *White Awareness*. Norman: University of Oklahoma Press.

Kirschenbaum, H. and Henderson, V. (eds) (1990) *The Carl Rogers Reader*. London: Constable.

Lago, C. and Thompson, J. (1996) *Race, Culture and Counselling*. Milton Keynes: Open University Press.

Lawrence, D. (1996) 'Race, Culture and the Probation Service', in G. McIvor, *Working with Offenders*. London: Jessica Kingsley.

Lewis, P. (1994) *Islamic Britain: Religion, Politics and Identity among British Muslims*. London: IB Tauris.

Matsumoto, D. (1994) *Psychology from a Cultural Perspective*. San Francisco, CA: Brooks Cole.

Murday, H. (1999) *Working with Difference and Diversity*. Unpublished: Lambeth College, London.

O'Brien, S. (1989) *American Indian Tribal Governments*. Norman: University of Oklahoma Press.

Paniagua, F. (1996) 'Cross-cultural Guidelines in Family Therapy Practice', *Family Journal: Counselling and Therapy for Couples and Families*, 4, pp. 127–138.

Paniagua, F. (1998) *Assessing and Treating Culturally Diverse Clients – A Practical Guide* (2nd edn), Multicultural Aspects of Counselling Series 4. London: Sage.

Pearson, G. and Lawrence, D. (1995) 'Race and Ethnic Monitoring: How not to do it', *Criminal Justice, The magazine of the Howard League*, 13, February.

Pederson, P.B. (1997) *Culture-centered Counselling Interventions: Striving for Accuracy*. Thousand Oaks, CA: Sage.

Rice, M. (1990) 'Black Feminists and Criminology' in L. Gelsthorpe and A. Morris (eds) *Feminist Perspectives to Criminology*. Milton Keynes: Open University Press.

Richards, A. (ed.) (1975) *Freud, The Psychology of Everyday Life*. Volume 5. Harmondsworth: Penguin.

Seager, J. (1997) *The State of Women in the World Atlas*. London: Penguin Reference.

Sherif, M. (1966) *Group Conflict and Co-operation: Their Social Psychology*. London: Routledge and Kegan Paul.

Smith, D. (1997) *The State of War and Peace Atlas*. London: Penguin Reference.

Thomas, H. (1992) *Explanation on Caribbean Migration*. Basingstoke: Macmillan.

Thompson, J. (2000) 'Intercultural Supervision', in *Race and Cultural Education in Counselling's Multi-Cultural Journal: Celebration of Difference for the Millennium*, 21, pp. 11–22.

Time Out (1999) The Race Issue – A Question of Color: A Week in the Life of Multi-racial London, *Time Out Magazine*, 10–17 November, No. 1525.

Tizard, B. and Phoenix, A. (1993) *Black, White or Mixed Race. Race and Racism in the Lives of Young People of Mixed Parentage*. London: Routledge.

Chapter 7

Counselling and cultural diversity in prison

Pam Williamson

This chapter is a personal perspective describing only a tiny part of Wandsworth Prison's history. It covers some of my work spanning about ten years.

Culture

Working inter-culturally in a counselling setting means a conscious decision, based on awareness and knowledge, to acknowledge how and when culture is influencing the interaction. The culture of the *setting* and the culture of the *counsellor* may be as important as the culture of the *client*. We have a number of *cultural identities* based on our belonging to different 'shared contexts': work, gender, sexual orientation, class, caste, tribe, race, ethnicity, religious beliefs. We follow the values, beliefs and behaviours that are held by the group. Much of this is unconscious, so it can be difficult to put into words. Culture goes beyond the surface attitudes that seem obvious to the outsider. It is largely invisible to those within it. The deep structures are 'felt' through interactions with others in the family or group. *Culture change* is recognised as something that can happen over time through the assimilation of different ideas from other cultures and from experiencing different events.

In the workplace legislation, market forces and ideals described by mission statements begin to force change at the behavioural level often out of step with underlying beliefs and attitudes of staff. This is especially relevant when trying to understand the dynamics at work between people from different races, genders, religions and social backgrounds as they find their place in British society today.

Lee's list of five dimensions (1999) is useful in capturing how we view the human experience based on our values:

1 *Human nature.*	Inherently evil ⟷	Inherently good
2 *Human activity.*	Doing ⟷	Being
3 *Relationship with* *natural world.*	Mastery/control ⟷	Harmony
4 *Relationship with self.*	Individual identity ⟷	Group identity
5 *Relationship with* *others.*	Individualistic ⟷	Collectivistic (I exist because the group exists)

Laungani (1999) has summarised similar dimensions contrasting behaviours and beliefs of British and Indian cultures:

Individualism .... Communalism
Cognitivism .... Emotionalism
Free Will .... Determinism
Materialism .... Spiritualism

These provide useful frameworks to explain cultural feelings and behaviour. Usually Western cultures would be at opposite ends to Eastern cultures. However, the dimensions represent a continuum rather than either/or, to allow for variability within cultural groups and individuals. For example, my family value *rational, logical* behaviour above *emotional* expression whereas I valued *intuition and feelings* and aspire towards *harmony* with the natural world.

The ways that I view the human experience are rooted not only in my upbringing but also in my counselling training and my work with clients. I believe people do the best they can based on their circumstances, knowledge and abilities. This view underpins my counselling and is now part of *my culture*.

My philosophy of counselling has its roots in existential-humanistic traditions from practitioners such as Gilmore, Egan, Yalom, Perls and Moreno and social theorist Boal (who started the Theatre of the Oppressed in South America). As human beings we need to make sense of things and as such are motivated to assign meaning to our experiences. This gives us a sense of control and safety and directs our behaviour.

The meanings we give originate from our values, and will have roots in our family culture, religious beliefs and the context in which we find ourselves (e.g. a relationship, a social occasion, a workplace setting). There is a circular relationship implied here as meanings give rise to values.

Distress occurs when we cannot find a meaning or the meaning assigned now does not fit. For example, 'I can protect my family from danger' now does not fit because something has happened which we were unable to prevent. In order to carry on we have to find a new belief incorporating the new event. For example, I will protect my family *whenever I can.*

We may have violated our values by our actions or decisions. Sometimes we have to choose between two of our values when a new situation means we cannot now hold both. For example, 'always tell the truth' and 'don't hurt others' when being honest would hurt someone.

People may seek counselling if their distress is unmanageable and 'new' meaning difficult to find. The person may become too afraid to cope with *meaninglessness.* Other conflicts and anxieties may surface linked to death, freedom and isolation (Yalom 1980). The defences used to overcome these anxieties will be culturally determined:

- *Death* – the conflict is the tension of knowing we will die and our wish to continue. Fatalism or religious belief in an afterlife will defend us and provide comfort.
- *Freedom* – the tension between knowing we are responsible for our actions and choices and our wish for structure. Individual-istic cultures may defend the anxiety by looking to shift blame to circumstances or others. Collectivistic cultures understand only limited personal choice and so defend the anxiety in terms of the group rules and structure.
- *Isolation* – the tension between knowing we are separate, unique and alone, and our wish to be in contact with others, protected and held. Our desire to belong. 'Doing' cultures will defend against this anxiety by engaging in work and activity which will ensure being valued by others in society. 'Being' cultures have individual identity embedded in the collective ego of the family and ancestral past.

The purpose of my counselling is to help the client to bring into their awareness these anxieties in order to face them and to learn to cope constructively with human existence. The use of the relation-ship in the process is an important component and distinguishes counselling from other forms of helping. When a working alliance is established clients can begin to explore their concerns. They may first need to release emotions in order to reduce the confusion they are experiencing. Only then can they begin to make sense of things.

There is a continuous spiral of increasing awareness as self-knowledge and activities evoke new meanings. Therapy ceases when *'meaning breaks'* have been restored: – meaning → being → meaning → doing → new meaning and so on (Figure 7.1).

Some people are unable to integrate experiences that challenge their current views or the sense they make of life (e.g. 'I can protect my family from harm'). Retaining a belief or meaning that fitted in the past feels safer. They deny events or feelings, including that death will happen. This can be represented in terms of a loop rather than a spiral, with death *outside* (Figure 7.2).

My English background and experiences in London prisons are part of *my culture* and have also influenced my understanding of the human condition described above. I started working part-time in London prisons more than seventeen years ago. I grew up in the Midlands in a white working-class family and moved to London to study industrial chemistry in the late 1960s. Some family rules will be seen as typically English: privacy is important, don't pry or gossip, work hard, be honest, kind and fair. Be an individual, value education and develop a social conscience: that contrast between being

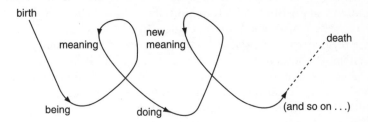

Figure 7.1

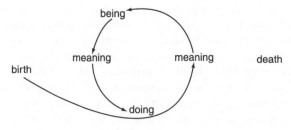

Figure 7.2

dutiful and yet protesting when injustice occurs; the reluctance to be labelled and being ashamed of what previous generations have done (Paxman 1999); a sense of humour that makes fun of myself and the English and yet can feel hurt by criticism when I did my 'best'.

Clients will guess some of these and may assume I am middle class because of my jobs: I worked in industry, education, cancer research and management before working as a counsellor. For the past seven years I have provided a counselling service to Wandsworth Prison staff and their immediate families for personal or work-related issues. I have delivered training to prison managers and staff on a variety of topics including understanding change; race relations; suicide prevention; assertion, harassment and health; critical incident debriefing and recognising traumatic stress.

My work with prisoners has been mostly in two London prisons where I taught basic education, self-development and psychology. I also facilitated group therapy for non-sex offenders and co-tutored on the National Sex-Offenders Treatment Programme (SOTP).

The prison setting

The Prison Service is traditionally a white male, hierarchical organisation using written rules to punish and control behaviour. It also has a paternalistic and protective side. These attitudes towards both the prisoners and the staff echo the processes of the criminal justice system. It knows it has to modernise to fight off market forces and changing social attitudes. There are no longer jobs for life. Prison staff live in the shadow of market testing and privatisation. Institutional racism has been acknowledged by the Head of the Prison Service along with the challenge to make *difference and diversity* a celebration rather than a problem.

The prisoner cultures in relation to race were studied in three prisons a few years ago (Genders and Player 1989). The 'pecking order' for different prisoners could be seen to mirror the outside criminal community with black prisoners forming an outside group. For example, in a prison holding long-term prisoners, the white professional criminals were at the top and sex offenders were considered the lowest of the low. The black prisoners operated as 'small businessmen' on the edge. In response to rigid and authoritarian attitudes, this hierarchy was replaced by prisoner solidarity against the staff. In a prison with younger, short-term prisoners there was no fixed power structure and black prisoners fitted in (or not) as they did in the outside local community. There was less prisoner solidarity against staff in the liberally run prison. Thus when two or more of our cultural identities are in conflict we have to choose the one that is the most important for the immediate situation. This is relevant when considering *the setting* in which counselling is offered, as it can have an impact on which cultural identity is to the forefront for the client.

Because many readers may have limited knowledge about prisons it may be helpful to provide some information about the architecture and the range of people who work in Wandsworth Prison. The prison was always seen as a tough place, dealing with some of the most difficult prisoners in the system. It had clear rules and authoritarian control. The regime is now more relaxed, providing prisoners with a range of facilities and challenging programmes to help them change their criminal lifestyles. Visible racism and bullying are investigated. Foreign National prisoners are provided with additional support.

The prison is situated in Southwest London. Although built in Victorian times many of the buildings have been refurbished and some completely rebuilt. The accommodation for around 1400 male prisoners is situated in two separate areas. The design viewed from above of both areas resembles wheel spokes radiating from a central hub. The larger one consists of six 'spokes' or wings that have four floors called landings. Prisoners who may be unconvicted or have sentences ranging from a month to life are housed here, i.e. a local prison serving some London Courts. The smaller site comprises three wings and accommodates prisoners convicted of sex offences. They will spend several years at Wandsworth following programmes that aim to reduce the likelihood of their reoffending and creating more victims.

Other buildings include a kitchen, industrial workshops, education classrooms and a library, gyms and places of worship for all religions. There is a hospital for prisoners taken ill during their time in prison and a drug therapeutic unit. There are visiting rooms for families.

There are some 700 staff which include managers, prison officers, doctors, nurses, catering staff, ministers of religion, work instructors, education tutors, librarians, psychologists, probation officers, administration and maintenance staff to cover 24 hours a day, 7 days a week and 365 days per year. There are also external professionals from different agencies who attend daily.

Over the past few years there has been a drive to employ a work-force that more truly reflects the local community. In London this would be 25 per cent from minority ethnic groups. In Wandsworth Prison there are currently nearly 14 per cent black and Asian staff employed. There are 25 per cent female staff. About one-third of the prisoners are from minority ethnic groups. In the national prisoner population it is 15.5 per cent. As in any other prison in England and Wales 'its purpose is to protect the public by holding those committed by the courts, looking after them with humanity and helping them lead law abiding and useful lives in prison and after release'.

In the early 1990s several important initiatives were started nationally which began to *change the culture* of the prison with reference to how *support* and *counselling* was regarded. One initiative was directly concerned with how staff would be supported after serious traumatic incidents. Following the Strangeways riot in 1990 there was to be a post-incident care team in each prison. Staff teams were to provide confidential colleague-to-colleague support after traumatic incidents. It was hoped that offering staff the opportunity to talk would reduce the likelihood of the normal temporary post-traumatic stress reactions developing into serious illnesses. The team members would also be able to assist staff in accessing counselling help when required.

At about the same time another initiative was being developed linked to the prevention of prisoner suicides. This was to be a co-ordinated response called the F2052SH procedure. The responsibility for identification and care of 'suicide at risk' prisoners would be a shared responsibility involving all prison staff and prisoners rather than viewed as a medical problem.

I mention these national initiatives together because they brought into the foreground not only feelings but the need for a *community response*. They triggered more understanding about and acceptance of the need for emotional support during times of loss and change. Other things contributed to this change of attitude, notably the introduction of the Sex Offender Treatment Programme and more recently addiction treatment programmes delivered by trained prison officers, psychologists and addiction counsellors. Counselling and other help is now part of prison life for both prisoners and staff.

In the past Wandsworth Prison had a 'macho' view about why help might be needed for individuals. 'Macho' here refers to 'don't show your feelings' and 'don't feel'. For example, attitudes such as 'If you can't stand the heat get out of the kitchen'; 'People are getting too soft nowadays'; 'Only weak people need help'; 'Pull yourself together', were common when counselling was mentioned. Nowadays there is the opposite view that counselling will be provided whenever people are stressed. This does not demonstrate an understanding of the purpose and methods of counselling but it is a shift in the right direction.

At the time when others were beginning to be aware of counselling, I was becoming more aware of the culture of the workplace and of the cultural differences of prisoners and staff.

Culture change and suicide prevention

Back in 1991 I set up a training workshop for staff and prisoners entitled 'How do you deal with unhappiness in yourself and others'. It contributed to the *culture change* mentioned. The one-day workshops were timetabled to run once a month for twelve new participants each time: six staff and six prisoners. I delivered them for two years to over two hundred people.

It was fairly unusual then to provide joint training and as far as I know it is still unique in the prison system. We would start at 8.30 a.m. with coffee and finish about 4.30 p.m., working through the whole day. We had a buffet lunch together at a time when it was not usual to have prisoners out of their cells at lunch time. The staff who attended were from all areas of the prison, the majority being prison officers. Senior and principal officers, governors, psychologists, civilian instructors, administration staff and teachers also attended.

The aim was to offer an opportunity to understand and gain skills in listening to someone who might be suicidal. We started with a contract about confidentiality and respecting differences. The participants first explored their own familiar feelings and the events that produced these feelings. They discussed their coping strategies and whether these were constructive or destructive. They identified common negative feelings linked particularly to loss and powerlessness. Then they practised 'counselling' each other using active listening skills. I would try and encourage everyone to use real experiences. This gave the 'listener' real practice knowing the 'client' was genuine. There were comments like 'I never told anyone that before' from staff after prisoners had 'counselled' them.

The workshop raised awareness of the feelings and needs of unhappy and suicidal people. It provided an introduction to listening skills. Some who attended realised that they were not comfortable as 'listeners/counsellors' but could now understand that listening can help. They were now happier recommending others to talk over their problems when they saw signs of anger or despair. They felt more willing to ask direct questions like: 'Have you thought of killing yourself?' 'How would you do it?' 'Have you thought how it would be after you are dead? Who might miss you? What will the world be like without you?'

Staff and prisoners allowed trust to develop between each other and their 'uniforms' were forgotten. Instead they were just people with life experiences that had affected them in some way. Over the two years and afterwards no one ever reported that confidentiality had been broken. A mutual respect for each other's role in the prison seemed to develop. Some examples from the feedback will illustrate this. Participants filled in anonymous questionnaires that included the following question: 'Has the workshop helped you in any way?' Some of the answers are given below.

- 'Yes, talking to prisoners in a personal manner is a first for me.'
- 'I was surprised how staff and prisoners mixed. In fact it's the first time in eighteen months I didn't feel like a prisoner.'
- 'It's given me a wider view concerning situations inside and outside prison.'
- 'Now I have a better understanding of the role of a counsellor. The importance of not offering solutions, instead letting the person reach their own decisions.'
- 'It's helped me understand underlying problems people keep hidden.'
- 'The workshop was good. It should involve more prisoners and officers to help break down barriers.'

The small closed group session also made it safe for both staff and prisoners to discuss their cultural differences in the practice sessions. It became clear on many occasions how these were important in understanding the reasons behind the different feelings experienced. For example, in the feedback part of the practice session, I overheard an African prisoner and a white prisoner discussing how they felt about having no visitors: 'I have brought shame on my family and country so I understand why they cannot visit me. For you it is different; you feel angry and want to hurt them. You expected support.' We discussed how our own family 'rules' and cultural attitudes about feelings affect how we view different emotions in others and ourselves. For example, in many British families being sad is often thought of as selfish. Children may perceive that 'if you are happy then you will be loved'. As adults they apologise for crying: 'I shouldn't be crying; you've been so kind.' They feel guilty because you may think they do not appreciate you: 'I don't know what's come over me.' They feel you may reject them because they are embarrassing you. They may avoid company because they feel unable to hide their sadness and this will upset others. 'Putting on a smile' is common in other cultures too (e.g. in Ghana). However, where bereavement is concerned in some cultures you will be expected to wail and shout rather than maintain 'a stiff upper lip'.

Following these workshops I tried to become more culturally aware in my counselling practice. I realised how different traditions can influence the meanings we construct and how these then direct our feelings and behaviour.

Around the same time prison staff in other prisons had also realised that training prisoners to listen and support their fellow prisoners may be a way forward in the prevention of suicide. To this end projects were started in many prisons which began to bring in the Samaritans to train prisoners as listeners. The listeners would be prisoner-Samaritans. This initiative spread throughout the Prison Service over the next few years. The recognition that suicidal ideation has to be a shared responsibility between all staff and all prisoners went hand in hand with the listeners' work.

Individuals want initially to be with someone they know or someone they think will understand: a family member, a friend, a colleague, a fellow prisoner. This has parallels with the philosophy behind the post incident care team, which is described below Accepting help from professionals can be difficult in any culture. It can mean giving up a belief related to themselves or their community (e.g. 'I'm strong', 'I can cope' or 'I accept my suffering'). It may feel like giving up control of their destiny or that someone is interfering with the suffering they must bear (Kleinman 1995).

Culture change and post incident support

The Strangeways riot in 1990 prompted the Prison Service to look at what it should offer staff after incidents in the workplace. Three types of confidential support would be put in place: post-incident care teams, group debriefing and post-traumatic stress counselling.

These would be in addition to the Management support and operational debriefs for staff. Each intervention would provide a continuum of care from different personnel as required. The acceptance of help may only be possible if it fits a person's cultural norm, but the offer began to change the macho prison culture. Staff are offered an opportunity to talk about what happened and how it has affected them. This can help to reassure and normalise their initial reactions and feelings. It is not unusual to spend time going over and over what has happened in order to make sense of it. The meaning the person assigns to the incident influences how they react to it and how they recover from its impact.

I will describe more fully the role of the post-incident care teams, as it highlights a *cultural change* in the prison.

Each prison has its own care team from within its own staff. The staff are trained in listening skills and recognising traumatic stress reactions. Care teams undertake to provide confidential listening and practical support in the form of colleague-to-colleague befriending. In Wandsworth prison, staff are given a leaflet that describes normal reactions and when to seek professional help. Counselling is available when necessary. I was involved in setting up the first post incident care team (PICT) in Wandsworth prison. Over the years it has included Asian staff, white staff and black staff from African and Caribbean backgrounds.

The team is currently made up of male and female staff from all grades, ages and cultures. It is important that staff who are approached after an incident feel that they are able to trust the person to understand their reactions and feelings. Sometimes staff will feel more comfortable with someone of a similar age or length of time in the job or wearing the same uniform, whereas for others it may be the same racial background or gender. Some of these expressed preferences can become unimportant when the person is overwhelmed by feelings and needs to talk. That is not to say that PICT members do not need to appreciate when there might be reluctance to accept help because they are the *wrong* person.

Different racial groups may have different reasons behind their unwillingness to accept help. When a white PICT member approached a black member of staff, he rejected the help offered, even though he was in distress. A black member of the team originally from Nigeria knew that his fellow countryman colleague would find it difficult to open up about how he was feeling unless he knew the person. Then it would not matter about the colour of the PICT member. It can also help to be approached several times and perhaps away from the formality of the workplace. In contrast some white male staff reject offers of help because they are denying their feelings. The white staff member is more likely to hold on to denial of any vulnerability or need, i.e. those with British 'stiff upper lip' and 'boys don't cry' family rules.

Several black and white staff have mentioned that off-loading to someone who is younger and appears inexperienced in life is more difficult. A black British Nigerian PICT member says that age difference is important in that 'if the person is only one day older' they are 'wiser' and so would be more acceptable. Feedback from a black member of staff with Caribbean roots suggests it makes little difference about age or colour if he believes the PICT member is genuine. This illustrates some similarities between groups and some differences concerning how the elderly are viewed.

Both black and white PICT members commented on their observations that male and female black staff were more willing to talk than white staff. They were less defensive about their feelings. There was less of a stigma associated with accepting support. White PICT members had also observed that black colleagues seemed to express more genuine gratitude for the offer of support. Perhaps some of this makes sense with respect to those male staff with African family traditions especially if they are the eldest in the family. My African colleagues tell me their role is to be strong and support the rest of the family, and ideally solve problems within the family. They would never break down in front of family members. It would be easier in front of friends they trusted. Thus any support they need for themselves would be readily accepted from trusted work colleagues whether black or white. They would also only use the services of a counsellor if a trusted friend had recommended the counsellor. I also know this from clients who came to see me after they first talked over the problem with many friends from the same background.

Gradually the offer of support from the staff on the PIC team has changed what is acceptable and appreciated by staff. The racial mix of the team has also encouraged different staff to seek further help when needed. Some people have reluctantly acknowledged that it does help to talk and it is all right to own up to having feelings.

The different interventions from a wide variety of people have the potential to offer culturally specific support *within the culture* of the prison setting. Although our understanding of traumatic stress reactions is based on studies around the world after wars and natural disasters, the assessment and treatment protocols have rarely taken cultural aspects into account. This has been criticised by several professionals (e.g. Baluchi 2000; Kleinman 1995; Young 1997). The British Psychological Society recently commissioned a Working Party to review Psychological Debriefing models (Tehrani *et al.* 2002), with a chapter considering cultural issues (Regel and Courtney-Bennett 2002).

Race relations – getting it wrong and getting it right

In recent years racism and racial tensions in Britain have been in the news. This has resulted in individuals and organisations looking closer at their attitudes and behaviour towards others. There has been training in race relations within the Prison Service for over ten years. However, at Wandsworth Prison a few years ago, we wanted to design and deliver our own training to provide staff with more information and examples which could directly relate to their workplace and the people in it. A multi-ethnic group of external trainers from NACRO and a multi-ethnic group of Wandsworth staff including myself developed a one-day course.

The course is interactive and includes small group work, quizzes and discussions. What has frequently engaged participants has been the sharing of knowledge about different religions, diets and cultural rituals. Staff began to share experiences and discuss differences in a positive atmosphere. They talked about situations at work.

Staff could get it wrong without realising. Behaviour and reactions they had seen could now be put into context. For example, understanding the significance of religious objects and who might touch the religious books was essential when staff were required to search cells and clothing. They now knew how the work could be done in such a way that did not compromise security and yet could respect the prisoner's religion. Once people understood why a person was reacting emotionally to a particular situation, it felt more manageable. Learning about these things in a brief workshop may be regarded as superficial, but it is a beginning. It can lead to less conflict as staff respond to cultural differences with more knowledge.

However, a difficult area for people can still be around recognising and challenging subtle harassment and indirect discrimination. Acknowledging that there is institutional racism requires a deeper examination of prison culture in terms of not only the written rules but also the common practices.

Being involved in this staff training has meant that my knowledge and awareness is increasing. It has also enabled some staff to make an appointment to see me. However, like others I can get it wrong, as I describe in the example below. Staff details have been changed to protect confidentiality.

A black member of staff approached me because she was not getting on with her white manager. The issues concerned her performance at work and she felt that her manager was racist. The manager had put things in writing and had suggested a course of action. She could not agree to what he suggested. She explained that there had been no problems with her two previous managers. One was white and the other black. Neither had indicated that her work had been poor. I offered to work with her as a counsellor or to facilitate a meeting between her and her manager. She readily agreed to the idea of a meeting with the manager. The manager was grateful for the opportunity to resolve things informally, as he had been hurt by the suggestion that he was racist. We then held a series of meetings where they explored their differences.

The meetings went some way to clearing the air but when it came to a resolution there was a stalemate. The manager felt his comments about her work were justified. The staff member wanted them withdrawn. I suggested they change roles and chairs, similar to role reversal or Gestalt chair work. I questioned them 'in the other role' to help them feel it was real. It was obvious both were truly connected to the other's position and were able to elaborate 'in role'. There seemed real understanding by both of them of each other. I was heartened. I moved them back to their original chairs as themselves and we resumed the work to resolve the problem.

Nothing had shifted. Their insights into the other provided no move towards the other. It almost seemed to reinforce to them why neither would compromise. Back in their own places they resumed the stalemate. Understanding how hurt the other is does not necessarily mean you can give up your own hurt.

Now I can appreciate how hard it is to resolve wars and conflict (e.g. Kosovo, Northern Ireland). Sometimes the pain is carried from generation to generation unconsciously and is played out in the present (Schutzenberger 1998).

I reflected on my work with them. Each had wanted the other to withdraw their opinion 'that her work was poor', 'that he was racist', and nothing else would satisfy them. They did not consider their own behaviour relevant to the discussion. I had hoped that they would acknowledge that there was some truth in the other's judgement of them and from this we could work out what was needed for them to be different in the future. There was no resolution because I had not taken into account their roles in the workplace, their cultural expectations of each other and their personal histories. If I had done so I would have known how much was at stake for each of them.

Some of the difficulty concerned the manager's confidence as a new manager in assessing others' work and in his relationships with the rest of his staff. He wanted to be seen as a good manager by them. Some of it concerned the member of staff's view of her own abilities in relation to the manager's abilities. She had been a manager in a previous job. She also felt that her family thought less of her because of her loss of status since being made redundant from her previous job.

What I had forgotten was that people cannot acknowledge their faults unless the setting is emotionally safe. I had missed this because both clients were willing to work on the 'problem'. I had assumed we were all defining the problem in the same way and therefore had a common goal. I had ignored not only their individual histories but also the culture of the setting. I had missed the existential anxieties triggered by the criticisms. Important parts of their respective identities were at stake.

Later an Indian Hindi man came to see me because he felt demeaned by his manager who was from the same ethnic origins. The client felt bullied and wanted me to talk to his manager. This time I decided to see if he would work with me individually. Perhaps then I could get it right. However, what was different for me as a white counsellor was that he first sought 'my expertise and knowledge' and also had no experience that people could change how they viewed a situation or how they might alleviate their own distress. His idea was for me to find a way of changing the manager.

He would tell me his problem and ask how long I needed to think about it before he came back for another appointment. He could not find any way to talk to his manager. He felt his manager had no worldly knowledge, he was 'just a young man', he spoke to my client 'as if he was a nobody'. The client felt the manager should show him some respect because he was older and married. The younger manager was single and appeared to have a more Western outlook towards work roles. The manager was third generation, which can produce many different conflicts (Eleftheriadou, 1999). The poor relationship between them seemed to be based on the manager feeling that my client was not interested in his work. The client did feel bored but he also felt undermined and isolated. As we worked together there were other examples in his life where he felt undervalued. His strategy was to put on a brave, cheerful face so as not to sink into depression. However, this seemed to even further annoy his manager, who had said to the client that he should take his work seriously. His culture was rooted in *relationship* rather than *doing and activity*. He had unconsciously assumed his manager would be the same. His existential anxiety concerned freedom and taking responsibility. Laungani (1999) comments that Indians defer to authority and seek precise guidance and direction when in need, which explains his initial demands of me.

Although I had started out with little knowledge of my client's background I was over time able to connect with him. I was genuinely interested to find out, and this helped him to begin to understand my role. He was able to use the counselling sessions because he trusted me in my professional role, even though I was younger and trying not to be an expert. I had shown him respect.

There have been white clients who have also wanted me to give them answers. For some it was related to the prison culture, of following orders and having rules, rather than their ethnicity. For others it was a lack of understanding of the purpose of counselling. With some black clients their expectation was not that I would give them the answer but that they believed I had knowledge and wisdom that they could not understand me withholding.

Although it can be difficult sometimes to know whether I have got it right, I will give another example. A fairly new black second generation African male member of staff came to see me because he was depressed about work. He did not feel that he fitted in. He seemed to have no friends from work and he had lost contact with other friends. He was constantly tired and began to dread coming to work. His manager had talked to him about his sick record and he just could not respond. He wished he could leave but felt worried about money. He dared not leave before trying for another job. He felt too low to look for anything. He knew that if he left this work his family would be upset. They had been so proud of him getting the job. He felt trapped. His colleagues and manager kept thinking he was being bullied. No one thought that he might not like the job because he was bored. He could not tell them. He had been living a lie and now he was exhausted and lost. No wonder he was depressed.

He was able to explore deeper issues with my help. The reasons that he had trained for the job were not his reasons but those of his family. He thought he had chosen but perhaps it was more complicated. He cared about his family, he cared about hurting them. He was able to talk to me because I was white and different. He felt I would not judge him. He could never let his family see him like this. He felt ashamed in front of his black colleagues. He felt he had let his white manager down.

We looked at how he might begin to face these issues rather than retreat into depression. How he might regain some meaning to his life that would enable him to face his shame and his fear of the future. Some of what he was experiencing were the conflicting values between the British individualistic work culture and his family collective culture. He fell between the two cultures. He did not know where he belonged and retreated into depression. We explored how that felt. After many sessions he was able to begin to talk about it to his family. He needed to do this before he could accept a new cultural identity.

These examples illustrate how my awareness of cultural issues grows. I began to study recommended books to increase my knowledge and to reflect on cultural aspects in my supervision. We are all culturally conditioned in ways that we are unaware and we all make judgements about others. It is essential to acknowledge this as a counsellor (Thomas 1992). Only then can I begin to help resolve another's distress from a non-racist position.

Inter-cultural counselling in prison

Much of the focus of this chapter has been around the themes of loss and trauma. These themes are very relevant in a prison setting and they are relevant to minority ethnic people. They may have experienced many types of loss. They may have suffered traumatic stress reactions in response to harassment, misunderstandings and discrimination. Staff may have had feelings of cultural loss as they adjusted to workplace values different from their family values.

These experiences can create a crisis of meaning and a sense of isolation. Fear and self-doubt can surface and become overwhelming. This may mean being more directive initially in order to try to provide a sense of safety as the person gradually regains control and enough ego strength to explore the feelings. Some clients are seen daily during a crisis and others weekly for several months. To illustrate, two fictitious clients are described below.

Bill

Bill came to see me after discussing with black colleagues the problems he was having at work. Some were in the post-incident care team and they encouraged him to consult me. Bill felt that his colleagues and manager were behaving in racist ways towards him. As we explored what had happened between him and the staff I realised he was seeing me in order to get a 'white viewpoint'. Bill's black African friends did not think it was racism and this distressed him even more.

He described how he felt humiliated by the attitudes of white staff. They thought he could not do his job. His white manager now gave him the easy jobs and still seemed to check his every move. He felt insulted. He had felt great pride when he passed his first year as a prison officer two months before. Now he believed the managers and white staff were hoping he would be sacked for making mistakes. It was important to discuss this as he was potentially testing my white response to his abilities and my understanding of racism. How Bill saw me became very relevant once I felt the reason he had come to see me was not because he perceived any 'expert' knowledge, not because he thought I could help him, but because I was white.

In the next session it emerged that the changes in attitudes towards him seemed to happen soon after he had been racially abused and hit by a white prisoner, six weeks before. He had not been physically hurt but now he admitted that he had not really got over it. Bill said he often thought about it when he least expected it. He felt uneasy when this happened, almost like fear. This confused him; it wasn't such an unusual incident in the prison setting so why was he thinking about it? Bill realised he wanted answers. He needed to make more sense of the incident and his feelings about what had happened. Bill was describing some traumatic stress reactions.

I explained that I would structure the session by asking him to go over the incident in a particular way. It was important to try to contain the incident memory by my being more directive. This could provide him with a safety net and minimise any re-traumatisation in order to help him move towards a resolution.

I believed it might help him answer his questions if we talked first about how he was before the incident. I wanted to establish some connection with the person he was when things were going well. I asked him to talk through some good times at work and at home. This helped me to assess his strengths and gave me an idea of his values. I might need to remind him of these aspects of himself as he remembered the assault.

I then asked that he start describing what had happened the day before the assault. I hoped he could again connect with the person he was before the abuse and assault. I guided him through the event several times in a fairly structured way so that he was able to feel some control as he recalled it. Bill's narrative became more detailed as he recalled facts, thoughts and impressions. He talked about how he was feeling at each stage, including what happened afterwards, which would later help him identify what the event meant to him. It was important that he realised that there was an end to the event by taking him beyond the time of the incident to the present.

Next we looked at his self-beliefs that it had challenged: 'I'm good at my job. I'm emotionally tough.' Now he felt weak and thought that others, white and black, were thinking he had dealt poorly with the prisoner so that it was his fault. Now Bill was not sure he had handled it well. These thoughts shocked him. He had not been aware of them before. Bill understood now how he had needed to hang on to his beliefs about himself. He could not replace them with the thoughts he had just identified. Bill could not be that person. During the next few sessions he began to be able to construct 'new beliefs'. He realised why others were treating him differently and what his black colleagues had meant. It was an uncomfortable process. Bill thought the prisoner had not affected him but the incident had triggered deeper existential anxieties.

Once he was able to make sense of his reactions to the prisoner, to his colleagues and to his manager he began to feel emotionally safe at work again. His relationships changed for the better. He could accept that he could make mistakes *within reason*.

We met weekly for eight sessions and in our final sessions we returned to the issue of racism. Bill knew he had changed. How he felt about himself had changed. How he felt about me had changed. We explored how others were treating him now. He could see some racism but he did not now feel that his manager was racist towards him. This helped him feel able to tackle the racism from some of his white colleagues. He wanted to try talking to them first. Bill now found it interesting to reflect on the fact that one person who was clearly racist, the prisoner, was the one he had missed out accusing. He realised he had not allowed the prisoner to affect him *because he was a prisoner* and therefore had less power. There was much to explore with Bill but he did not feel he wanted to continue at present. Bill had allowed me to understand him. He had showed himself in a way that he might not have done with his black colleagues or perhaps with a black counsellor.

Steve

Steve came to see me after his manager suggested it. Steve was distraught because his girlfriend had left him. He was in tears. Steve, who was 32, said they had been together for three years and they had a 2-year-old girl.

We met twice a week initially and over several sessions he experienced hurt, anger and then fear, which ran deep. This unsettled him so much that self-doubt emerged and led him to want to look closer at his whole life. Steve questioned what he really needed from a relationship. Why was it so important to have a family? He could not bear to lose his child. Had he ever loved his girlfriend? Why did he react to things the way he did? Who was he really?

During sessions over the next six months Steve was able to explore these questions. Gradually he was able to make sense of the current crisis after he had talked about his past and his sense of being in the world. It was very painful to confront himself like this. He knew his family saw him as selfish and he thought it too. Steve also re-examined his behaviour with others at work. He was grateful for the support of his manager throughout this time but realised that 'he expected' it, as if it was owed to him. He made sense of his past behaviour because he had believed he was the centre of the universe.

Steve had lived with his grandparents who he said had spoilt him. Even now they would give him money whenever he had been frivolous. Even now he found it difficult to accept that a woman had shattered his whole world. He did not believe it could happen to him. Steve had always 'played the field' and felt in control of his emotions. His grandparents had always been on his side before. Now because he had a daughter they were reacting differently. They 'wanted him to grow up'. His mother had left when he was a baby to pursue a career in America. Gradually Steve was aware of the hurt and anger that he had not realised was there. His grandparents had tried to shield him from the loss by giving him whatever he demanded. He had felt invincible. Now he realised how fragile he was.

There were periods when Steve felt down, but he was able to use the counselling time to work through the feelings. Having a 'safe space' meant that he did not feel so alone or so desperate. He gradually came to understand himself better and to understand the way he had used people. He eventually felt stronger and less affected by everyday frustrations. He began to take responsibility for himself and his actions. Steve was ready to change. With Steve it was important not to be directive. It was important that he discover his true self, or recover himself, through a relationship that was consistent but could not be manipulated selfishly by him. I could care about him without being in his power. Steve was black from a Caribbean background but had lived all his life in Britain. He was an only child. He came to me because his manager 'sent' him and because at first he wanted my perspective on his girlfriend's behaviour. That I was female was more important to him than that I was white, as his girlfriend was black.

However, our racial differences were important in the relationship, as was the culture of the workplace. I needed to keep in mind his view of himself as a black man growing up with his Caribbean grandparents in a predominantly white neighbourhood. Steve's attitudes towards his manager and his colleagues were linked to his pride in his black identity in a predominately white department and workplace. They were also linked to his need to stay 'out of relationship' with those around him. I was part of that *normality* for him as a white woman. Now he let himself experience a different type of relationship with me. This enabled Steve to feel safe enough to look at how he had been with his black and white friends and colleagues.

Celebrating diversity

I have defined inter-cultural working as the awareness of cultural issues between the client, the setting and myself. Sometimes this means being specific about cultural differences and attitudes. Sometimes it is subtler, with me noticing what is happening in terms of different cultural frameworks, ready to bring issues to the forefront when necessary.

To do this I have to be aware how clients might see me within the prison culture:

- *As white*, and therefore part of the majority racist culture.

- *As female*, and therefore as having less power in a male-dominated society but also as being more likely to be sympathetic to those with problems. Perhaps they would see me as less competitive than the males in the prison.
- *As older* (sometimes) and therefore as having more experience and wisdom. Deserving respect.
- *As younger* (sometimes) and therefore having less experience and knowledge.
- *As a Northerner (having an accent)* which may produce class prejudice.
- *As a professional (an expert, clever, educated)* which might also produce class prejudice or an assumption of power.
- *As a counsellor* having no power because I am not a manager.

To do this I have to be aware how clients see themselves within the prison culture. I have to be aware of the culture of the setting in which counselling takes place. I have to be aware of any changes that individuals and the prison are experiencing.

I have mentioned the shift to *peer and shared responsibility* that is particularly appropriate for *loss and trauma*.

In 2001 another initiative was launched. This was the Respect Staff Support Network, a network for minority ethnic staff that also welcomes white staff. I value being part of this network. It is another step towards challenging a hierarchical culture by focusing on peer support managed by staff for staff. As Ghandi said, 'we must become the change we want to see'.

People need different types of help at different times. For some the most important is their family, for others their colleagues and for others professional support. For most of us a combination of these is needed. This is why it is important to be open to a variety of ways of introducing help to people. Then we will have a greater chance of providing culturally specific help.

The post-incident care team has facilitated acceptance of a staff counselling service at Wandsworth Prison. My being involved with training has also helped. Some staff need to see me in a non-counselling role before committing themselves to coming to counselling. The fact that I have worked with prisoners and am inside has influenced some staff more than the fact that I am a different race, gender or age. The predominant concern for them was that I understand the culture of the workplace. However, it is my responsibility as the counsellor to be aware and as knowledgeable as possible about the clients' culture in order that I do not miss what might be the real issues for them. This is not an easy task. *Culture* is not a fixed thing. For many this can create the crisis, as society changes, as workplaces change and as different generations settle into new identities carrying the knowledge and pain from these collective pasts.

So what about the future? What vision do I have? What vision do others in the prison have?

The first thoughts that spring to my mind are *teamwork, respect, valuing and celebrating differences and diversity*. I asked other staff. One black member of staff gave strong views about not distinguishing the counselling or support needs of non-white people from the needs of white people. He felt it would encourage separateness rather than promote wider understanding *as if* black people have strange problems which only others of the same race could deal with. He felt that the sources of stress may sometimes be different but the symptoms were the same. Other staff said that the issue for them was not the quality of care by professionals but rather about how to work closer with colleagues and prisoners from all cultures.

It seems to me that the challenge is to take cultural diversity and *use it* to improve individual and group achievements, and subsequently well-being. Perhaps this means looking beneath the surface to the way that different cultural values create tensions and misunderstandings. If we can harness these differences creatively then we will truly celebrate diversity, rather than just acknowledge them and then carry on as if that acknowledgement is enough. Understanding is not enough to change behaviour, as I have learned through work with my clients. True teamwork is *valuing equally* the different contributions each person brings. Let me outline some situations that staff have mentioned to me. They may illustrate how we can begin to shift to a more sophisticated level of awareness.

The discomfort experienced by African staff when 'high-flyers' are denigrated. Do managers or others notice this tension in the group? Similarly, the attitudes to those staff who volunteer for courses and further training; some staff view them as if they are trying to be better than everyone else or that they are 'professional course takers', always leaving others to do the *real* work. In African cultures this will be seen as demonstrating taking responsibility for the benefit of the family or group, rather than trying to be above others or avoid group responsibility. It is responsible to learn to your maximum capability in order to benefit the family or group. It would be selfish not to learn: i.e. a collective value. Another example is where staff may make frequent trips to their family's country of origin. Again this may be seen as selfish, as if they are holidays, whereas they are an obligation, a family responsibility (e.g. if you are the eldest male you will have to take care of the extended family's finances and problems).

A situation that I have noticed concerns reactions to criticism about poor work. For some people it will trigger deep shame while others are indifferent. These different emotional responses have immense impact on work relationships and future behaviour within teams. Understanding this can explain some tensions and group dynamics.

Perhaps by focusing on these thoughts and questions, staff, managers and counsellors can try to understand everyone at a deeper level. This may eventually create supportive and productive teams where all can feel safe *to be themselves*.

In the future I also want to keep in mind some of Yalom's (1980) comments about different cultures producing different meanings. In the West the belief is that 'life must have a point' or 'life is a problem to be solved'. In the East there is the view that 'life is a mystery to be lived'. By my asking the client which is closest to their view, or how would they complete the phrase 'life is . . .', I am not unconsciously imposing my culture on them. I may begin to discover what otherwise I would miss about them and about their needs. By being conscious of my own culture I will be clearer about its impact on the counselling relationship.

I am reminded of a time when I was travelling in Indonesia and staying with a village family. I never heard a baby cry though I saw many. They were always wrapped around their mother or an elder sibling, even at night-time. They were never alone. In Britain babies spend a lot of time crying and alone. Western cultures encourage independence. There can be a negative side to this. It discourages people from accepting help from others.

Therapy helps people by providing another person *for a while*. Clients are 'held safely' by the relationship. How I 'hold' my clients in the relationship should depend on our inter-cultural norms, the *meeting* of our respective cultures. I need to acknowledge what my culture might mean to them by knowing something of the clients' culture. Within this context if I 'carry' some clients until they can safely walk it will not inhibit their healthy growth and can help them face what is troubling them.

*

The recommended books can help counsellors reflect on their own inter-cultural practice. The other chapters will also provide a rich source of information and food for thought.

References

Baluchi B. (2000) Beyond Urgent: A Strategy for Refugee Health. *RACE* 21, pp. 28–30.

Eleftheriadou, Z. (1999) in Palmer and P. Laungani, *Assessing the Counselling Needs of Ethnic Minorities in Britain.*

Genders, E. and Player, E. (1989) *Race Relations in Prison.* Oxford: Clarendon Press.

Kleinman, A. (1995) *Writing in the Margin.* Berkeley: California University Press.

Laungani, P. (1999) Culture and Identity. In Palmer and Laungani, *Counselling in a Multicultural Society.* London: Sage.

Lee, C.C. (1999) Cultural Diversity in the Workplace. *RACE* 20, pp. 6–9.

Paxman, J. (1999) *The English.* London: Penguin Books.

Marsella, A., Friedman, M. and Spain, H. (1993) Ethnocultural Aspects of PTSD. *Review of Psychiatry* 12, pp. 157–181.

Regel, S. and Courtney-Bennett, H. (2002) Cultural issues with an impact on psychological debriefing. In Tehrani, *Psychological Debriefing.*

Schutzenberger, A. (1998) *The Ancestor Syndrome. Transgenerational Psychotherapy.* London: Routledge.

Tehrani, N. (ed.) (2002) *Psychological Debriefing.* Leicester: The British Psychological Society, (in press).

Thomas, L. (1992) Racism and Psychotherapy. In Kareem and Littlewood, *Intercultural Therapy.* Oxford: Blackwell.

Yalom, I. (1980) *Existential Psychotherapy.* New York: Basic Books.

Young, A. (1997) *A Harmony of Illusions – An Ethnographical Account of Post Traumatic Stress Disorder.* Princeton, NJ: Princeton University Press.

Recommended reading

Boal, A. (1995) *The Rainbow of Desire.* London: Routledge.

d'Ardenne, P. and Mahtani, A. (1989) *Transcultural Counselling in Action.* London: Sage.

Kareem, J. and Littlewood, R. (1992) *Intercultural Therapy.* (2nd edn 2000.) Oxford: Blackwell.

Krause, I.B. (1998) *Therapy Across Culture.* London: Sage.

Lago, C. and Thompson, J. (1996) *Race, Culture and Counselling.* Buckingham: Open University Press.

Palmer, S. and Laungani, P. (1999) *Counselling in a Multicultural Society*. London: Sage.

Williams, B. (1996) *Counselling in Criminal Justice. Counselling in Context*. Buckingham: Open University Press.

Chapter 8

Working inter-culturally with probation and forensic clients

Lennox K. Thomas

Most people who have contact with the Probation Service through the criminal courts are increasingly those from poorer sections of the community and those who persistently offend with drugs or alcohol as a large part of their lives. It is much more difficult to separate out those who commit theft, violence or acts of dishonesty without the influence of addictive substances. This is particularly so among the young and poor who are perhaps the most visible. The affluent young also offend but are often not living lives on the streets and are not often known to the police, having the protection that their social class status provides. The reason why people break the law has always been an interesting area of study for psychiatrists and social scientists. Rather like the study of disease, scientists wanted to know about the social, demographic and psychological factors concerned with mental state and crime. While there is some correlation with youth poverty, unemployment and purposelessness, it is harder to determine why an individual offends and becomes a persistent offender. It is baffling when two families sharing similar social and economic status living next door to each other can produce one home of law-abiding offspring and the other a family of law-breakers. Even within the same sibling group where values and social conditions are communal, it happens that offenders and non-offenders are found. When this takes place, it could be that individuals make choices or are influenced by the values and morals of those whom they hold in high esteem.

Those individuals who take their values from the gangs in the street and not from law-abiding homes present a fascinating picture because one wonders when and how their conflicting positions get worked out, if they ever do. Older generations of parents from the Caribbean and Africa are often at a loss to understand why their children have rejected their hardworking religious values to choose the values of the street where hard work and honesty mean little. Some of these families have to face the painful truth of having their industriousness and sacrifice rejected by their children as a waste of time. Many of the young black people who were born in the UK have been disillusioned by the fact that the racism that their parents were up against has also confronted them. Some of these British-born blacks feel a sense of being cheated by an assailant whom they cannot readily identify. Accompanying this is a grudging black British identity which serves to place them at the bottom of the social and economic pile. Many feel that their parents' efforts were in vain, and forty-five years later, they as the children and grandchildren are not materially in any better position to those who came as citizens from the Crown Colonies as immigrants.

A major generational difference is that older Caribbean people who came as immigrants to the UK were a great deal less likely than their children and grandchildren to break the law and come into contact with probation officers, social workers and others. A similar picture appears with regard to mental health and related psychological problems. It is more likely that British-born blacks present for treatment than the older generation born outside the United Kingdom. Sometimes the problems of offending and mental health appear together. For some people their mental health problems would be a factor at the time of their offending. The task of assessing and dealing with mentally ill offenders is a specialist area (Thomas 1991). In recent years there has been some concern about the after-effects of Care in the Community, a policy with good intent which inadvertently led to many people with psychiatric problems being made unintentionally homeless and living on the streets. Those clients who, while not having a prior mental health diagnosis and who appear to function reasonably well in the community, have a variety of interpersonal and other problems. Presenting these to probation officers and others in the forensic field for assessment has not always met with success.

The profile of offenders has however changed considerably in the past fifteen years or so. Chronic unemployment, a lack of social stability, homelessness and addiction to drugs and alcohol appear to be features of the young. What is consistent is the persistently large numbers of young people who have histories of family breakdown and institutional care. These experiences will leave young people with long-standing difficulties in forming lasting relationships and problems of self-worth and self-esteem. The number of young black and mixed parentage people in this category is disproportionately large and growing. Given the fact that these patterns of behaviour are often passed on to the next generation and repeated if left unchecked, there is concern about the future of black and dual-heritage young people and the formation of an underclass.

The therapeutic treatment of black offenders is not often debated. This absence is probably due to several distinct factors. Meeting the therapeutic needs of black people in the mainstream is relatively new after many years of neglect; it probably follows that inter-cultural forensic counselling might be able to inform and address the complex issues. There is a scarcity of writing on this subject in the UK. The view that those who offend should be locked up and punished is now prevalent, but there were times when there was a climate of reform. While hanging and flogging has always had support, another view was that behaviour is not easily modified by a treatment model and no attempts should be made to sentence offenders to therapy. While objectionable to some, Bottoms and McWilliams (1979) considered probation counselling an infringement of the offender's civil rights. Alongside the latter view is the notion that increasing the severity of sentence was the most reasonable solution. It is argued that this way the offender is making a rational choice, and imprisonment is simply an occupational hazard for the persistent offender. Working with offenders has been surrounded by this debate for many years, seemingly rational yet at variance with the basic principles of probation practice of advising, assisting and befriending. Counselling is an opportunity for offenders to think differently about themselves and their situation, to open up choices, however limited, and to think through the consequences of their actions.

Psychodynamically derived ideas for working with offenders have sometimes met with limited success because they are often based on classical psychoanalysis, a model of psychological treatment developed for working with patients suffering from hysteria and neurosis. Schmideberg (1975), one-time head of the Association for Psychiatric Treatment of Offenders, sees the psychoanalytic model as inappropriate for working with offenders. While this controversial view overlooks some types of offenders whose difficulties have some neurotic origins, there is a need for counsellors and psychotherapists to reappraise therapeutic methods for working with offenders. The usual psychodynamic model is the main theoretical base from which counselling originated, yet this approach does not work for everyone.

Offenders are very different psychologically and socially from the private practice neurotics; they must be treated within the penal-legal system and the methods of therapy must be geared to their mentality and situation. Offender therapy, though still in its early beginnings, has already gathered many interesting observations. It enables middle class therapists to glimpse into a world so very different from their own.

(Schmideberg 1975, p. 22)

Schmideberg convincingly argues that the cohesiveness of psychoanalytic theory leaves much unexplained, particularly in the field of psychopathology. It must be said that Dr Schmideberg, a forensic psychiatrist and former psychoanalyst, had much experience of working with offenders. Her apparent repudiation of the psychoanalytic method must be seen in the context of her relationship with her mother, the eminent psychoanalyst Melanie Klein with whom she had many professional disagreements and public skirmishes. While Freudian theory paid little attention to antisocial tendencies, this aspect was well developed by those who came after Freud. Many of these clinicians have a view that modifications of classical analysis could be of use to some offenders (Bowlby 1947; Glover 1960; Winnicott 1967). It is noticeable that these psychoanalysts worked in the public sector as paediatricians or psychiatrists and were able to use psychoanalysis in applied forms with good results. The unmodified use of a classical theory developed in the context of late nineteenth-century western Europe for working with neurotic wealthy people in psychological pain is not guaranteed to bear favourable results with offenders in twenty-first-century multicultural Britain. The seeds of theory have been usefully sown by some eminent therapists who have had the courage to select what might be of use. The debate about psychopathology and method in counselling and therapy with offenders is an interesting one. Having passed the hurdle which questions the treatment model for psychologically disturbed offenders, the next is which of the counselling approaches would best fit offenders. Any successful approach would require the counsellor to take into account a broader user group and a more flexible theoretical base.

The Inter-Cultural Therapy Centre, Nafsiyat, was set up in 1982 in order to provide a clinical service to black and ethnic minorities, and received referrals from both the criminal and civil courts for assessment reports and treatment. Already taking a particular position

(Kareem and Littlewood 1992) in relation to the application of psychoanalysis and its derived ideas to work in the context of race and culture, the staff with experience in the forensic field were bringing their own ideas to bear on the meeting of the judicial process with race, culture, social context and counselling. Certain pertinent questions needed to be debated around assessments for treatment and assessments for sentence in the criminal court in order to present a picture of a person who has offended against the law and society. In doing so, how much do we take into account the cultural, social and racial differences in the process of counselling and therapy? In thinking about this, are we opening a hornets' nest or are we doing a disservice to clients and patients if we are not able to chart not only individual pathology and adjustment issues, but also the effect of discrimination and racial assault? In short, pathogenic issues in society at large which touch the material and psychic lives of black and minority individuals and groups (Thomas 1995). Researchers and therapists in the forensic field like others are keenly interested in the very different effects that environment has on members of the same family who have by and large been exposed to the same social and familial factors. Frequently, enquiry reveals that subjects report the most appalling privations which they believe have doomed their lives to crime, broken relationships and psychological problems. Yet they inform us of siblings whose lives have been successful and seemingly unaffected.

The interplay of culture, race, environment and individual psychopathology has proved to be most interesting and fertile ground for therapeutic work. What has been of particular interest is why some clients from black and ethnic minorities have sought out a minority psychotherapy and counselling service, or why counsellors have chosen to refer their clients. Those who seek this service, one suspects, have an idea about how their individual problems mesh with their social context and have come prepared for the long task of dealing with them. Other clients may have come to check out or to measure up against another who may have had firsthand experience of making sense of their minority experience. These clients are not only marginalised by their ethnicity but also by their experience of law-breaking. In addition, the particular understanding of psychological problems coupled with culture that these groups present often leaves inexperienced counsellors and probation officers feeling unskilled and unaware. So many of the stereotypes that persist in our society about African Caribbeans, particularly males, are around law-breaking and lack of control. Even those who are subjects of the stereotype are aware of the way they may be viewed by others and this can play its part in the struggle for their identity development (Hutchinson 1994; Madhubuti 1990). The struggle for a positive identity for the black individual in a predominantly white society is not an easy one (Thomas 1995). This struggle can lead to clients referring themselves for counselling help.

Although counsellors are advised to occupy a neutral position, the experience of racial, cultural and value difference often provokes strongly held views. The professionally desired neutrality in the counsellor is couched only in the neutrality of the counsellor's own culture. It could be said that any therapeutic contact between two people from very different cultures is an inter-cultural therapy. Moreover, when the values that those people subscribe to conflict, it is inevitable that the therapy will be affected. Counselling and psychotherapy cannot be culture free; nor can it be neutral, because the taught concepts are derived from our beliefs and interpretations about human nature and how people live their lives. A young, white, British-raised person, for example, may have a very different view of the world as compared to a young person raised in India. Apart from the possibility of not having a common language, they may have different belief systems about many aspects of life. While helping a person in need of counselling is not impossible, to be able to offer a more finely tuned intervention requires counsellors and probation officers to consider the transferential issues around difference. In recent years counsellors have considered the importance of cultural, ethnic and other differences for the counselling relationship (Kareem 1988; Dupont-Joshua 1991).

There has been a discipline of transcultural psychiatry for the study of symptom presentation and diagnosis for some years and a United Nations World Health study into the worldwide incidence of schizophrenia (World Health Organisation 1973). Similarly, social anthropology has made a great contribution to understanding human behaviour, in particular child-rearing and life cycle matters with transcultural studies (Mead 1949). Given these differences, some therapists wanted to test the notion of the universality of some of these ideas. Some questions posed were, for example: Are the symbols which are relied upon in therapy the same for those raised in different cultures, and would an interpretation be very different? Are our emotional responses different and are we trained to behave differently? Given the social differences that exist between ethnic groups in society and the conflict that sometimes arises between them, what happens in therapy between counsellor and client when they enact these splits? Inter-cultural therapy and counselling has so far been interested in ways to help counsellors understand these differences and work with them rather than try to deny or ignore such differences. Psychodynamic counselling and therapy has always been interested in engaging with the unconscious process, and inter-cultural approaches are often interested in the denied and therefore unconscious issues surrounding the meeting of difference, and to discover the extent to which the counselling process is affected by it. The interest in inter-cultural therapy has inevitably attracted those who have a personal curiosity about many aspects of difference in the consulting room, notably those who in some way see themselves as relative outsiders, or on the margins of mainstream society. Many clients have expressed the view that their story is little known to those outside their culture or lifestyle. Their unfamiliarity, it is feared, contributes to their marginalisation and runs the risk of their being pathologised. For those who belong to minority ethnic groups and offend against the law, they are a minority among the minorities. Counselling probation and forensic clients from minority ethnic backgrounds will always be a meeting place of dynamic psychology, forensic therapy and inter-cultural ideas. A synthesis of these different influences will not necessarily make for a comfortable fit, yet practice and careful analysis of clinical examples will make it possible to develop forensic inter-cultural counselling and psychotherapy.

The man of good character who feared that he would become a criminal

Wesley, a 36-year-old British-born man of African Caribbean heritage, referred himself for psychotherapeutic help. He was a successful man, newly married and a senior employee in an accountancy firm. He said that Francine, an old friend from university who was herself in therapy, had suggested that he might benefit from some help. They had spoken on the telephone frequently after her move to another city with her job. He said that Francine had found him supportive during her depression and she was surprised to learn about his unhappiness, which he told her had been with him for many years. He explained to his therapist that since his teens he has feared that he might commit a crime and end up in prison. This fear began when he was studying for his A levels. He had little money and frequently avoided paying his fare on the London Underground. After being caught, humiliated and eventually cautioned by the inspectors, he had nightmares of being locked up. He said that he was angry when the inspectors told him that 'his sort always tried it on'. He said that those words would come back to him, particularly when things were not going well or when he was in low spirits. He said this sense of shame prevented him from ever telling anyone about the incident until he told Francine.

Wesley described a fear of being caught for stealing or even being wrongly prosecuted, criminalised and becoming a social outcast. Taking his cue from the inspector he always wanted to know what 'his sort' was and always wished he had the presence of mind to ask eighteen years earlier. It had crossed his mind many times that it might have been a racial insult, but he was not entirely convinced by this and tried to put the thought out of his mind. He felt that the comment could have been about his age, apparent student status, social class, or indeed all of these. Wesley believed that his present law-abiding status was no guarantee against a similar insult or of being wrongly perceived by others. 'They just have to see black and man together in one package and you are guilty'; he paused for a moment and said sadly that he did not really think differently when he saw groups of black youths. He was sure that something bad was going to happen to him and was fearful that he might cause such a terrible scandal that Dee his wife would leave him. He said that he could see the headlines. Wesley it seemed, was not only trying to prove to himself that he was a decent person; he was trying to prove this to others in society and to white authority in particular. While he had been raised in a Christian family and had no dealings with the police, he feared that his badness would usher in disaster. Having brooded on this at times of depression his ultimate presentation for therapy was to check out if he was going mad like so many other black people he knew. He said that an abiding childhood memory was seeing an ambulance and police outside the gates of the Pentecostal church that his family attended. They were called to take away yet another distressed and blameless church member.

This man's self-doubt seemed to have been sparked off by his law-breaking and a humiliating comment made many years earlier. At a second glance it is possible to see that Wesley's family values and codes were policing him internally and the incident on the London Underground seemed a recapitulation of what he had known in earlier years: that right was right and wrong was wrong. His shaky sense of his own identity appeared to have preceded the incident so that his sort was something that was unclear to him. Wesley, like so many young black people, has found difficulty in locating himself in the British economic and social class system. Many have identified with, or have lived out, the stereotype that has placed them firmly in the 'underclass'. Wesley's family's middle-class identifications felt inauthentic to him and seemed to offer him no buffer of security from the disaster that would cast him into the abyss. Having had a protected life as a born-again Christian, Wesley did not seem to have developed the resilient skin which to some extent serves to protect against negative projections. Moreover, his unworldliness left him vulnerable to the teasing and undermining that he endured from young black contemporaries at university who ridiculed his Christian faith. His father had referred to these young people as Kicksters, and had cautioned his children against mixing with them. It seems that this prohibition served as an irresistible lure for Wesley who found these people interesting and attractive. They were as unfathomable to him as he was to them, but they had a liveliness and daring that he lacked.

Wesley was at university to learn and to better himself, while the Kicksters seemed to be there to have a good time. It seemed that meeting so many different people gave Wesley an opportunity to explore different ways to be; however, this made him feel more insecure, as though the fortress which protected his goodness and decency was under constant attack by his impulses to be exciting and different, what he called his badness. Not being good at self-regulating, Wesley relied on the church and its doctrine to actively keep him on the right path. He had a punitive super-ego which controlled him, yet he secretly enjoyed the idea of being daring from time to time. Avoiding payment of his fare represented the most rebellious act that he could possibly carry out, and he reported being in a state of fear while he sat on the train visualising how he was going to get away with it. He was not only fearful but also in a heightened state of excitement.

How low self-esteem and guilt had served to sabotage him

Wesley had not only taken upon himself notions of his badness from religion but he also took on the social projections that many young black men are given in societies where they occupy minority status. The African-descended young males in western societies have become convenient containers of those societies' projected badness (Thomas 1997). Thomas cites the case of a black men's psychotherapy group with a black therapist where most of the members, after a few weeks of attending the group, come to realise that the group did not have a good start. It transpired that the men had a fear of each other. The fear was voiced by one man as 'Black men could not be trusted because of their uncontrollable ferocious violence'. Shock that so many of them felt this way led them as a group to think about how they had acquired this prejudice about black men and ultimately negative views of themselves. Internalising such a poor image of themselves is not unusual for black men. In pre-civil rights America this notion of black male badness resulted in the lynching of countless numbers of black men and boys by white women and men who did this with impunity. These projections of badness have a similar effect of socially and economically 'killing off' young black men in contemporary Britain in a variety of ways. The very complex discussion on both sides of the Atlantic states that the demise of black boys begins in schools. Many black men do not have a full awareness of the part that their gender and ethnicity have played in their lives.

As well as offence-focused work, forensic psychotherapy and counselling with probation clients from ethnic minority backgrounds requires that particular attention is paid to the social context of their life, cultural or ethnic identification, and subsequently their personal identification. Such attention paid to the client will have transference implications whoever the counsellor may be. How transference relationships manifest themselves across ethnic and culture boundaries needs to be understood by counsellors who may not chose to work in an elaborate way with transferential material. Traditionally it has been the technique of probation officers and clinical social workers to approach transference relationships in a particular way, more often to elucidate rather than encourage them with clients (Ferard and Hunnybun 1962; Irvine 1963) The offence which brought the client to the worker's or counsellor's attention must always be borne in mind as there are often motives for the offence or related attitudes in the transferential relationship. For example, the convicted violent or threatening client whose menace is never seen in the counselling room should give the worker some cause for concern because of its absence. While the offensive behaviour may be a contained, encapsulated part of the client's personality, therapeutic help must be considered to be in its early stages if dealing with this material in the room has not yet taken place. The worker with the dishonest client will witness dishonesty even in some small way in their presentation during counselling or therapy. Sometimes working with offenders in a group setting can make patterns of behaviour more easily recognised by peers in a way that individual therapy can sometimes miss. In a group the client cannot disregard it, telling you that you must have misheard them, nor can they play the part of the wounded and wronged. The selection of method is very important, and no single blanket approach which suits the counsellor will achieve good results. Many counsellors and probation officers emphasise the importance of flexibility and adaptation.

> The third factor, the method to be applied depends both on the type of case and the art of the therapist. I believe that the therapist should be in the position of choosing between various approaches, selecting the most suited for the given case.
>
> (Engel 1975, p. 12)

Engel describes delinquency as the expression of a variety of different mental attitudes, and he considered neurotic offenders to number some 5 per cent of delinquents as compared to those who are motivated by the pleasure of law-breaking. He mentioned that different types of offenders needed different approaches, even though he regarded delinquency as merely a symptom (ibid., p. 15).

A similar point is made by an eminent consultant psychotherapist from the Portman Clinic (Welldon and Van Velsen 1997) that assessment for psychotherapy requires a modification of terms and concepts from those used when assessing neurotic patients. It is clear from several texts that a classical psychoanalytic model may not be the best method of choice yet dynamically informed ways of working have great value. In the following case example the client's drug use appears to serve as a mask, or as a symptom of long-term family and racial identity problems.

The drug supplier who was pressured into change by fear of imprisonment

Melvin, a 34-year-old British man of mixed Caribbean and English heritage, rang a counselling service demanding that an appointment be given to him over the telephone for him to see a counsellor the following day. When the procedure was explained to him he was abusive, telling the administrator that he would try elsewhere because she was useless. A week or so later Melvin wrote to the counselling centre apologising for his behaviour over the phone the previous week. His letter explained that he had attended a hearing in the Magistrates Court and the probation officer there suggested that he sought help for his drug addiction problem while he awaited his case being committed to the Crown Court. It was implied that he would be seen in a much better light if he was drug-free when he returned to court. He said that he was lucky not to be locked up and that he did not wish to be. When seen for assessment Melvin was a drug dealer and user who had made a frenzied attack on a young man whom he employed as a street dealer. He had attacked him with a large spanner, damaging his cheek-bone. He said that the young man was trying to move in on his territory and was trying to squeeze him out. Melvin had indeed got to his position by doing the same thing with an older dealer to whom he was apprenticed. He began to use drugs recreationally in his teens. He said that he had been a mixed-race child living on a rough white East End council estate. His family was the only family on the estate that was not white and had to run the gauntlet of racist abuse on the landings and to put up with swastikas painted on their doors and windows. He remembers how his mother was relentlessly abused by other white people and how she tried to keep his father from knowing this, possibly to protect him or because she was so ashamed that the white people around her were so cruel. He remembers his father's advice at the time to keep away from these people, but it seemed so useless then. He said that he soon realised that there was no way that he could avoid them so in his own way he joined them.

Melvin had two brothers and one sister. He was the youngest, with a gap of seven years between him and the brother preceding him. He said his early childhood was dominated by his fear of being attacked or bullied in some way by white kids, or worse, by their older brothers or parents. The only way that he survived on the estate was by doing errands for the older boys who came to see him as useful. He said the racial abuse became terms of endearment for him because at least he was not being beaten up. Eventually the other black or mixed-parentage children in the area or on other estates became their target. He admitted to having no sympathy for these other children and to some extent he felt secure in his favoured position as one who was singled out. It was not long before Melvin was sent to buy drugs or to hide stolen goods in his parents' home. While his brothers and sister disapproved of the time he spent playing out, his mother, a locally born person, thought it fine that he had his own friends. As he grew older Melvin threw himself completely into a strong cockney identity which was a great source of irritation to his father who had for years worked on the night shift of a local motor manufacturing plant. Melvin was very different from his siblings who were more strictly brought up and who kept closer to home. He believed that they were resentful of the freedom that he had and they did not have when they were the same age. He in turn felt a little disliked by them and particularly by his sister, who often said that he was a spoilt child.

At age 14 Melvin first got into trouble with the police for breaking into cars. Other difficulties arose from truanting, a prosecution for burglary, possession of stolen goods and affray. It was not until his late twenties that his drug use became apparent to his parents. Before that they considered that his friends were to blame for his difficulties. He said that he had been successful in fooling everybody, even his girlfriends with whom he lived from time to time. He said that his mother and probation officer should have been able to guess what he was up to. His belief was that they should have stopped him getting into the serious trouble that he is in now. Typically, he could see that everyone else was to blame for the actions he chose to take.

Counselling as a chance to save himself

Melvin wanted to start counselling immediately and tried to convince the assessor at the counselling centre that he was no longer addicted to drugs. He was told that as a long-term user who had never before attempted to give it up, he needed to enter a detox programme before he could be considered for long-term therapy. With this he went away and completed an eight-week detox where he attended several groups and was held to account as a dealer for the part that he played in other people's addiction. After what he described as a rough ride, he persuaded a rehab social worker to refer him for therapy on completing the programme. He said that he could not cope with all the things that were going on in his head any more and was worried that he might be 'going mad'. He was again assessed by the same senior therapist who thought that he could now make good use of counselling and seemed determined to stick it out. He began individual work with a black male counsellor, a thoughtful and sensitive man. After some initial doubts about not being understood and feeling criticised by his counsellor, he settled down. Weeks later he told his counsellor that he had a secret which he needed to tell him but hoped that he would not be looked down upon. He said, with a great sense of shame, that he visited prostitutes and had done so since the age of 18. He said that his relationships with girlfriends were fine until they wanted marriage or to settle down together. Even worse than this was his fear that he would be expected to be a father or have to be responsible for anyone. He described his time spent with prostitutes as a release, mentioning that he liked wild sex but giving no further details. His discomfort in talking about this part of himself was visible to his counsellor and he quickly added that his visits were not because he did not like women who were interested in him. He actually spoke of his visits as treats, for example: 'I had a bit of money so I could afford a couple of visits last week.' The women who provided him with this apparently much needed release seemed no more than commodities to him. Melvin seemed to live in a world that did not value women, nor the values that women might bring into his life. Women's bodies served the function of offering him comfort and release but they had little other significance for him. The idea that his girlfriend could become a good friend and companion seemed a totally alien notion to him.

From the developmental history that his counsellor took from him, and which developed over a little time, Melvin was a clingy child. Until his early school years he cried at the school gates and could not get to sleep at nights. He shared his mother's bed until he was 8 years old while his father was at work. When his eldest brother left home he shared a room with the other brother. While he was on the one hand a tough street kid, it seemed a mask for the outside world. His obsessive and ritualised sleeping pattern with a stuffed cuddly elephant contrasted starkly with his tough guy street persona. The fact that his brothers and sister had no dealings with estate people ensured that the other side of him would never be disclosed. He said that the present offence for which he awaits trial was a source of surprise to his family because he seemed a calm and controlled person to them. His vicious attack on the street seller was uncontrolled, revealing a side of himself which was as frightening to others as much as it was to himself. Conscious of his need to keep some sort of order and discipline, he felt that he had to do something in order to maintain his position at the head of his enterprise. However, his drug dealing came to an abrupt halt after his arrest and two weeks of imprisonment before being bailed.

Melvin's counsellor was surprised at his ability to make good use of the counselling. This was particularly so because of his poor relationship with his father whom he had discarded as useless during his childhood. His counsellor, like his father, was black. During the ten months of therapy pending his Crown Court appearance Melvin worked very hard both in his therapy and in the employment he had secured as a van driver. He developed a close and attached relationship with his counsellor which served as a vehicle for him to work through feelings about his distant father. He said he always believed that he would have got on better with his father had his father been white. He always wished that his father was white so that his mother and siblings would have been spared the racial abuse which had dominated their early lives on the estate. As the years passed his mother became more accepted where they lived, and refused to move away when it was possible for them to buy a house elsewhere. He saw his father as an aloof and unforgiving man who would not change his attitude to those on the estate. Disclosing his childhood shame of his father was uncomfortable for Melvin and he wept as he realised how similarly isolated he now was. He could not remember a time when he felt close to his father and he admits to times when he avoided being seen talking to him when in the company of his friends. He was successful in the secret hatred of the part of himself that was black, and his father as a representative of that blackness. Melvin's closeness to his mother was, it seems, at the expense of forming a good trusting relationship with his father. As a child born after a long gap, he was claimed by his mother as her own. From an analysis of the novel *The Murderer* by Roy Heath (1999), Fletchman-Smith discusses the main character Galton Flood whose mother does not hold men in high esteem and whose father was not supportive of his growing son.

> However, I believe that many of the problems which require attention are just as much 'internal' as they are 'external'. For instance, in Heath's novel we encounter Galton's father, who cannot (or will not) help extricate his son from the clutches of the mother. Yet it is vitally important that fathers – or someone carrying out the father function – takes on this task.
>
> (Fetchman-Smith 2000, p. 49)

Melvin had not been extricated from his mother and his father appears to have given up on forging a meaningful relationship with his son. It could be said that Melvin developed his masculine identity on the streets, where it was a dog-eat-dog world. His mother objected to him being scolded by her husband, complaining that he was being too hard on the boy. Melvin became a comfort to his mother during her periods of isolation at home and likewise she could always be relied on to support him in arguments with his older brothers and sister. While he would have enjoyed the close relationship with his mother and the physical assurance of snuggling into her in bed, he also felt a sense of shame.

Melvin was able to change albeit with the threat of imprisonment hanging over his head. Some professionals see this period as a time of crisis and a good time for offenders to change. Others feel that such external pressures to change produce false starts, and would prefer to work therapeutically with clients who make a decision to seek help after they have initiated an evaluation of their lives and see good reasons to change.

The boy who lived in a world of his own

Manjeet was unusual in many ways. He was one of few young men of Asian descent at that time to have been found guilty and referred to the probation service for reports. He seemed a lonely figure sitting in the waiting room. Manjeet was a quiet 15-year-old who had been arrested for holding up a local tobacconist shop with a large knife. Barely disguised with a stocking over his head, he managed to escape with the takings of some eighty pounds. To his great surprise he was caught that afternoon with all the money intact in his room. It was his first offence in the Juvenile Court and he was in no doubt that he had brought shame on his family, but he seemed not to care. At interview he seemed to have been lost in a fog, at times unable to hear the voice of the probation officer who was talking to him. He gave a bland, flat picture of his childhood which had no texture to it. His probation officer noticed that he was one of the few young people he had met who did not attempt to plead innocence, nor indeed to offer mitigation by way of excuse for the offence they committed. He did say that he needed some money, but when asked why he needed it he was unable to say why. Exploration of other motivation revealed that Manjeet seemed to get pleasure from holding the knife and making the shopkeeper frightened. Asked why he wanted to see fear in the eyes of this man, he replied that the sub-postmaster who was from the same part of India as his parents had always looked down on him and his brothers ever since they were very young. He appeared to have a belief that the shopkeeper was pleased at his father's death, but could not support this in any way. It seemed likely that Manjeet had fantasies which led up to his enactment of the offence, probably avenging the death of a father with whom he had identified (Bailey and Aulich 1997). Apart from making little response Manjeet might have been considered polite and pleasant. He would have appeared to have been the quiet boy in any school: able, yet showing little interest in school work, present, yet in many ways absent. Recognising what appeared to be his depressed state he was referred for assessment with a view to receiving some brief counselling help.

This young man had quite a powerful effect on his probation officer who spent much of his casework supervision time talking about this client. Although it was clear that Manjeet had difficulties relating to others and was probably not a good candidate for probation super-vision, the emotional hooks of concern for him were already in the probation officer, who argued that it was precisely because he was poor at relating to others that he could benefit from probation help. On assessment at the local centre for psychotherapy and counselling he was offered twenty-four weeks of counselling as part of his super-vision order. Occasionally, in counselling he would smile and make contact that way. Alternative smiling to himself created in the coun-sellor an eeriness and a concern that he might be abusing a sub-stance. His smiling to himself also seemed to be evidence of some secret amusement or a mode of lapsing into his fantasy world. His probation officer made valiant attempts to get into Manjeet's fantasy world, considering this to be richer than his actual life. However, this was resisted by Manjeet who was quite skilful at evasion. In Court Manjeet was eventually given a supervision order, but this did not create in him any sense of joy at not being sent into custody. He attended probation supervision and began his counselling. He began to feel at ease and was able to talk more easily with the probation officer. In taking his social history Manjeet's life seemed grim and tragic. The youngest of three sons, his father died when Manjeet was 3½, having suffered from a terminal illness. Manjeet said that his fam-ily did not have photographs of his father around the house because it was not thought to be good; he was not sure why this was the case other than it was a custom. His mother was alone in this country with her children apart from some minimal support from her brother-in-law and his family who lived in another part of London. She had no other family in the United Kingdom and she was not fluent in English. Her eldest son usually spoke for the family due to his mother's lack of confidence in dealing with authority.

A disclosure of childhood abuse

The family did not attract the interest of the social services or the school. Manjeet said that sometimes he wanted to tell his teacher about what happened at home, especially being hit by his older brothers. He was afraid of his brothers for most of his childhood because of their violence. He had begun to discuss this with his counsellor but their time together came to an end, and it was suggested to him that he continued to explore some of his past with the probation officer. It was not for several months that his probation officer was to learn about the extent of his abuse and humiliation, both physical and sexual. This began at an early age, being ridiculed and made to perform sexual acts. He said that his older brother stopped it, but his middle brother continued for some time longer. Although he has no clear memory of when the abuse began, he remembers that it ceased when he was about 10 years old, before attending high school.

Recognising the solitary nature of Manjeet's life, the probation officer referred him to a social skills group but he refused to attend. He said that he did not want to attend because he did not feel that he could say anything in the group. He had changed little during the course of the year, expressing no view about his past nor about his future. He seemed to have passively accepted what life had in store for him, not feeling able to make an impact on his own destiny. Manjeet had a limited social life and his only hobby was collecting *Spiderman* comics. He would update his probation officer on his latest acquisitions from time to time. His world was sparsely peopled and consequently he spoke of few friends and little about his brothers whom he disliked. His mother merited little mention; she was always there but had no direct influence on his life or little relevance. Angry at his mother always taking the side of his eldest brother, Manjeet said that this brother was allowed to do what he wanted. Manjeet's robbing of the tobacconists had an interesting effect on members of his family, who now appeared to notice him and treat him with a grudging respect. From the contact that the probation officer had from home visits he developed a picture of the home as offering little emotional nourishment. This new regard for

Manjeet appeared to have been a sort of hostage to hope that he would not further disgrace the family. He was told by his mother that what he had done might make it difficult for the family to secure good marriages for his older brothers.

When Manjeet completed his work with the counsellor, she was disappointed because she felt that she knew as much about him at the end of the counselling as she knew at the beginning. She had worked sensitively with the partial disclosure of his abuse but had felt that he could not connect with it and behaved as though it had happened to someone else. Like with most things Manjeet was indifferent. Always polite, he would convince both workers that he agreed with what was being said to him yet in reality he had an invisible shell around him. Both workers were concerned about his silent retreats which made him inaccessible and lost in time and space. When he became aware of his absence in the room he would smile and apologise. He seemed to be aware of his apparent daydreaming.

Closing his case file his probation officer wrote in the notes that Manjeet was an unknown quantity and that he was capable of serious, unpredictable violence. Because of his experience of repeated sexual abuse and humiliation he was distanced from feelings, his own in particular and other people's in general. Because he was not able to speak about the violence perpetuated against him it seemed that Manjeet had to 'show' what he had learned about violence. Perhaps speaking about it made his passive part in it seem too real and frightening.

Three years after the ending of his probation supervision Manjeet was arrested after two tourists were robbed at knife-point in the West End of London. In an attempt to get away, one of the victims was hit by a passing car and was killed instantly. Manjeet and his accomplice were tried and convicted for manslaughter. As well as feelings of sadness, his counsellor and probation officer were left feeling that they should have done more to reach him emotionally.

Using inter-cultural ideas

Counselling in the criminal justice system can have its rewards when client behaviour is affected. Placed within an institution that relies heavily on facts and evidence can leave those working with emotions and irrational behaviour on the sidelines. The powerful coexisting systems of the legal field and the psychological world can be a source of confusion for both clients and workers. In addition, those who have not worked in a public service agency as counsellors will find themselves applying their counselling skills in a way that is very different from private practice. These three clients all presented with different problems that were in the field of probation and forensic counselling. One, Wesley, came to counselling entirely of his own free will. Manjeet's contact with probation and counselling was as an order of the court and he had no choice, and Melvin's fear of imprisonment led him to reconsider his life. What motivates people to get counselling in the probation and forensic field differs. This sector of the population is not usually considered to be the most willing of clients but intervention at a time of crisis can help to make changes in their lives, as happened in the case of Melvin. Given that all three had at least one parent who was born outside the United Kingdom brought aspects of another culture to the task of raising their children in the context of another culture. All three were to varying degrees on the margins of the flow of British society. Only Melvin took up a negative position in relation to his father's culture and background. Manjeet and Wesley did not bring negative issues about their culture or upbringing to their counselling, but inescapably their culture had an effect on their lives. It was while in a traditional hierarchical relationship of obedience to his older brothers following the death of his father that Manjeet was terrorised by those charged with his protection. Similarly, the fundamentalist Christian ideas of his family and culture contributed to Wesley's fascination with and revulsion at the idea of criminality. It would not be reasonable to assume that all people from Caribbean backgrounds develop psychological problems around moral and religious beliefs, yet undoubtedly there would be some religious motive in their psychological presentation. The centrality of Christianity in this community makes it unsurprising that individuals will have to struggle with a sense of their goodness and badness from time to time.

Having an understanding of some of the cultural issues that are brought by clients and being willing to engage with them helps to develop trust in an inter-cultural contact. For the second or third generation children of people who came to this country as immigrants, being on the margins not only describes their relationship to British culture, but also the culture that has been passed on to them by their parents. The apparent ethnic sameness and difference between the counsellor and client did not seem to be an obstacle in the counselling relationship experienced by Wesley, Melvin or Manjeet. The real issue with these clients was that of being understood, and the counsellor being able to make a connection with them so that some sense could be made of their whole experience. The histories of all three clients played its part in equipping them to see the world and forming their attitudes to others in it. Raised as a person of mixed parentage having an African-Caribbean father and London East End mother, Melvin felt that given his environment he had little choice but to play down or at any rate ignore his black Caribbean heritage. He favoured the white part of himself, despising black people probably as much as did his friends. In order for him to survive, Melvin had to split off the black part of himself and to remain partly unaware of it. A counselling relationship with a black African male counsellor presented a considerable challenge to both Melvin and his counsellor because he was constantly reminded of the black part of himself, that which had previously been consigned to the rubbish heap. Manjeet had a culture that was very different to that of his probation officer and counsellor, both of whom were white British, while he was British born of traditional Asian parents. The roles, relationships and patterns of behaviour in Manjeet's family differed greatly from those which were familiar to his counsellor and probation officer. Although one of his most important issues was the loss of his father, it was difficult for Marjeet to both observe his traditional culture of neither wallowing in the memory of a lost loved one nor keeping images of them on display. In order for the counselling to be helpful the counsellor not only has to help the client to recognise the difficult situation they may be in (for example, living between two cultures) but also the impact that this might have on their offending behaviour. Counselling should help the client to think about ways to overcome the belief that they are compromising their culture.

Although Wesley and his counsellor both came from a Caribbean background, they were nevertheless very different. Unlike his counsellor, Wesley was born in the United Kingdom, and the counsellor on an island almost a thousand miles away from Wesley's roots. In terms of their culture, black clients and counsellors can at times have little in common because their communities are as equally complex as white British culture in how they are stratified class-wise as well as in other ways. For many African and Caribbean people the only commonality between them can sometimes be the colour of their skin. Even here skin tone is the site of old battle grounds between black people, and in part remains one of the principal means of being separated, the light skinned separated from the dark who were treated in an inferior way. This device to create division on the plantation still survives as shameful hidden attitudes. Indeed, the black client and black counsellor cannot assume that they have a common culture, and may need to explore and clarify issues of their sameness and difference and what these might symbolise.

The counsellor who is able to ask for clarification over matters of culture that are misunderstood shows a greater degree of respect to the client than one who ignores what is not understood. Working from a position of curiosity about the client and their lived cultural experience is not helpful unless the counsellor can think about their own experience and how this might impact on the client in terms of attitudes and preconceived ideas. Counsellors also have to be aware of how they might be affected by the client's culturally based views and attitudes which may be very different to their own. As more is learned about minority ethnic cultures and counselling, it will be more likely that we will see all cultures as more complicated than we might have first thought. It is very important to be aware that we each learn cultural messages consciously and otherwise, and that even professional counsellor and therapy training will not completely wipe out or obscure our histories or bias. Ethnic culture has an impact on our values and often dictates how children are raised in one culture or another. Identification with a particular cultural group can provide not only a sense of inferiority in some, but a false sense of superiority in others. It is from our own personal development as counsellors that we will learn about the ways in which our past and present experiences are entwined with those of the clients with whom we work. We even have to locate and know the delinquent parts of ourselves, however latent this may be, in order to cope with the powerful feelings that might be evoked in us when working with forensic clients.

The more recent move in probation is for counsellors to view their task as law enforcement, which runs the risk of reducing the original aim of probation, that of exercising personal influence and guidance through a counselling relationship. It is however possible to do good offence-focused counselling with clients from minority ethnic groups. In the past, black and ethnic minority offenders did not receive the same or equal treatment in the criminal courts (The Hood Report, Commission For Racial Equality 1992; Home Office S.95 CJA Race and The Criminal Justice System 1990). In more recent years the Courts, probation and the Prison Service have made some attempt to take action to prevent disproportionate numbers of black offenders from being sentenced to custody. The Hood Report in its findings concluded:

> All else being equal, Black offenders had a 5–8 per cent greater possibility of being sent to prison than Whites, and Asians a lower probability of about 4 per cent. These percentages put a sizeable number of Black offenders at a disadvantage each year, particularly when combined with the longer sentences following not-guilty pleas.

Conclusion

While some of these clients' acts of law-breaking can be straight-forwardly understood and dealt with similarly, there are some aspects of their offending which may be hard to understand. Although Wesley apparently lived a comfortable, law-abiding life, he was very bothered by a fear that he might end up in prison. This fear was not only fuelled by his past fare-dodging, but also by his punishing and guilt-ridden inner world. While Wesley was so fearful of his criminal impulses and wanted to stay on the right side of the law, Manjeet and Melvin were able to cross the line of what was socially acceptable and did not have the same degree of internal conflict, or at any rate what might have been apparent at the time. Struggling under a weight of guilt Wesley seemed driven by neurosis and fear; on the other hand, Manjeet in particular and Melvin less so showed little trace of guilt or concern for others. There is an enormous variety in the personalities and attitudes of those who come to the attention of probation officers and forensic psychotherapists, and each person needs to be assessed before an appropriate model for work is selected from the worker's repertoire.

Some assessments are made by probation officers who ask the client a variety of questions. For example: Does the offender admit to the charge, Was there a victim involved, Is there any concern for the victim and how the offence might have affected their life? Further assessment questions might be put to the client, but the assessor could ask themselves and conclude from their own observations. Would the offender be prepared to make restitution? Do they feel that they have done anything wrong? Is there a history between the offender and the victim? Can the offender give their account of the offence, and how does it differ from the prosecution or other accounts? Does the offender see this offence as part of a predestined mission of some sort? Can the offender see the offence as a significant event or turning point? Can they describe the effect it has had on them? What do they regret (apart from being caught)?

Coupled with an ability to take a social or developmental history, open-ended questioning can help to build a picture of the offender in his or her social context. Individual motivation or pathology is important to ascertain, but peer group behaviour and family attitude and values are equally important. Some people are raised in homes where the most respect is conferred on the most prolific and lucrative thief, in which case growing up to be like them can be an ambition. In these circumstances breaking the pattern of offending will be difficult. Traditionally the social casework approach has been used by probation officers, and in more recent years the focus has been on offending behaviour. Both are broadly based and rely on a variety of social and psychological theories. Unlike individual casework, offending behaviour programmes might be group or theme based and tend to work on behavioural change.

This is a move away from the more insight-giving and awareness-raising endeavours of individual casework which had the relationship as its central purpose. The influence of the probation officer and what they might represent to the offender is considered to be an important aspect of relationship-based casework. Each having their place, both approaches are useful and need to be selected with clients after assessment. Save for the misdemeanour for which he was cautioned as a young student, Wesley was a good and upstanding person. He was well versed in the feelings of guilt and the fear of sin, having spent all of his youth in the church. He even saw himself as having been born with sin, and learning to repent and be forgiven as the only way. He began therapy not because of criminality but because of his fear of committing a crime, and being caught and shamed. He feared the consequences that this might have on his life. He did not feel easy about having children with his wife Dee for fear that she would have to raise them alone. Like Raskolnikov in *Crime and Punishment* (Dostoyevsky 1865), Wesley felt that he did not have sufficient control over his life. The individual who presents with fears of becoming a criminal is unusual, and is often very different in terms of attitude and personality to the habitual offender. The over-burdening sense of guilt for an act that Wesley fears he might commit puts him in stark contrast to the antisocial person who appears to be addicted to law-breaking. While at first sight it might seem that Wesley felt profound feelings of guilt for fare evasion committed many years earlier, it could also be argued that his guilt and shame might have its genesis in his early understanding of his Christian faith, or indeed that he picked up these feelings of being black and poor in a society where black and poor are relegated to the bottom of the social pile. Wesley's shame was such that the London Underground inspector's comments appeared to unearth something that was deeply buried. The way that Wesley had been affected seemed disproportionate to what was said.

In the case of Manjeet it was difficult to discover the presence of guilt or regret. Although it was hard to find out what he felt or thought, what was certain was that he spent much of his young life being concerned for his safety and survival in his family. He learned from his experience how hurting and abusing was carried out and, more importantly, how not to be victimised any more. Information about his offence without some knowledge of the treatment he received in his family and the grudge he harboured over many years for the post office worker could leave the probation officer or counsellor perplexed. Given his experiences, it is hardly surprising that Manjeet had such an impoverished inner landscape. He had a limited understanding of the effect that his actions had on others, and similarly his capacity for concern for others seemed to have been killed off if it was ever alive.

Melvin by comparison did well in his counselling; it seems that many factors came together which enabled him to use the counselling and the person of the counsellor in a positive transferential way. It is not always the case that the course of counselling, psychodynamic or otherwise, runs smoothly. The counselling in his case was probably effective because he was very motivated, and his counsellor was very experienced and had learned to exercise great care with the use of interpretations of the transference. Melvin was also at a developmental crossroads in his life and this was an important time for change. He had lost status and with it his trade as a small-time drugs dealer. Getting rid of his drug habit was an achievement for him.

Working therapeutically with offenders has been greatly influenced by the Institute for the Study and Treatment of Delinquency and its clinic, the Portman Clinic as it is today. There are publications which have discussed some of the training issues for working with offenders (Andrew 1978; Bhui 1999; Welldon and Van Velsen 1997). Little attention has been given in recent times to the importance of teaching psychopathology to social workers, counsellors and psychotherapists. If this is not adequately done, professionals will have problems of assessment and therapeutic method selection. With the proliferation of counselling and therapy courses it is important that students are taught and prepared for the challenging task of working with offenders.

References

Andrew, J.M. (1978) Values in Counselling Probationers. *International Journal of Offender Therapy and Comparative Criminology* 22(1): 11.

Bailey, S. and Aulich, L. (1997) Understanding Murderous Young People, in Welldon and Van Velsen, *A Practical Guide to Forensic Psychotherapy*.

Bhui, K. (1999) Cross Cultural Psychiatry and Probation Practice: A Discourse on Issues, Context and Practice. *Probation Journal* 46(2): 95

Bottoms, A.E. and McWilliams, W. (1979) A Non-treatment Paradigm for Probation Practice. *British Journal of Social Work* 9(2), pp. 159–202.

Bowlby, J. (1947) *Forty Four Juvenile Thieves, Their Character and Home Life*. London: Baillaiere, Tindall and Cox.

Dostoyevsky, F. (1865) *Crime and Punishment*. London: Penguin Books, 1979

Dupont-Joshua, A. (1991) Inter-Cultural Therapy. *BAC Counselling* August pp. 203–4.

Engel, S.W. (1975) Some Basic Principles of Offender Therapy: 1. *International Journal of Offender Therapy* 19(1): 12.

Ferard, M.L. and Hunnybun, N.K. (1962) *The Caseworker's Use of Relationships*. London: Tavistock.

Fletchman-Smith, B. (2000) *Mental Slavery, Psychoanalytic Studies of Caribbean People*. London: Rebus Press.

Glover, E. (1960) *The Roots of Crime*. London: Imago Publishing.

Heath, R. (1999) *The Murderer*. London: Picador.

Hutchinson, E.O. (1994) *The Assassination of the Black Male*. Los Angeles, CA: Middle Passage Press.

Irvine, E.E. (1963) *Transference and Reality in the Casework Relationship*, in *Relationships in Casework*. London: Association of Psychiatric Social Workers.

Kareem, J. (1988) Outside in. . . . Inside out. . . . Some Considerations. *Inter-Cultural Journal of Social Work Practice* 3(3).

Kareem, J. and Littlewood, R. (1992) *Intercultural Therapy; Themes Interpretations and Practice*. Oxford: Blackwood Scientific, reprinted 1999, p. 57.

Madhubuti, H.R. (1990) *Black Men, Obsolete, Single, Dangerous?* Chicago, IL: Third World Press.

Mead, M. (1949) *Male and Female*. New York: Morrow.

Schmideberg, M. (1975) Some Basic Principles of Offender Therapy: 11. *International Journal of Offender Therapy* 19(1): 22.

Thomas, L.K. (1991) *Magistrates Courts and the Mentally Disordered Offender: An Exploration of Professional Viewpoint and Local Practice.* Unpublished manuscript, Department of Government, Brunel University, London.

Thomas, L.K. (1995) Psychotherapy in The Context of Race and Culture: An Intercultural Therapeutic approach, in S. Fernando (ed.), *Mental Health in a Multi-Ethnic Society.* London: Routledge.

Thomas, L.K. (1996) Organisational Change in the Probation Service, in A. Cooklyn (ed.), *Human Systems, Issue on Systems and Organisational Consultation.* London: KCC.

Thomas, L.K. (1997) Reworking Stereotypes for Self-Identity in a Black Men's Psychotherapy Group. *RACE Journal*, p. 25.

Welldon, E. and Van Velsen, C. (1997) *A Practical Guide to Forensic Psychotherapy.* London: Jessica Kingsley.

Winnicott, D.W. (1963) Psychotherapy of Character Disorders, in *The Maturational Process and the Facilitating Environment.* London: Hogarth Press, 1982.

Winnicott, D.W. (1967) Delinquency as a Sign of Hope, in *Home is Where we Start From.* London: Penguin Books, 1986.

World Health Organisation (1973) *The International Pilot Study of Schizophrenia.* Geneva: WHO.

Chapter 9

Inter-cultural counselling in a social services setting

Elaine Arnold

Introduction

> Basic to the profession of social work is the recognition of the
> value and dignity of every human being, irrespective of origin,
> race, status, sex, sexual orientation, age, disability, belief or con-
> tribution to society. The profession accepts a responsibility to
> encourage and facilitate the self-realisation of each individual
> person with due regard for the interest of others.
>
> (BASW 1977)

My involvement in social work followed ten years of teaching in
primary schools in Barbados and Trinidad in the West Indies. It was
always of interest to me to discover the background of the children
who presented with behavioural challenges in the classroom and
invariably it was found that they were reacting to problems within
the family. There may have been the birth of a new sibling or the
separation from a member of the family through death or migration,
or the child may have been shifted from his or her family home to
another. What was rewarding was that after a number of visits to the
home and getting to know the family and they to know me, the
child's behaviour improved and so did the educational attainment.

The change to social work occurred after teaching for several years
in the school attached to an 'orphanage'. This was home for a
number of children, some of whom were orphans, some placed by
parents whose economic situation prevented them from providing
adequate care or others inclined to be delinquent and considered as
'beyond control'. Here the children were physically cared for and
their educational needs were being met, but their social and emotional development lagged far behind their physical development.

When an 'uncle and aunt' scheme was introduced in order to encourage members of the community to take an interest in some of the children and provide home life experiences, the all-round improvement was very marked. This was an indication that they were less troubled and felt wanted and appreciated.

The decision to change from teaching to social work was based on the premise that as a social worker, there was the opportunity to study the whole context in which individuals functioned, and to raise awareness of behaviours at different stages of development of human beings, and the impact of certain factors within the environment on them and their families.

In most societies there are those who feel committed to help others who for a variety of reasons are unable to cope effectively with personal problems, which may be of social, financial, political or emotional origin. The help may be given by social workers through government organised or funded social services, and in voluntary organisations. Social work has a history of varied interests which include direct work with individuals in attempts to assist them to cope with living in their communities and to experience a maximum of comfort to themselves, and to enable them to establish and sustain relationships. There are times when social workers have adopted a more radical stance as advocate for the clients who are unable to challenge the social, economic or political systems. Whatever the focus has been, there is usually the belief by every committed social worker that the welfare of the individual is paramount.

Volunteers, in the course of helping individuals to cope with problems arising within their families and communities, became aware that practical solutions were not always appropriate or effective. Frequently the problem presented to the worker was not the 'real' problem. It may have been a cry for help emanating from a more deep-seated emotional difficulty.

The ideas of Sigmund Freud greatly influenced social workers in America during the 1930s. Using Freudian concepts and techniques, a psychological method of work developed and was known as casework. The writings of American social caseworkers (e.g. Hollis 1964; Towle 1945) were used in British social work training and in practice over many years. There were critics who ridiculed social workers as wanting to know the entire background lives of clients and criticism from the clients themselves, before helping them with practical problems (Timms 1964). Gradually social work training focused on the

development of skills, such as inner skills which process the information clients bring and make sense of it, interactional skills which
facilitate dealing with feelings of clients, group skills when more than
one client is involved and 'Strategic skills for use with special issues'
(Middleman and Wood 1990, p. 14).

The British Association of Social Workers defined social work as

> The purposeful and ethical application of personal skills in
> interpersonal relationships directed towards enhancing the per-
> sonal and social functioning of an individual, family, group or
> neighbourhood.
>
> (BASW 1977)

Congruent with all social work, its aim is to raise and undergird the
level of human competence and satisfaction in daily living. This
definition provided scope for the worker to attempt to form a working alliance with the client in order to develop trust and so enable
them to try together to find a solution to the problem.

According to Howe (1995, p. 2), the best laid plans of social
workers can easily go astray unless there is good knowledge of
the human condition and a sound understanding of how and why
people behave the way they do. Howe appreciates the fact that
increasingly social workers attempt to form relationships on rational,
logical, systematic grounds, but he warns against ignoring the psychological, irrational and emotional; this last will affect the scope of
the practice adversely. There are times when clients, because of their
overwhelming problems, try to force social workers into roles which
they think would bring about a solution. When their demands are
unmet they leave, disappointed with social workers and disillusioned
with the service. It is therefore necessary that from the beginning of
the relationship, clients are informed of the parameters of the agency
and the role of the workers.

Clark (2000, p. 1) describes the contentious nature of social work
and states what social workers are not.

> Social workers are not health professionals but they seek to
> promote individuals' well being. They are not formal teachers
> but they must try to teach people new ways of thinking about
> the issues in their lives. They are not lawyers, but they have the
> practical responsibility of applying some particularly sensitive
> aspects to the law; and they are not ministers of religion, but

they use their influence to promote or suppress certain ways of human living.

The social worker as an inter-cultural counsellor

The demographic nature of society in Britain has changed over the past few decades, and in the communities where the social services are established the clients are people of varied ethnic and cultural backgrounds. All social workers and especially those who are ethnically and culturally different from the client need to be sensitive and understanding of the client's cultural norms. It is also necessary to recognise when some behaviour attributed to the client's culture may be detrimental to the welfare of a member of the family (e.g. excessive punishment of a young child). It would be imperative for intervention to be taken to safeguard the child and a thorough explanation given as to why this was necessary. Kareem (1992, p. 19) stressed the point that 'beyond the fact of our shared humanity, individuals are unique and distinct from each other and thus there is always an interpersonal and "inter-cultural" dimension to any encounter between two people including that between therapist and client'. This is applicable to social workers and clients. Jafar Kareem founded Nafsiyat,[1] an inter-cultural therapy centre. Having worked in the National Health Service as a psychotherapist, he observed that black and ethnic minority clients were not responding to the type of therapy being offered. Some social workers, realising that a small centre did not have the capacity to work with all of the clients they could refer, took the opportunity of training offered by Kareem and his training team to add inter-cultural counselling to their skills.

Kareem believed that the worker needs to take into account the whole being of the patient – not only the individual concepts and constructs that are presented, but also the patient's communal life experience in the world, both past and present. He advocated that 'when working with difference in human beings, one must seek the very universality that exists in diversity' (Kareem 2000, p. 20). The powerful social factors which impinge on the individual and cause severe pain are poverty and social disadvantage; also discrimination, on the basis of culture, gender, disability, race, religion, sexual orientation, are real to the client.

The people who approach the social services come from diverse backgrounds. Some may refer themselves when relationships in the immediate family break down, or they suffer loss of a family member. Some may be referred by other agencies, while others may be unwilling clients who are sent by the Courts and the judicial system. Since Britain is a multiracial country, it is evident that among the would-be client group there will be individuals of different races and cultural backgrounds. Some may be second or third generation offspring of immigrants, some may be refugees or asylum seekers who are unfamiliar with the system and who speak a different language. Some individuals may have experienced racism in one or all of its forms, namely individual racism, cultural racism, institutional racism, and the experiences have left them with diminished self-esteem.

Counselling usually begins with the client and the social worker meeting in the social worker's territory (the office). This immediately establishes the power imbalance between the two. The client may feel anxious and may have a biased view of the function of the agency. The perception may be that it is bureaucratic and unsympathetic to the group to which the client belongs, or the client may be optimistic that the social worker is able to solve the problems presented. The worker in social services has duties and powers to which he or she must adhere. What is important is the style of performing those duties and exercising those powers to create an atmosphere in which the client will feel safe and trust the worker in order to enter into a working relationship. The social worker in a social services setting needs to inform the client of what is permissible within the legal framework and so avoid unrealistic expectations about the help available.

The working relationship

Before the working relationship can be established, it is important that social workers know the backgrounds of their clients. Johnson (1989: 9) states:

> To understand the environmental factors, a social worker needs to have considerable knowledge of the culture of the ethnic and racial groups with which s/he is working. This involves knowledge of a cultural group's history, values, and morals, family and community patterns, attitudes and thinking patterns, religious traditions, child-rearing practices and ways of coping with change and stress. Also important are the group's experiences in relating to the dominant culture, which involves social

and economic factors and acculturation experiences and their results. This may seem an onerous task, but it is a necessary one if the worker is going to work in any depth with the client and help effectively.

Poor and disadvantaged clients may be distrustful of how a well-educated, middle-class worker whose life experience may have been so different from theirs will be able to understand and identify with them. These clients may be of a similar racial and ethnic group. A black or other ethnic minority individual may have doubts about whether a white worker who has not experienced discrimination on the basis of skin colour is able to understand and empathise if he or she expresses feelings about having been discriminated against.The white client meeting a black worker may wonder whether the service given will be adequate since he or she may have a stereotypical view of the inferiority of black people.

It is impossible for social workers to know the cultural norms of all the clients with whom they work but it is important for them to ask the client rather than to make assumptions. There may be some broad areas of behaviour within a group that are common; for example, child-rearing, care of the elderly, ways of worshipping, dress, preparation of food and so on. However, some young individuals within that social/cultural group may deviate from the norms and incur the wrath of parents or other members of the community. If these individuals seek help from a social worker, it is absolutely necessary that the worker does not try to fit them into what is considered to be normal for a member of the particular ethnic group but listens to them and helps them to consider what support systems are available to them before making a complete break. If abuse is disclosed there may be occasions when individuals need protection outside of the family.

Assessment

Before deciding to counsel a client, the worker needs to make a thorough assessment of the client in order to discover the meaning he or she attributes to the problem. The social worker needs to be genuine and empathic and above all be a good listener. He or she needs to acknowledge the client's discomfort and try to reduce the feeling of vulnerability. At times this means having to listen to material which seems to bear no relevance to the problem as stated in the referral, but it may be the client's way of testing the worker's willingness to empathise, to listen and also to test the safety of being in the worker's presence. The skilled worker will gradually help the client to focus on the problem.

The use of interpreters

In inter-cultural counselling, sometimes there may be the necessity to communicate through an interpreter. Before the interview it is necessary to check that the interpreter speaks the client's language. This may appear to be stating the obvious, but workers who confuse race and culture may not pay attention to detail of the client's place of origin. The worker may know that the client is from Africa or India but does not pinpoint the region and therefore the language spoken. When thorough preparation is not done before the interview and the interpreter is unable to help, this can lead to frustration and embarrassment.

Interpreters need to be briefed and have impressed upon them that their views must not be given, and that the client's words must be translated exactly. In the early days of working with clients who spoke different languages, social workers used members of the family. This was found to be unacceptable as it undermined the dynamic of the family, especially when children were put in a superior role to their parents who were finding it difficult to cope with the strange environment. Husbands who perhaps had preceded their wives to the country and were better equipped linguistically spoke for them, and this sometimes served to diminish the women's self-esteem.

Following the assessment and the decision to counsel, the client and the worker need to establish the boundaries, such as time and duration of the session. Confidentiality in counselling is a fundamental principle. In social work it is important that the client is made aware that confidentiality is not absolute because the worker works within a legal mandate. If the material disclosed poses a serious threat to the client's life or that of the child, the worker must share the information within the agency and with the relevant professionals outside of the social service. The worker needs to help the clients to accept the principle and realise that they can take part in the decision-making.

Separation and loss

For many clients, separation and loss have been the basis for most of their difficulties. They may have been separated through adoption or fostering, through immigration, or by virtue of being an asylum seeker or refugee in England. They may have experienced the death of a loved one or parted through divorce. Whatever the circumstances, separation and loss are very traumatic for those who have experienced them.

The knowledge of attachment theory is very relevant for social work in this respect. Bowlby (1979) emphasised that people's sense of security is adversely affected when loss of significant figures occurs and often the anger that is felt for being in the situation is suppressed. Because of individual differences, people react to loss in a variety of ways. Some may withdraw from life situations and become apathetic and depressed; others may use aggression as a defence against accepting sympathy.

Case study I

The following case study illustrates the social worker's ability to utilise theory to enhance practice.

Miss B, age 34, was referred by her doctor. In the letter of referral it was stated that over the years when Miss B was being seen at the surgery she was a cheerful, highly motivated young woman. She had a daughter aged 12 and had struggled to care for her without the help and support of the father. She had been married but the relationship had lasted only two years and she was not in a relationship at the time of referral. Recently she had been attending the surgery complaining of lack of sleep and indefinable pains. The doctor had tried to find out what significant changes had occurred in her circumstances, and had discovered that her 12-year-old daughter had gone to stay with a friend and had said she preferred her friend's mother to her, and she did not want to return home.

When Miss B arrived at the social services office she was very angry, and demanded that the social worker did 'something' about her daughter. She was anxious that with all the news about children being abused, her daughter could be at risk. The social worker acknowledged her concerns and reassured her that she would visit her daughter, that she would check on her daughter's safety and try to discover her reasons for wanting to stay at her friend's house. She also suggested that Miss B and her daughter should be seen together. This was intended to observe how mother and daughter interacted with each other.

Miss B agreed and the social worker saw mother and daughter for three sessions. It was agreed that her daughter could visit her friend and her friend could visit her daughter, and proper agreements were made with both sets of parents when they would be able to stay overnight.

The social worker observed that Miss B's mood was low, and after discussion with the supervisor, the social worker invited her to return for brief counselling and she accepted. The social worker listened carefully to Miss B's story and learned gradually that she had been privately fostered from the age of 2 as her mother had wanted to complete her studies, and there were no members of her family living in this country. The foster-parents were white English and lived in one of the home counties. Miss B had become attached to her foster-parents and did not want to leave them, but at the age of 6 her mother was able to have her back. The circumstances under which her biological family lived in the city were very different from those of her foster-parents. She did not see her foster-parents until she had grown up and was able to visit them. She had felt the separation from them very keenly. Miss B had felt angry with her mother who now had a second child, a boy, to whom she felt her mother showed preference. Her father worked abroad and visited home periodically, so she never formed a relationship with him. She had grown up being very much a loner, did not make friends easily and had concentrated on doing well at school.

At first Miss B did not see the relevance of having to talk about her early life, but she persisted in attending the sessions and was able to form a working alliance with the worker, and was able to complete the twelve sessions that were offered.

It was evident that Miss B was lonely and felt very keenly her inability to sustain relationships with friends or a partner. She acknowledged that her feelings of jealousy, resentment and marginality which she felt as a child had resurfaced when her daughter left home. Miss B acknowledged that she had always wanted to be close to her mother but had never been able to do so. She would value her support now that her daughter is growing up. As she became more in touch with her feelings the relationship with her daughter improved, and she realised that that she could not be dependent on her daughter for companionship. She began to look for other interests. Miss B realised that she had become fearful that she was losing her daughter. She appreciated that the social worker was empathic and understanding, and so working together with the family had helped.

Helping clients to acknowledge their need to mourn their loss is crucial and involves skilful work on the part of the social worker. As in all counselling situations, the counsellor must start with knowledge of self. Workers need to be aware of the values and prejudices they hold, of stereotypes of other people and how amenable they are to changing views when they are presented with evidence contrary to earlier understandings. There is a need for the social worker to be able to strike a balance and to differentiate between cultural traditions and clients' responses to pressures within society.

The worker must be able to sacrifice some of the power intrinsic in the role, and admit to a client whose racial and cultural backgrounds are different, that he or she does not know everything about his or her culture but is willing to learn. A show of interest in clients' country and cultural norms and their families' ways of reacting to these norms can facilitate the development of the relationship. Information is more forthcoming with honesty and openness and there is an acceptance of boundaries which clients do not overstep. The outcome of the interaction is more likely to be successful.

There are of course some clients who may not be prepared to share information, and the worker needs to be helped by the supervisor to examine whether the working alliance between the two is possible. If this is not the case, the client needs to be offered a choice of another worker where possible; but sometimes the client may choose to terminate the counselling sessions. This could undermine the worker's confidence in working inter-culturally. However, careful and sensitive supervision by a supervisor with experience of working inter-culturally becomes invaluable for the worker.

Case study 2

Mrs A, aged 32, a mother of West Indian origin who had recently arrived in the country with her husband who was a student, was referred by the nursery manager, who was concerned that in recent weeks, on most evenings when Mrs A arrived to collect her son Carl, there was a scene, with him demanding to be taken shopping and wanting to take a bus home when they lived within walking distance. After reasoning with him, his mother would forcefully take him by the hand and walk home. That morning Carl had arrived at the nursery limping, and the worker asked him what was wrong; he said, 'Mommy beat me'. Mrs A was confronted by the worker and she explained that Carl had been very overactive, jumping on the furniture, taking away toys from his younger sister and refusing to be dressed to come to the nursery. She warned him that she was getting angry with him and if he did not stop jumping about, she would punish him. She hit him with a narrow belt and the buckle had caught him and caused the wound. She had washed it with antiseptic and had apologised to him, and they had 'made up' as he quietened down and allowed her to help get him ready. Mrs A became tearful and said that she did not want to be thought of as abusing Carl. The nursery worker explained that there was evidence of Carl having been struck, and that it was mandatory for her to report the incident to the social worker and Carl would have to be seen by a doctor. The social worker would visit her at home to assess the family.

The nursery was situated in an area where few of the children were from black or other ethnic minority groups. The staff was white British and may have had a different understanding of the use of the word 'beat' from that of a child from a Caribbean background who described any physical punishment, whether light or severe, as a beating. In this instance the punishment appeared to be serious as there was a wound.

Mrs A had come from a culture where it was accepted that mothers loved their children and vice versa. She was willing to co-operate with the social worker, and accepted an appointment.

Issues to be considered

One controversial issue is that of corporal punishment. There are many parents from the indigenous ethnic group and from minority groups who believe that it is their right to punish their children in ways that they think fit. Often this entails corporal punishment, and this is justified by parents claiming that their parents punished them in that way and it did them no harm. They resent being labelled as abusers but if they are not helped to look at what they do and the effect on their children and why they do it, they run the risk of the children being taken from them to be looked after by social services.

A second controversial issue is that of time-keeping by black and ethnic minority clients. The worker needs to set clear boundaries of time and not accept that black clients are unable and unwilling to keep time.

If the worker is going to enter into a counselling relationship with Mrs A, in the initial assessment there are two areas of concern. First, the client's wish to be co-operative may cause her to identify with the majority culture and to say what she thinks the worker wants to hear, thus presenting a false self (Thomas 2000). Second, Mrs A, being a new comer to the country, is isolated, and could easily adopt a position of helplessness.

From the beginning the social worker needs to have clear objectives, most importantly to develop a trusting relationship with the client. This will entail a great deal of patience and empathic listening.

Inter-cultural counselling is psychodynamically based and so the counsellor needs to take account of the client's unconscious. Mrs A has lost the support of members of her extended family and that of her husband. She has had limited experience of interacting with people of different races and cultures in the context of the university student group. This did not prepare her for the impact of a mass of people who were different from herself. Besides, she has read and seen the news of racist attacks on minority groups, and may be fearful lest she becomes a victim when out with the children, without her husband who spends long hours at the university. The worker needs to help her to acknowledge her fear and her loneliness.

These questions are relevant in the social services setting

If the worker is white, how threatened does Mrs A feel in this situation when child abuse could be levelled at her? How much trust will she be able to summon to form and sustain a working alliance? How does the white worker feel about working with a black client who does not fit the stereotype of a socially disadvantaged black client? Kareem believed that it was the responsibility of the workers to identify the differences between themselves and their clients and to ensure that they are comfortable about acknowledging the difference (Kareem 2000).

If the worker is a black woman and older than Mrs A, there may be a temptation for them to enter into a collusive relationship whereby Mrs A could become dependent. Will she think of her as a maternal figure and how will the transference be handled? On the other hand, the black worker may be inclined to be ashamed that a black client has found herself in this predicament.

The black client, who has internalised racism, may believe in the superiority of white people, and if assigned a black worker may feel that the service given to her may be inferior. How does the black worker cope in this situation? Thomas has highlighted the point that for some black clients the fact that a black person has achieved professional status may somehow mean that they have sold out to white values (Thomas 2000, p. 158). In this instance, Mrs A has grown up in a country where she has experienced black people in positions of power. She could be challenging to a young black worker who may not have encountered a self-possessed black individual, and thus the initial interaction may be unsatisfactory to both of them. A black worker in such a situation needs appropriate supervision in order to persevere with trying to create a working alliance.

Conclusion

Social workers in the social services have been deterred from counselling and pressured into short-term work and closure of cases because of the demands upon the service. It is important that social workers have knowledge of resources in the community, to which clients who need further help and who agree may be referred for long-term counselling. Recently, there has been a decisive shift in social work from the social worker working directly with clients and utilising interpersonal skills to that of care managing.

Social work is about helping individuals to cope with problems which prevent them from living fulfilled lives, and workers need to assert their right to practise the profession for which they are trained. Perhaps they need to alert clients to the part they can play in getting the authorities to realise that they value the individual relationships which social workers provide. It is important that social workers impress upon their managers that they want to counsel clients. In this changing society, there are many vulnerable people who are in need of counselling.

Notes

1 The word 'Nafsiyat' itself comprises three different syllables, each coming from a different ancient language: they stand for mind, body and soul. 'This name was chosen to indicate that in this approach to patients,

we try to look at the whole person, as a social as well as a psychological being' (Kareem 2000, p. 14).

Bibliography

Allen-Meares, P. and Burman, S. (1999) 'Cross-Cultural Therapeutic Relationships: Entering the World of African-Americans', *Journal of Social Work Practice*, 13(1): 49–57.

Arnold, E. (1998) 'Anti-Racist Practice Teaching Equipping the Practice Teacher for the Task', in H. Lawson (ed.) *Practice Teaching-Changing Social Work*, London: Jessica Kingsley.

BASW (1977) *A Code of Ethics for Social Work*, British Association of Social Workers, 16 Kent Street, Birmingham.

Bessell, R. (1971) *Interviewing and Counselling*, London: B.T. Batsford.

Bowlby, J. (1979) *The Making and Breaking of Affectional Bonds*, London: Tavistock.

Clark, E.L. (2000) *Social Work Ethics*, London: Macmillan.

Cootes, R.J. (1968) *Britain Since 1700*, London: Longman.

Egan, G. (1990) *The Skilled Helper, A Systematic Approach to Effective Helping*, New York: Brooks/Cole.

England, H. (1986) *Social Work as Art. Making Sense of Good Practice*, London: Allen & Unwin.

Hillman, J. and Mackenzie, M. (1993) *Understanding Field Social Work*, Birmingham: Venture Press.

Hollis, F. (1964) *Casework: A Psychosocial Therapy*, New York: Random House.

Howe, D. (1991) *On Being A Client. Understanding the Process of Counselling and Psychotherapy*, London: Sage.

—— (1995) *Attachment Theory for Social Work Practice*, London: Macmillan.

Jarry, D. and Jarry, J. (1991) *Dictionary of Sociology*, London: HarperCollins.

Johnson, L.C. (1989) *Social Work Practice, A Generalist Approach*, (3rd edn), London: Allyn & Bacon.

Jordan, B. (1979) *Helping in Social Work*, London: Routledge & Kegan Paul.

Kareem, J. (2000) *Journal of Social Work Practice*, 14(1): 146–160.

Kareem, J. and Littlewood, R. (1992) *Intercultural Therapy* (2nd edn), London: Blackwell Science.

Lago, C. and Thompson, J. (1996) *Race, Culture and Counselling*, Buckingham, PA: Open University Press.

Middleman, R.R. and Wood, G.G. (1990) *Skills for Direct Practice in Social Work*, New York: Columbia University Press.

Perlman, H.H. (1957) *Social Casework: A Problem-Solving Process*, Chicago, IL: University of Chicago Press.

Preston-Shoot, M. and Agass, D. (1990) *Making Sense of Social Work, Psychodynamics, Systems and Practice*, London: Macmillan.

Robert, W. and Nee Robert, H. (1970) *Theories of Social Casework*, Chicago, IL: University of Chicago Press.

Thomas, L.K. (2000) 'Racism and Psychotherapy: Working with Racism in the Consulting Room, An Analytical View', in J. Kareem and R. Littlewood (eds), *Intercultural Therapy* (2nd edn), Oxford: Blackwell Science.

Timms, N. (1964) *Social Casework*, London: Routledge & Kegan Paul.

Towle, C. (1945) *Common Human Needs*, Washington, DC: National Association of Social Workers.

Chapter 10

The impact of multi-cultural issues on the supervision process

Angus Igwe

Introduction

My aim in this chapter is to explore the impact of multi/cross-cultural issues on the supervision process for supervisors, supervisees and clients. In order to do this I begin by placing my work and myself in an identifiable context, and follow with a brief discussion of just what comprises culture, and multi-cultural issues. I then take a look at some current thinking on the process of supervision, illustrated with some examples from my own practice that highlight the complexity and challenge of this work.

A supervisor in context

I supervise, primarily, with an EAP (Employee Assistance Programme), which services a very large county council (Hampshire), with more than sixty counsellors. I am directly responsible for supervising about half of these, both on an individual basis and in groups. The supervisees represent a cross-section of all the popular theoretical counselling backgrounds, ranging from psychodynamic to transactional analysis. I supervise them in mixed groups dictated by the county/town boundaries in which they work and live, rather than in terms of their counselling orientations. I also supervise for other organisations, among them the University College, London counsellor training course, which is psychodynamically based, with a predominantly female, white, middle-class mixed age, (adult) student body. I also have a private practice that contracts with some twenty-two therapists across a breadth of orientations: I monitor their work with individuals and organisations within both the public and private sectors. I am currently the only black male counsellor and supervisor in this county, which means that all clients/ supervisees requiring such a counsellor/supervisor (multi-cultural) are referred to me.

I was born in an African country which has many tribes (cultures), and married into an English (if there can be said to be a solely 'English') culture; I raise a family of mixed-race children, living in a part of Great Britain where people of my colour make up only 0.0011 per cent of the population. In my working life, I am one man to ten women, a black counsellor to 100 white counsellors, one black male counsellor to 200 to 300 female counsellors, a male supervisor to ten female supervisors, and as a black male supervisor I am one in 400 to 500. Most of the time I work with people of a different gender, social setting, ethnic background and other distinct elements of 'opposing' cultures, although of course, this is also true, to some extent for all counsellors.

Heading towards a definition of culture

It is relatively easy for my (English) family and myself to acknow-ledge and celebrate our different holidays – 1 October (Nigerian Independence Day) vs. 5 November (Guy Fawkes) – and it is not particularly how we celebrate that makes a difference, but *that* we celebrate. It is less easy however for me to explain how uncomfort-able I feel when young children address me as Angus. I am respond-ing in both a generational way to this – to me – discourtesy, and in a (my own country's upbringing) cultural way, preferring to be addressed as Mr Igwe, or as Uncle (a courtesy title). Nevertheless, after many years in Britain I have become more used to it, but it still amuses me to note my instinctive (negative) response to what I see as a breach of good manners.

By the early 1960s there were more than 160 different definitions of 'culture', and it is now regarded as one of the two or three most complicated words in the English dictionary. Of all these definitions, the ones I find easiest to work with are:

> Culture means the total body of tradition borne by a society and transmitted from generation to generation. It thus refers to the norms, values, standards by which people act, and it includes the ways distinctive in each society of ordering the world and rendering it intelligible. Culture is . . . a set of mechanisms for survival, but it provides as also with a definition of reality. It is

the matrix into which we are born, it is the anvil upon which our persons and destinies are forged.

(Murphy 1986, p. 14)

It is a collective mental programme of a people in an environment.

(Hofstede 1980)

To understand culture we need also to recognise that 'Culture is an immutable fixed property of social groups'.
And,

Ethnic is a mixture of cultural background and racial designation which includes religion, skin colour, language, food, of yourself and or family of origin. It is not the same as nationality.

(NHS Management Executive 1993)

Thus, by implication:

An individual cannot through introspection and self examination understand himself or the forces that mould his life without understanding his culture.

(Thomas and Sillen 1972)

All of the above imply some notion of culture being static – 'an immutable fixed property'. Although culture is of itself a real and identifiable entity, it is the fact of culture that is immutable; the facets that make up each separate culture are never wholly static; they change from individual to individual, environment to environment and generation to generation as new ideas (economic pressure, racism, even military might) permeate the group concerned. We need to explore with an open mind the assumptions contained within cultural issues (which give structure to our way of perceiving and form the basis of our conceptual system), starting with an awareness that cultural issues are often so deeply entrenched in the unconscious that they dictate all our behaviours, with or without our knowledge, and with or without our permission.

A new health visitor called on a woman from a Trinidadian background. She was concerned to see that the woman was still in her nightdress at 11 a.m., and wondered in her notes if the woman was exhibiting signs of depression. She was not aware of the common (to her client's culture) behaviour that the woman was engaging in: she had been brought up to scrub the house from top to bottom each day in her nightdress, and then to bathe and dress ready to go out before noon.

The awareness of difference

Each counsellor who comes to supervision brings not only an internal belief system about the world and how it operates, but also his or her own family background, educational background, and all life experiences to date – a powerful cultural cocktail to imbibe when each of the other supervisees has their own individual cocktail to sip.

In a knowledge-based way, having attended many seminars and conferences on the subject, I believe that most professionals are aware of cultural issues; yet there is a difference between this and having the sort of awareness and sensitivity which leads to a reduction in the inappropriate use of certain models of counselling/supervision. Rather, real awareness is a process of examining and being open to the possibility of changing principles and beliefs where and when necessary.

An exposure to and experience of clients, supervisees and organisational culture is part of what is necessary to create a shift from abstract to real awareness. Supervising a counsellor without an examined awareness of one's own, the client's, the supervisee's or the organisational culture – 'why we do what we do' – may lead, unknowingly and unintentionally, to 'abuse' of the counsellor. The possible consequences of this abuse are low self-esteem in the supervisee or client, or worse, a feeling of not just guilt – which often means 'I made a mistake' – but shame, which can translate as 'I *am* a mistake'.

My first training supervisor had no idea of my feelings of dismay and disillusionment arising from his treatment of my ventured interpretations and theoretical understandings; not only was he dismissive of them but he was also somewhat punitive in his dismissal. As a new counsellor I was very confused, and felt left out, overlooked, and so often just plain wrong. I did not know why he was acting that way. (Now, I would say that he belonged to the school of thought which says that being colour-blind is the same as being non-racist.) I wanted to explore my own assumptions about my colour and cultural background and my client's colour and cultural background – and he was adamant that they played no part in 'good' counselling. It took me many years to overcome that experience – to be able to recover confidence in my own thought processes about race and counselling. And now I think: What was the impact on the others in the training group – have they too taken away the implicit message that race and culture do not matter, are of no significance? An unintentional act however does not render us guiltless as supervisors. We need to be aware of the consequences of ignorance.

In my own practice, it is imperative that issues of culture and race have a high priority. We often do some simple questioning of each other, and when I ask, 'What does it feel like to be supervised by a man, and a black man at that?' there is often a stunned silence. The responses range from a hesitating 'I hadn't really noticed', through 'I know you're a man and a black man but I think my professionalism would prevent me from letting it make any difference', and 'Some of my best friends are black men', to 'Well, I've always wondered if what they say about black men is true'. (That last comment brought the group to a complete stuttering halt, and the counsellor herself looked hugely embarrassed, not quite believing she had said it out loud.)

Another gambit is to ask each member of the group to introduce themselves culturally. This they do readily in terms of their counselling tribe, but less readily in terms of their social setting. When I ask them if they have an awareness of which class they belong to, or if they believe that Britain is a classless society, the conversation again grinds to a halt. They are further challenged when asked if, despite their non-judgemental training, where they were born/grew up/ educated/worked/significant others/family context could influence the way they work with, and relate to, any client, to each other in the group, and to me.

Is it enough to acknowledge the blind spots, and then leave well enough alone? Beck (1967) said that entrenched belief is not altered by fact, which would seem to suggest that the confrontation of erroneous beliefs about other cultures will not necessarily be changed by learning the 'truth' from someone of that culture. There are three distinct voices to be taken note of here – the supervisor, the supervisee, the client – all of whom will feel the repercussions of the above discussion and how it was dealt with, although the client's voice will be somewhat subdued and tend to be interpreted through the material brought back to the supervision group.

Some current views of multi-cultural counselling supervision

Multi/cross-cultural supervision is the most recent important new idea in supervision to shape the field of counselling. It is still a relatively new field, an unexplored gold-mine – or a land-mine, depending on your own experiences of supervision. Cross-cultural counselling supervision has been defined as any counselling relationship in which two or more of the participants differ in cultural background, values and lifestyle (Sue *et al.* 1982). This definition represents a broad view in which much of counselling supervision becomes cross-cultural in nature. All counselling relationships may be viewed as cross-cultural or multi-cultural to some degree, since all humans differ in terms of cultural background, values and lifestyle. However, multi-cultural counselling supervision has been conceptualised in much narrower terms, referring primarily to the counselling relationship when the supervisor is from one racial background, and the supervisee and/or client is from another.

The potential differences between supervisors and their supervisees, and supervisees and *their* clients, are myriad: race, gender, sexuality, educational background, class, social milieu, marital status, nationality – all could be different, making for a very interesting if sometimes volatile mixture. For some of these differences, the visible nature of them makes it easy to think that there will be an overt awareness of potential conflicts or collusions, but for others, not only the ones that are not visible – but are readily determined (are you divorced, married, cohabiting, single and so on) – but also the ones that are not visible and are also unconscious, there will need to be constant monitoring of the transference and projective identification.

The term *cross-cultural* would seem to imply a comparison between two groups (the 'standard group' and the 'culturally different group'), leading all too easily to thoughts of a normative group and a non-normative group. A broader view, therefore, of what constitutes cross-cultural issues would ensure that language and terminology reflected the perspective being taken. Consequently, the term *multi-cultural* is used because it seems to be more reflective of this broad and inclusive view (Fukuyama 1990), that in fact every working alliance is multi-cultural. What is then noticed and worked with is the degree of supervisor, counsellor and client similarity or dissimilarity in terms of race, ethnicity, sexual orientation, gender and cultural background.

Lago and Thompson (1996) have developed a theoretical model (of triads) of these similarities and dissimilarities, which graphically illustrates the complexity that can and does emerge when one, two or three of the working party (supervisor, counsellor, client) are different initially, and visibly different. This complexity increases the more invisible the difference. A Nigerian counsellor is earmarked as the perfect person to see a Nigerian client, but they may not, almost certainly do not, share a common tribe, religion, language or educational background. A critical question has always been 'How can a supervisor, counsellor and client who differ so much from each other work together effectively?' This question led to the birth of Race and Cultural Education ((RACE) the multi-cultural training part of the BAC) which has contributed to a great and much needed understanding of the difference among various racial, ethnic and cultural groups.

It could be said that the primary task of the supervisor is to ensure that certain beliefs and understandings which may be, or appear to be, unconscious are brought to consciousness for the group to examine. Yet it is not likely that the supervisor him or herself is always aware of what he or she believes or understands about multi-cultural issues. And because of the power imbalance inherent in the supervisory process (reflecting the power imbalance inherent in the counselling process), a partial identification with the omnipotent figure of saviour offering a hand to the suffering (Carotenuto 1992, p. 51) is possible, particularly in the case of a supervisor who feels multi-culturally aware already. This supervisor may be responsible (unintentionally or not) for creating a new 'supervision culture' that is damaging to clients and supervisees alike.

A good supervisor welcomes the opportunity to work on both the conscious and unconscious understandings and misunderstandings in his or her group – a kind of shifting from an unconscious incompetent state (I do not know what I do not know) to a conscious incompetent state (I know what I do not know) (Figure 10.1).

Supervisors, with the best will in the world, cannot divorce their supervisees and clients from their social and cultural background, nor should they; they are, after all, a specific group of people who have reacted in specific, often unique ways to their problems – a human being does not live in a sterilised plastic bubble (Cooper 1984).

One way of thinking about the sometimes fixed nature of beliefs is to visualise a 'belief window' (Figure 10.2).

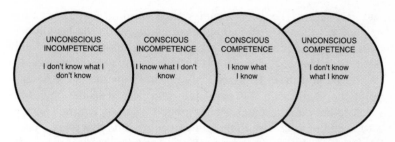

Figure 10.1 Model showing how we move from a state of unconscious incompetence (unaware of what we do not know) to unconscious competence (where we have internalised what we know so well that we are no longer aware of knowing it)

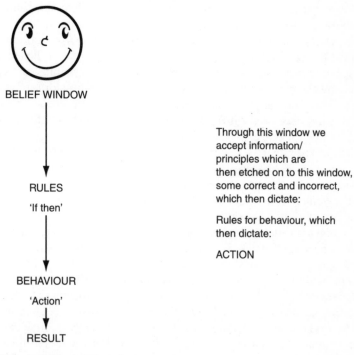

BELIEF WINDOW

RULES

'If then'

Through this window we accept information/principles which are then etched on to this window, some correct and incorrect, which then dictate:

Rules for behaviour, which then dictate:

ACTION

BEHAVIOUR

'Action'

RESULT

Figure 10.2 The belief window

A young man complained about food wastage by his wife (who is a good cook) when she cut off the knuckle joint of a ham. When he enquired as to why, she replied, "If you don't cut that end off it won't taste very good." "Who told you that?" he asked. "My mum" was the reply. The young man waited until his wife's mother next came to lunch. After complimenting his mother-in-law on her cooking he then proceeded to ask her why she cut the knuckle joint off a ham. Her response was, 'If I don't it won't taste very good.' 'Who told you that?' he asked. 'My mother' was the reply. At this point the young man was perplexed, and picked up the phone to speak to his wife's grandmother, asking, 'I hear you cut the knuckle off the end of your ham joint before cooking it. Is that true?' 'Yes I do' she replied. 'Why do you do that?' he asked. 'Because if I don't it won't fit in my oven.' Three generations on they are still cutting the knuckle joint off the ham (even though our ovens today are bigger). We've forgotten why we did it in the first place.

When each of my new supervision groups is formed, we look at some of our entrenched beliefs. Since these are sometimes difficult to identify or own consciously, I ask my supervisees to participate in some statement completion exercises – a kind of free association in print. One partial statement about dogs (All dogs are ____) elicited a range of responses: wonderful, happy, stupid, loving, vicious, perfect pets; but there was little in those responses to give pause for thought about whether the particular belief was going to prevent a supervisor, supervisee or client from doing some good work. (Although I did have a supervisee with a client who doted on her dogs to the extent of keeping herself without adequate food in order to feed her beloved Yorkie. My supervisee did not like dogs, and would not have done the same thing at all, but it did not stop her being sympathetic to the woman's plight.) However, three other partial statements: (All men are ____; Black people are ____; White people are ____) elicited some answers that were disturbing to those who had made them. One supervisee remarked, 'I didn't know that I thought that way, I thought I was free of those prejudices.'

The ability to work with another individual who is distinctly different is a rare gift, one that needs constant nurturing with self-challenging. Sue *et al.* (1982) note that the best possible counselling scenario is one in which cultural differences between the participants are minimal; that is when the supervisor/counsellor/client are similar in a number of important racial, ethnic or cultural dimensions. The holy grail of therapists is to come to each session without memory and without desire (Bion 1976). The worst counselling scenario is one in which the cultural differences between the participants are numerous and there is a resistance to the awareness of these differences, whether non-judgementally motivated or not.

Compelling arguments have been made in support of cultural matching (Vontress 1971), as exemplified by the Triad model (Lago and Thompson 1996). Yet the matching triad model somehow reduces individuals into relevant cultural characteristics along the lines that Asian clients should see only Asian counsellors, and gay male clients should see only gay male counsellors. One difficulty with a matching approach begs the question: Who do we match to whom? Supervisor to counsellor, counsellor to client, supervisor to client? Casas (1985) suggests that 'Caution be exercised in drawing any definitive conclusion about the effect of race/ethnicity similarity between participants on counselling effectiveness'. Margolis and Rungta (1986), in their criticism of multi-cultural training, recommended a more integrated approach to training counsellors to enable them to work with a variety of special populations. How can this integrated approach be deployed in an environment or setting where there is covert prejudice and an unwillingness to confront the inability of all different schools of theory to work together?

Two conceptual systems – East meets West

The difficulty in interpreting multi-culturalism through a eurocentric conceptual system is that the dominant European culture fosters an either-or type reasoning, whereas Western approaches in theory are usually focused on control (for example, of symptoms) or understanding by analysis (for example, in psychotherapy and counselling). In cultures that emphasise harmony, balance and integration within the individual, acceptance (of problems or symptoms) is more important than control. Understanding by contemplation supersedes the need to analyse feelings, and problems do not automatically call for solutions; rather they need to be understood and worked with or worked around.

I acknowledge and emphasise that there is a large overlap between the different systems/theories, and of course there is constant interchange of ideas and views. However, the balance in the interchange is often determined by power, prestige and economic advantage, rather than validity (of concepts, therapies and so on), or the *usefulness* of different ways of coping with human problems. This is where institutionalised racism comes into play, resulting in the imposition of Western ways of thinking, as the basis of 'superiority', 'scientific worth' and so on. We bandy about this sense of superiority without thinking, or being insensitive in its use because we assume that 'our' disciplines, 'our' font of knowledge, 'our' theories of the psyche (and of the soma), all these are 'scientific', basically because they stem from cultures that happened to dominate the world, linked to races that presumed superiority.

A Caribbean woman comes into therapy to talk about her relationship. As her story unfolds, the counsellor comes to know that her client was left behind in the Islands when her parents came to England to find work. She and her brother lived with her grandmother. The parents had two more children and then sent first for her brother, and then for her. How relevant was it going to be to talk of issues of attachment and abandonment when, in her culture, the client was like many others who had been left behind when a family looked for a better life; she could not find within her the sense of loss that 'should' have been there – her culture had trained her to celebrate the separation as necessary in order to 'get on' in life.

The range of therapeutic theories in use today has been numbered as 481 distinct models (Karasu *et al.* 1984), though it is widely recognised that there are three or four categories or approaches into which the large number can be fitted. Often described as the first, second and third forces in psychology/counselling, they represent psychoanalytic, behavioural and humanistic ways of viewing human beings and their problems (Mahrer 1989). The contention is that, parallel to these Western approaches, other approaches seem to have been swept under the carpet in favour of the dominant cultural approach.

Jackson and Meadows (1991) set up three hypotheses to help understand the world view:

> The European System, with an emphasis on material gains, the consequence of which leads to PERFORMANCE = WORTH.

> The Asian system emphasises cosmic unity, with an integration of Mind, Body and Spirit, the consequence of which produces an identity and self-worth based on BEING.

> The African Conceptual System emphasises spiritual and material matters, together with gender relationships, and is based on the knowledge of symbolic imagery and rhythm; the consequence of which produces an identity of self worth that is INTRINSIC.

Lee *et al.* (1992) concluded from their research responses that the major causes of psychological distress and behavioural deviance are based in three areas:

Family Dynamics – The family elders are seen as the wise ones and that's not negotiable. Stigma and shame are strongly attached to mental illness, and consequently only when family efforts have failed would the "sick" member seek other forms of help, but first it must be from within the extended family, then friends, then community, which is often an extension of the extended family.

Fate – Dominates all approaches, with spirituality and religion the fulcrum (centre pole), e.g. the (Nigerian) Muslim will take everything to 'Allah' and say it's 'His' will. Here there is a very high level of acceptance as a way of 'resolving', 'dealing' with or 'coping'. There are also Christian Spiritual Churches (Healing Houses).

Possession by the Evil Spirit is Traditional – The Traditional Healers are identified by different names, e.g. Medicine Men, Shamans, Black Magic Experts, etc. They operate in many ways, some of which include entering an altered state of consciousness; prescribing herbs and other traditional medicines; using verses of the Koran; and using special 'magic' words to ward off or to cast spells even in someone's absence. Other traditional methods include sufism; kung hunter-gatherers; altered states of consciousness ('Lain' Dance Rituals); the Sioux sun dance; the gourd dance; mediumship and spirits.

Most Western therapies have an individual emphasis, while others described here have a community or family focus. Most Western therapies are also delivered in a one-to-one setting, while others may use several healers who may work in group settings. They do not involve friends or family members in the therapeutic process, and they do not induce deliberately altered states of consciousness through ritual dancing and chanting. But some contradictions to the above assertion include group therapies of creative dance, movement, art, sound – and Alcoholics Anonymous.

Therapists are urged to respect and take very seriously their culturally different clients' wishes and views in relation to what they conceive as helpful. Some issues that have arisen in my own practice need to be looked at in at least two ways.

Case study 1 – Sylvia

Sylvia, 45, came to therapy because she was unhappy in her marriage, but did not wish to leave it. She thought that therapy might provide some understanding of her husband's behaviour, or provide some means whereby his behaviour might be changed. Her husband, Sunny, was Filipino. He had been married before in his home country, and worked as a merchant seaman, cooking for the crew. One year, when they docked in Southampton, he jumped ship. Sylvia met him when he served her a meal one night in the hotel where he worked. She was instantly smitten, thinking him a very good looking man, even though a bit younger than herself. Sunny seemed to find her equally attractive, and they began a sexual relationship that very night, when Sylvia took him home with her. To all intents and purposes, he never left, and they were married three months later. Sylvia noticed that he flirted with other women, but initially at least, found it quite charming, thinking that although he flirted with them, he went home with her.

Sylvia too, had been married before, but described her husband as 'a bit of a freak'. Sexually, he did not want to penetrate her, and in all the ten years of their marriage he never did, saying that it was 'not the done thing'. Eventually they divorced, and Sylvia had both a handsome financial settlement from him, and also an inheritance from her mother, who died about the same time as Sylvia's divorce was being made final.

Sylvia's concerns were many. Not only did Sunny appear to believe in 'black magic', but he seemed to think that black magic was being practised on him from a distance – from his home in the Philippines, and possibly by his former wife. He was concerned about the effects of this on Sylvia, and insisted that she wear an amulet around her ankle to protect her. He had begun to reminisce about his former wife, and Sylvia was feeling both insecure and jealous. Sunny was also full of rage at times, against quite who or what she did not know. Often, it seemed to be directed at her. He insisted on being able to go out on a Friday evening and not return home until the Monday morning, no questions asked. If he arrived home late from a night out, he expected her to be waiting up with a meal ready, and if she had gone to bed, he wanted her to get up and cook his meal there and then. Sunny was also badgering Sylvia to have children, even though she was 45, and when they went to the Philippines on holiday, Sunny treated her as his queen, a prize won abroad, which she found somewhat disturbing.

After a session with Sylvia, Jane, my supervisee, was often left feeling furious with Sunny, and also quite angry with Sylvia. She tried hard to respect Sunny's differentness and his dominating ways. She was alarmed too about the black magic, believing as a Catholic that there was possible evil afoot. But she disliked his behaviour even more, and she also disliked Sylvia's submissiveness. When I challenged Jane about her lack of empathy for Sunny, she looked discomfited – was she wondering if I too might be demanding of the woman in my life, being a male from another (less Western) culture? That, being so black, I too might practise black magic under a full moon? In addition, I understood Sunny's treatment of Sylvia as a queen, and did not lack an understanding either of why Sylvia felt objectified: she *was* an object – a white woman prized by a darker-skinned group. I had married a white woman, and although, to the best of my knowledge, I did not choose her for the colour of her skin, I had to acknowledge that it may well have played a part. Should I reveal this information to Jane? The visible differences were causing some difficulties already, and now the invisible differences were resonant in the background.

Sylvia had never told Sunny that the sessions were about their marriage; since she had been referred through an EAP scheme, she let him assume they were work related. What actual progress was being made in the sessions with Sylvia? Each time she was challenged to reflect on Sunny's behaviour, and how, at least in part, her tacit acquiescence promoted more of the same, she would somehow miss the following session. Her original six, which one assumes would take six weeks, took almost four months. Jane was fed up, I was puzzled – it seemed that just as Sylvia's first husband did not penetrate her sexually, Jane and I could not penetrate her with a different point of view. Although Jane and I were both hopeful that Sylvia could be encouraged to acknowledge Sunny's culture without bowing down to it, and that Jane could affirm Sunny's seemingly chauvinistic ways without condoning them, there was no way to keep any links in the foreground. The pattern of being challenged and then disappearing continued in its disruptive way. In working with this couple it was exceptionally important to be aware of all the various elements of difference – gender, country, culture, religion – and to be knowledgeable enough to confront them without being dictatorial. Sunny needed to be well informed and supported in the impact of separation from his culture, and the psychological issues and realities of living where he now lives. Sylvia in turn needed to be educated about his cultural and gender-based differences. He may have been an unpleasantly demanding young man by her (Jane's and Sylvia's British) standards, but he was not pathologically ill.

The ways in which people cope, attempt to solve their problems and seek assistance are shaped by their social and cultural norms, and by the symbolic meanings within their culture. Different authors do agree that differences exist between cultures on what is deemed as problematic. Westwood (1990) and Torrey (1972) identified five crucial elements to successful helping in any culture (within the non-Western approach).

1 The client's problem is named.
2 The personal qualities of the counsellor/helper are extremely important.
3 The helper must establish credibility through the use of symbols, skills or power.
4 The client's specific expectations must be met.
5 The counsellor must apply certain techniques designed to bring about relief to the troubled client.

Case study 2 – Trevor and Janice

Trevor and Janice were sent for therapy by their case social worker. They had been married for sixteen years and had ten children. They were always in financial difficulties, constantly rowing because of it, and at the time of being seen Trevor was once again on the verge of bankruptcy. The social worker could not understand why Trevor and Janice refused to think of curtailing their large family. Janice was pregnant again.

The counsellor was herself confused. It seemed a simple equation to her – if you cannot provide for your family, you should not be trying to increase it. Yet she also acknowledged a woman's right to dominion over her own body. Was Janice happy with this state of affairs, or was she being coerced by Trevor? The counsellor was an only child, a single parent with two children who thought two was more than enough, and who struggled to raise them on her salary. What must the home conditions be like for Trevor and Janice's family? Trevor spoke of their Covenant with God, and said that all children were a blessing and would be provided for. His place was at the head of the family, he was responsible for dictating family life, and

Janice's place was at his side and at home, and it did not matter what happened to them as long as God loved them and they kept their Covenant with him. My supervisee was concerned about some of Trevor's language – were Trevor and Janice part of a cult religion? And what did cult religion mean exactly – was it relevant to the marital work? I recognised some of Trevor's phrasings, and it soon became clear to me that Trevor and Janice were Latter Day Saints (LDS) I had been LDS too for a time, so understood their adherence to the teachings of the Book of Mormon. Should I declare my knowledge, and my former religious affiliation? Should I also reveal that I have five children – not a large family by Trevor and Janice's standards, but larger than many people's today. I wondered if the disclosure of my former faith would be a help or a hindrance to my supervisee, and through her, to Trevor and Janice. In fact, how could they as a couple be supported in their faith, and also challenged to see that certain of their beliefs were disadvantageous to them, that the rows were not only about the chronic shortage of money, but also about the strains of looking after so many children.

The common denominator here in both cases was that the assumptions made, which were invariably made by professionals trained in a Western setting, were those of a Western style of emotional differentiation or expression; and that this was the norm against which all other cultures are judged. Such assumptions are inherent in the adherence of most professionals to 'illness' models based on Western thinking, whatever the context and whatever the cultural background of the service user. In clinical situations this often leads to a pathologising of the culture itself.

The content here may have given the impression that issues of race and culture are overwhelming and impossible to grasp. An attempt has been made to indicate that the problems are often very basic and that we need at all times as therapists (helpers) in all shapes and forms to grapple with the cultural differences that divide us. But there is another side to this. Divisions that impede communication across cultural divides are no different in quality from the divisions between us as individuals or families or groups of people.

Living and supervising with difference

There is an assumption that counselling supervisors already know their own assumptions! Within a multi-cultural/multi-racial society, and, as a consequence, the counselling setting, counsellors and supervisors need to recognise the danger of any closed biases and a culturally potentially encapsulating system that promotes domination by an elitist group. In a multi-cultural society we really have no option but to live with these differences, and to learn how to do this in a constructive, peaceful and decent way.

A young African man had gone into therapy as part of his social work training requirement, and had become silent when the counsellor asked him to talk about his mother. He stopped going to therapy because of the confusion this brought. He explained: 'As a child I had three "mothers". I was breast-fed by six breasts. In my country it is usual to be passed from breast to breast, depending on who is free and "milky" at the time of demand. Which "mother" should I talk about?'

Yet differences do not need to be discerned as problems; it is differences – cultural differences – whether between individuals or groups that make for a healthy and vibrant society, which in turn gives rise to development and growth (whether economically or in the arts or sciences), all of which makes life worth living. Our differences, then, are a society's main asset. It has been said that as each wave of immigrants arrived in Britain, so they joined a great melting-pot. There was assimilation. Then, in the 1970s, there began to be seen a different style of adaptation, and it was soon no longer a melting-pot of different nationalities and cultures, but rather better described by the term *mosaic*, each group living separately, but still nestled next to each other. And now perhaps, moving into the twenty-first century, there is once again more cultural overlap between groups and individuals. Tiger Woods defined himself as a Cablanasian, a new word he coined to reflect his parentage and their distinct and different cultures. Of course in this setting, the question of identity (ethnic identity) becomes extremely complicated, though still a crucial issue for counsellors to try and understand.

Moving forward

If we are to circumvent cultural divisions (in counselling supervision), or celebrate cultural diversity, or understand cultural difference, if we are to do any of these things, we must first and foremost learn how to identify and counteract racism (which is currently very covert in the helping professions). To do this we must start with our own self-discipline, our own work, within our own selves (adapted from S. Fernando RCP).

To gain the fullest understanding of individuals it is necessary to explore the unique and simultaneous influence of cultural specificity, individual uniqueness and human universality. In the case of the couple who came for marital therapy, their cultural specificity dictated that they have many children without regard for being able to provide for them. Their individual uniqueness resided in their adherence to their Covenant with God, and a human universality was expressed in their great love and care of their children. Although the contribution of each of the spheres is important, it is only in combination that we can begin to capture an understanding of the richness of each individual. The whole really is greater than the sum of the parts.

Implications for multi-cultural training

Lessons learned from counselling supervision would result in changes in the current approach to training, placing more emphasis on self-knowledge to enable a more diverse understanding and appreciation of others. The trainees through the programme would require considerable introspection as they bring into conscious awareness their feelings, thoughts, assumptions and biases. A major developmental task for all would involve the discovery and integration of the personal and socio-political meaning of one's ethnicity, culture and race as these affect oneself and others.

Practitioners/supervisors

Little was known about how supervisors assume the supervisory role, and the full extent of the supervisors' responsibilities and legal liabilities were not necessarily evident to supervisees or supervisors themselves (Loganbill *et al.* 1982), even though supervision was one of the top five activities psychologists engaged in (Garfield and Kurtz 1976), and more than two-thirds of counselling psychologists provided clinical supervision (Thompson 1991). In 1982, Hess wrote that only 10 to 15 per cent of supervisors had any specific training. And Carroll (1988) notes that supervision was still tied to counselling theory despite its efforts to become a discipline on its own, hence the BAC code of ethics and practice for the supervision of counsellors.

Some key issues when supervising or being supervised

One of the most fundamental questions that was never asked of me, and which I insist on asking my supervisees, is how they feel about being supervised by me. This is particularly important if they have been 'sent' by their organisation, although if they have chosen me directly themselves there are still likely to be many projections and phantasies.

If you and your supervisee are from the same cultural background, are you engaging in some collusion over shared (unspoken/invisible) assumptions? Or are you able to acknowledge both the good and the bad aspects of your culture without idealising or denigrating it? Jackie was born of a Jamaican mother and a Ghanaian father. She was educated privately, studied hard and won a good law degree, married a white man, and did not consider herself to be particularly black. When she and her husband were unable to have children and put themselves forward to be considered as adoptive parents, Jackie was shocked to be asked by a counsellor to explore her feelings about being black in Britain today. My supervisee was herself of mixed parentage and could not really understand how Jackie, whose skin tone was very dark, could have avoided noticing that she was black in such a white culture as Britain. And I as the supervisor, raising mixed-parentage children, also wondered how she had been so colour-blind for so long.

The effective supervisor for cross-cultural counselling

I conducted a small sample survey, asking clients and supervisees how and why they had chosen their counsellor/supervisor. If the counsellor/supervisor had been chosen for them, why had they stayed put? What were the qualities they looked for? I thought they might mention skills, intellectual knowledge, self-awareness, cultural similarity/dissimilarity or natural personal warmth. Most said that they had chosen on the basis of the counsellor/supervisor's (perceived) level of self-awareness. A few believed that experience had been important. However, very few had thought about cultural issues at all. Does this mean then that cultural issues are irrelevant? Not at all. Perhaps the questions asked could have been put in a different way; for instance, how has having someone of the same cultural background been a help or a hindrance to you? An effective supervisor needs to be aware and willing to accept a level of conscious and unconscious incompetent/competent awareness, and not become inflexibly stuck in the 'I know everything about multi-culturalism – after all, I am from a different culture'. It is good also to have a working knowledge of the ethnic and cultural background of your supervisees and their clients. It would not be possible to know something about every different ethnic group, but it is good practice to ask about the things you do not know. Here, you are looking especially to understand what is normal in anyone's culture. A young Englishman was put into an African mental institution for observation because an over-zealous, and culturally illiterate, health professional had heard him say 'It's raining cats and dogs'.

I have found one of the most rewarding aspects of my work as a supervisor to be that everyone learns how to be both supportive and challenging of each other's culturally held ideas and beliefs, and I am always proactive in initiating discussions of multi-cultural issues that arise between a supervisee and his or her client. All these points are geared towards ensuring that the supervisors/therapists do not misuse their power (personal, gender-related, cultural, racial, institutional) with clients/supervisees, and that they also do not impose culturally biased views or procedures for action that will, in effect, be harmful to participants.

Conclusion

Once racial prejudice is embedded within the structure (of counselling/society), individual prejudice is no longer their problem. Today, racism is fashioned by racial prejudice and underpinned by social factors. When implemented consciously or unconsciously through the institution (e.g. counselling) of society, racism becomes institutionalised and entrenched. Combating this is always difficult, like trying to capture a cloud, but the supervision group is a good place to start.

It seems clear that the best way to ensure the best possible supervisory experience is to remain open to the nuances that come to the relationship from all quarters: individual differences as well as cultural ones. Racial and cultural identity is an issue for everyone, whether they are acutely aware of it or not, with many experiences that connect them to their own racial and cultural group. Such common bonds can greatly influence the therapeutic and supervisory relationship, and provide a model of exploration, acknowledgement, challenge and acceptance to take with them at the end of their time of work. There are skills-based methods to learn – interpreting accurately what you see, hear, feel; simple mantras to memorise – just because I speak English does not mean that I am English; and the more subtle complexities of examining our clients'/supervisees' expectations and belief systems, as well as our own.

References

Beck, A.T. (1967) *Depression: Clinical, Experimental and Theoretical Aspects*. New York: Harper and Row.

Bion, W.R. (1976) Notes on Memory and Desire. *Psychoanalytic Forum II* (3): 271–80. [Reprinted in Bott Spillius, E. (Ed.) (1988) *Melanie Klein Today, Vol. 2, Mainly Practice* (pp. 17–21). London: Routledge.]

Carroll, M. (1988) Counselling Supervision: The British Context. *Counselling Psychology Quarterly* 1(4): 387–96.

Carotenuto, A. (1992) *The Difficult Art: A Critical Discourse on Psychotherapy*. Wilmetter, IL: Chiron.

Casas, J.M. (1985) A Reflection of the Status of Racial/Ethnic Minority Research. *The Counselling Psychologist* 13: 581–98

Cooper, C. (1984) Individual Therapies: Limitations, in W. Dryden (ed.) *Individual Therapy in Britain*. London: Harper & Row.

Fernando, S. (1988) *Race and Culture in Psychiatry*. London: Croom Helm.

Fukuyama, M.A. (1990) Taking the Universal Approach to Multi-Cultural Counselling. *Counsellor Education and Supervision* 30: 6–7.

Garfield, S. and Kurtz, R. (1976) Clinical Psychologists in the 1970s. *American Psychologist* 31: 1–9.

Hess, A. (1982) *Psychotherapy Supervision: Theory, Research and Practice*. New York: Witney.

Hofstede, G. (1980) *Cultures Consequences: International Differences in Work Related Values*. Beverly Hills, CA: Sage.

Jackson, A.P. and Meadows, F.B. (1991) Getting to the Bottom to Understand the Top. *Journal of Counselling and Development*, Sept/Oct: 72–6.

Karasu, T.B. *et al.* (1984) The Psychiatric Therapies (Part I, The Somatic Therapies, Part II, The Psychosocial Therapies). APA Commission on Psychiatric Therapies. Washington, DC: American Psychiatric Association.

Kareem, J. and Littlewood, R. (1992) *Intercultural Therapy: Themes, Interpretation and Practices*. Oxford: Blackwell Scientific.

Lago, C. and Thompson, J. (1996) *Race, culture and counselling*. Buckingham, Philadelphia: Open University Press.

Lee, C.C. *et al.* (1992) Indigenous Models of Helping in Non-western Countries: Implications for Multicultural Counselling. *Journal of Multicultural Counselling and Development* 20(1): 3–10.

Loganbill, C., Hardy, C. and Delworth, V. (1982) Supervision: a Conceptual Model. *The Counselling Psychologist* 10(1): 3–42.

Mahrer, A. (1989) *The Integration of Psychotherapies: A Guide for Practicing Therapists.* New York: Human Science Press.

Margolis, R.E. and Rungta, S.A. (1986) Training Counsellors for Work with Special Populations: (a second look). *Journal of Counselling and Development* 64: 642–4.

Murphy, R. (1986) *Culture and Social Anthropology: An Overture*, Second Edition. Englewood Cliffs, NJ: Prentice Hall.

Sue, D.W., Bernie, J.E., Durran, A., Freinberg, L., Pederson, P., Smith, E.H. and Vasquez-Nuttall, E. (1982) Position paper: cross cultural competencies, *The Couselling Psychologist* 10: 1–8.

Thomas, A. and Sillen, S. (1972) *Racism and Psychiatry*. New York: Brunner/Mazel.

Thompson, J. (1991) *'Issues of Race and Culture in Counselling Supervision Training Courses'*, unpublished MSc Thesis, Polytechnic of East London.

Torrey, E.F. (1972) *The Mind Game: Witch Doctors and Psychiatrists.* New York: Emerson-Hall.

Vontress, C.E. (1971) Racial differences: impediments to rapport. *Journal of Counselling Psychology* 18: 7–13.

Vontress, C.E. (1979) Cross-cultural counselling: an existential approach. *The Personnel and Guidance Journal* 58: 117–22.

Westwood, M.J. (1990) *'Identification of human problems and methods of help seeking: a cross cultural study'*, paper presented to the Comparative and International Education Society. Anaheim, California, 29 March to 1 April.

Index

Note: Page numbers in *italics* refer to diagrams; page numbers in **bold** refer to tables.